THE

CRACK-UP

OF THE

ISRAELI LEFT

THE

CRACK-UP

OF THE

ISRAELI LEFT

MORDECHAI NISAN

mantua books

2019

Published by: Mantua Books Ltd.
Canada
www.mantuabooks.com
Email: administration@mantuabooks.com

Library and Archives Canada Cataloguing in Publication
Nisan, Mordechai, author
    The crack-up of the Israeli left / Mordechai Nisan.
ISBN 978–1–927618–11–0 (softcover)

    1. Right and left (Political science)--Israel. 2. Israel--Politics
and government--1993-. 3. Israel--History--1993-. I. Title.

DS128.2.N57 2018   956.9405'5   C2018-906367-X

Dedicated to the Memory

of all the Israeli victims of savage Palestinian terrorism, who were callously betrayed by treasonous and defeatist policies; and to all the many hundreds of Israelis slaughtered and maimed with the launching of the delusional Oslo peace process in 1993.

Among them:

~ *Sam Eisenstadt, 80, assaulted with an ax in Kfar Saba on February 2, 1994;*

~ *Madhat Yusuf, 19, border police captain, shot by Palestinians and left to bleed to death by the Israeli army at Joseph's Tomb in Shechem (Nablus), October 1, 2000;*

~ *Dr. David Applebaum, 51, murdered with his daughter Naava, 20, on the eve of her wedding, by a suicide bomber in Café Hillel, Jerusalem, on September 9, 2003;*

~ *Tali Hatuel, 33, and her four daughters—Hila, 11; Hadar Simcha, 9; Roni Sarah, 7; and Meirav Rachel, 3; who were shot and murdered at close range in their car near the Kissufim crossing in the Gush Katif area of the Gaza Strip, May 2, 2004.*

Love Truth and Peace

Zechariah 8:19

CONTENTS

PREFACE

~ As this book is about truth, it was virtually impossible to write. For so many reasons and in so many
ways, truth is not to be spoken; obfuscation, mendacity, nuancing, distorting, and concealing, are the
ways people—and the media—present things today. A book is written with words and words were
exceptionally inadequate for the task of describing
the Left in Israel and its collaborators abroad. To
give a precise picture of the Left requires plumbing
the depths of a school of thought which is detached
from the national historical moorings of Jewish
peoplehood and devoid of political reality attending
Israel and its surroundings. Certainly Politically
Correct thought-terror confines our ability to portray and expose the Left in the fullness of its
warped manifestations. It is unreasonable, unrealis-
tic, and shameful to the core. It must surely be one
of the most astonishing cases of cognitive dis-
sonance—when facts contradict ideas—in human
history.

But another level of the repulsion of leftism is that it has given itself a
good name. Leftists are described by its adherents and fellow-travelers
as idealistic, humane, wise, moral, responsible, and meritoriously inclusive. All of their defects are white-washed and certified as sanitized by
normalcy. This is a second rung of leftist ignominy.

Some forty years ago I began to collect newspaper articles on items
gleaned from media coverage. I slowly added slips of paper with my own
thoughts. I didn't know when or if I would eventually collate these
materials to write a book on the Left, in particular, but also about the

Right. I would prefer, instead of the Right, to call that camp—patriotic, traditional, realistic, sensible, nationalist, loyal, and conservative. The Left could be labeled hallucinatory, delirious, treasonous, puerile, and psychotic. Perhaps it has good intentions. Leftists near and far will undoubtedly release a torrent of crabby criticism of my forthright exposure and polemic against their world-view.

I am attributing the term Left in Israel not therefore to its conventional definition as a political ideology merely favoring a set of values: equality, sharing economic wealth, radicalism, and liberalism. It has become a term of controversy and disparagement over the years. In Israel the Left signifies solidarity with the Arab enemy, dissent from a traditional code of national principles, and bashing the country. Those who love Israel are considerably more likely to be on the Right of the political map.

In Israel, where freedom of speech still requires legal grounding, you can land in jail if you defame someone by accusing him of treason. This is the state of PC thought-control which is one of the engines of cultural power to hide the truth from people. In one brief brush-in with the law, I spent a night in a Jerusalem detention facility for no misdemeanor; just for wanting to exercise my civil right to demonstrate at a political protest, which actually never took place.

Yet I use the conventional (Israeli) terms Left and Right out of convenience acquired since the revolutionary French Assembly's political seating arrangements. The word Crack-Up in the book's title is, however, more precise and less circumstantial in capturing the era in which, with God's munificence, the Left alone will crack up—but not Israel herself.

I wrote this book in English and not in Hebrew though its subject is Israel where I live and work; because my long experience has taught me the difficulty in finding a mainstream publisher for my works in Israel. I did write two books in Hebrew and they were published in Israel, but I failed to interest a major publishing house. I was inspired somewhat by the history of the anti–Stalinist anti-communist samizdat dissident literature which was self-published; might this be the fate of this book, I wondered. Evading leftist censorship and literary oppression can lead a writer to write in an elliptical way when faced with political persecution. But I chose the straight path here.

My professional and academic experience at the Hebrew University of Jerusalem provided me with a lesson of political bias of which I was a victim. I taught Middle East Studies for 35 years, published quite extensively and wrote 10 books. Class evaluations attested to my satisfactory distinction as a lecturer. But I was consistently marginalized in terms of academic recognition, advance, and opportunities. I was ignored and deprived of the chance to address conferences or participate on other public platforms, as for example in a seminar on Middle East minorities which was a subject about which I had written a major text. I suffered this injustice with resilience and gratified that I confidently expressed my views, though not in the classroom. Meanwhile the partisan establishment locked its castle of doctrinal faith from free debate and intellectual pluralism. Two university colleagues told me in discretion, that they were keenly aware of certain professors who definitely would or did block any chance of my advancing academically at the university. I was probably one of the most ostracized Israeli academics in the country, and in my university. It wasn't that when I entered the physical perimeters of the university on a rather daily basis that I felt I was in enemy territory; but admittedly I was something of an outsider. I was playing the game on somewhat foreign turf. I would hear, but not respond to, a snide allusion about Kiryat Arba, the focus—in my eyes— and product of commendable Jewish idealism and courage. I knew of lecturers who freely shared their leftist opinions with students in class. Fellow-workers and colleagues knew who I was: religious, Zionist, rightist, and a settler in Samaria (for a brief few years). But I rigorously refrained from politicizing my lectures. I was friendly and accommodating without compromising or abandoning my own convictions. I suffered neither from melancholy nor arrogance. But the shabby and insulting treatment I received was part of my life at the university, as when denied co-authorship for a book despite a signed contract which promised me that status.

My personal experience of this demeaning treatment as lecturer, researcher, and author, was an instance of the history of leftist loathing and abuse against its ideological and political rivals. In 1948 the Labor Party (Mapai) under Ben-Gurion instituted a policy of ostracism by blocking former underground pre-state Irgun and Lehi members from jobs and opportunities. Israel Eldad, a leader of the Lehi group, was fired by orders given by Ben-Gurion from teaching in a high school, and later denied tenure teaching Humanities at the Technion Institute in Haifa. This was probably the most infamous personal case of blackballing the Right in Israel. It was rumored that Professor BenZion Netanyahu, a prominent Revisionist, was denied an academic position at the Hebrew University due to his political views; for lack of a position, he was forced to leave the country to work in the United States.

A standard operating procedure of the Left included removing books that were irritating to its radical dogma. Two come to mind: *Perfidy* (Julian Messner, 1961) by Ben Hecht which raised the suspicion of the Labor Party preferring its affiliates from among Hungarian Jewry for salvation from the Holocaust; and the exceptional work by Joan Peters, *From Time Immemorial* (Harper & Row, 1984), which detailed the origins of the Jewish–Arab conflict in the land and the foreign origin of many "Palestinians." These two books were banished from book stores as the Left padlocked the gates of the free market of ideas.

If you didn't possess a red medical card identifying you as a member of the Histadrut Workers Union and Sick Fund, and you were known as a Revisionist, Herut Party adherent, or Lehi devotee, then your options were limited. Many such people left the country, others lived in poverty. Only in 1977, when Likud led by Menachem Begin took power, were the disaffected finally given recognition and the job market began to open up. In my case, I had a foot in the door but I was not permitted to pass the gate to a normal academic career.

To admit that my political preference was the Right and not the Left, and to which I gave expression in other than the classroom setting and purely academic contexts, assured my virtual excommunication from the scholarly community. My personal life as a Gush Emunim settler in Samaria magnified my political heresy in the eyes of the elites at my beloved Hebrew University. Yet I didn't break any law, I didn't harm any Arab, I didn't tangle with leftists on the hills of the homeland. At Neve Tsuf (Halamish) our family enjoyed an exhilarating and challenging experience of participating in the adventure of building a new settle-ment, with idealistic people sensing that something dramatic though dangerous was taking place in a part of the land where Jews hadn't lived for thousands of years.

This book is not encyclopedic in its scope and detail. Its purpose is to scan the field of persons and their ideas that feature in the Left and Right camps in Israel and abroad. It serves as a handbook that guides one through the thicket of a cultural fissure in the Jewish world, and in Israel above all else. Let this monograph remain as a testimony telling a story, minimally part of a story.

For those readers who until today are perplexed as to whether they are on the Right or the Left, this book will hopefully resolve their dilemma. If it doesn't, then you should read the book a second time.

Alas, we are committed to the solidarity of the Jewish people and the unity of Israeli Jews as an unshakable value never to be squandered in the name of petty politics and ideological quarrels. The integrity of the Jewish people is a sacred trust that our forefathers have bequeathed to us as a tribute to the glorious history of our people. The Right–Left rift must be transcended, somehow. Truth is important and no less is peace.

I must make it clear that this book was not written in order to shame the Left for its arrogance and prejudiced approach toward other views and persons. It was also not motivated with personal vengeance on my part, nor to promote a partisan position for the Right. That the Left strayed from the path of reason and loyalty is clear; while the welfare and security of the state of Israel is my only concern.

I choose to acknowledge R. Emmett Tyrrell Jr., whose singular writing style in *The American Spectator* came my way in the past. I subscribed to that witty and entertaining political journal, and it flew across the ocean all the way to Israel. I was then a conservative, later an Israeli nationalist. The titles of Tyrrell's books, *The Liberal Crack-Up* and *The Conservative Crack-Up*, were inspiring in my choosing the title for this book. I hope RET will not be displeased with my choice.

I thank my publisher, Howard Rotberg founder of Mantua Books, for bringing his courage and convictions to this project, in addition to providing important editorial assistance; and thank Ann McDonald who guided and meticulously prepared the book for publication. For all this I am exceptionally grateful.

To err is human, and I take personal responsibility for any omissions, misrepresentations, and other sins—for which I preemptively apologize—in composing this book.

Mordechai Nisan
Jerusalem, 2018

Chapter One

THE NOBLE LIE AND ISRAEL

We read in Plato's *Republic* that a myth which contains a kernel of truth serves as a great lie in human and political affairs. Socrates explained that the beginning of relying on falsehood starts "by telling children fables, and the fable is, taken as a whole, false, but there is truth in it." A good or efficacious lie always includes some truth. Thus the Big Lie, wrote Eric Voegelin, is subtly transformed into the Great Truth.

Israel as the Jewish national renaissance in political form is in itself a Great Truth. That truth rests on the biblical notion of God's special people, the seed of Abraham and keepers of the Law of Moses who traveled through the tragedies and dramas of their extraordinary history. Jews became Zionists in modern times and energized the wondrous dream of return to the Land of Israel, leading to the establishment of the state of Israel, now 70 years old.

A myth as a transcending tale embedded in collective memory and faith weaves people together: this is the story of the Jewish people in history. A myth combines a truth and a fable, like restoring the Kingdom of David and building a Third Temple in Jerusalem. These images are the stuff of dreams and actions.

In Zionist days, the truth became a myth and the Zionist fable won a most notable rank in the tales of human achievements. Zionism liberated the Jews from exilic reek and mire, and juxtaposed the myth of Zionist history to the eternity of the Jewish saga. Incredible feats were achieved in overcoming the drawbacks of nature—"making the desert bloom"— and blocking the genocidal intents of the Arabs.

Although parading and proving patriotism, Israelis yet craved internationalism and cosmopolitanism. At home socialism became the doctrine of a pseudo-totalitarian utopian vision whose ethic of state responsibility and control of the citizens necessarily denied aspects of human liberty and dignity. Likewise the mantra of peace with the Arabs was transparent proof that Israelis denied reality. Yet, the Great Lie(s) of Zionism, which included more than a kernel of truth, merged with the Great Truth of Israel.

The fanfare of Israeli demagogic personalities served to exhilarate people far and wide, Jews and Gentiles, while intimidating enemies within and beyond the borders of the state. The fable of Israel was a stupendous success story to the credit of capable and innovative elites who, while acquiring fame, continued to pursue policies partly inimical to the fundamental beliefs and interests of the people.

A few examples of ideological deviance and political practice can illustrate our point. David Ben-Gurion, despite his extraordinary role in the Zionist renaissance, was a primary agent of intra–Jewish conflict, demonizing his political opponent Menachem Begin and leaving a legacy of a most profound rift between the Left and the Right in Israel. Ben-Gurion was a statesman without ceasing to be a callous politician. His contributions for better and worse in both roles were inestimable.

Teddy Kollek, the renowned mayor of a united Jerusalem, its builder and advocate after 1967, served ignobly as a liaison between the pre-state semi-official para-military Haganah and the British Mandatory authorities. He spied on Irgun and Lehi fighters, and then turned them over to the foreign occupying regime in Palestine.

Yitzhak Rabin as a prominent Palmach commander carried out an order, under the aegis of the newly-founded Israel Defense Forces, to fire upon the Altalena Irgun arms ship in June 1948 off the coast of Tel Aviv. Sixteen Irgun men on the ship were killed; Begin, to avert a civil war, ordered his Irgunists not to return fire. Later as prime minister, Rabin scathingly demeaned Jewish settlers in Judea and Samaria, and authorized Israeli recognition of the terrorist PLO while handing over parts of the Land of Israel. This surrender was appended to a hope for peace with the Palestinians and the termination of the conflict. This was the essence of the Oslo wager in 1993. Rabin's arch-nemesis Shimon Peres, who succeeded to establish an atomic reactor in Israel with the assistance of France, was a serial saboteur against political rivals. He was also the primary subversive force behind the reprehensible Oslo Accord. His personal fanfare was designed to conceal his political felonies.

The above personalities—Ben-Gurion, Kollek, Rabin, Peres—were, while making remarkable contributions to the Jewish national revival, all affiliated with the Labor Party. Three others are worth adding to the list. Former IDF Chief-of-Staff Haim Bar-Lev opposed Jewish settlement in Judea and Samaria, once offering a military opinion to invalidate an embryonic site (Elon Moreh/Rujeib) in Samaria in 1979; and on another occasion in 1980 blaming young Jews murdered in Hebron for their very presence in the City of the Patriarchs, cut down by Arabs on a Sabbath eve. Chaim Herzog, serving as president of the state of Israel (1983–93), was unrelenting in propagating the primacy of democracy, implying Israel was not a standard and valid democratic state; maybe sporting too much of a Jewish national character. And Golda Meir, prime minster during the 1973 Yom Kippur War, would go to her grave, she said, with pain in her heart for not having prevented or preempted the Arab military assault against Israel on the holiest day of the Hebrew calendar.

Israel is the objective fulfillment of a transcending prophetic promise and vision that has come to fruition in modern times. It is also the partisan enterprise of Jewish individuals who, while advocating, defending, and leading the struggle, at times mangled it for their own diverse and nefarious purposes. Their impulses were not always pure, though the fruit of their labor blossomed and ripened at the appropriate stage of history. Israel is a fable and a myth, but also a Great Truth.

Netanyahu: the Rise of the Right, the Decline of the Left

In 2017, the Right was unrelenting in its effort to balance the Supreme Court membership. It sought to appoint justices who oppose leftist-slanted interventionist judicial activism, and represent sectors of society—the religious, the nationalists, and Sephardic/Oriental Jews—who were always marginalized on the bench. Justice Minister Ayelet Shaked from HaBayit HaYehudi (the Jewish Home Party) was pushing for reform against the entrenched judicial establishment. Two new justices appointed in February 2017, David Mintz and Yael Wilner, were identified as part of the nationalist camp. Some on the Right sensed it was time to accelerate the struggle for a more ideologically diversified Jewish Israel. A year later, in February 2018, another two new justices were chosen, one of whom, Professor Alex Stein dubbed a conservative, was the minister's favored choice. He is known to be an opponent of judicial activism.

But before the final autopsy of the Israeli Left, it is critical to comment briefly on its incremental decline in national politics. The hardcore dogmatic Left, at times Mapam and Meretz, was never the dominant force in the political domain. It was marginal in parliamentary representation, never winning an election. It participated in coalition governments but never formed a government. The Center/Left historically held power, identified as Mapai/Labor, until the Right under the Likud Party rose to preeminence in 1977.

During the forty years from 1977 until 2017, there were only seven years of singular Labor Party rule. From 2009–2018 Likud governed under Prime Minister Benjamin Netanyahu (and not for the first time); interestingly his two immediate prime ministerial predecessors, Ariel Sharon (2001–2005) and Ehud Olmert (2005–2009), were renegade Likud politicians who bolted from the party. Sharon had established Likud in 1973 and Olmert had been one of its early ambitious shining lights.

The landscape of Israeli politics was transformed after 1967 and more visibly so after 1977. The extraordinary military victory and territorial conquests in the Six Day War energized national sentiments into an ideological collage on behalf of Eretz–Israel (the Land of Israel). The heartland of Judea and Samaria ("West Bank") had returned to its historical-biblical sons and daughters and, moreover, its retention was no less a security imperative than it was a spiritual wellspring for identity and pride.

The Left and Center-Left chose, however, to live in denial, parade a policy of pragmatism, and promote peace with the Arabs. Obsessed with pleasing the hostile international community, and bewitched by the mantra of "taking risks for peace," this approach only partially appealed to the Israeli public. On the Palestinian issue, the Labor Party ignored the reality of Arab duplicity and blinded itself from the incompatibilities and fundamental issues that prevented and would prevent full reconciliation and a final resolution of the conflict. Likud, elected to office from 2009, in particular testified that the 1993 Oslo paradigm for Israeli–Palestinian peace and reconciliation was moribund, and the two-state solution a foolhardy and virtually impossible blueprint to execute.

The malady in the Leftist camp in all its parts was seemingly irremediable. When Menachem Begin introduced the Golan Law in the Knesset in December 1981, the Labor Party was divided and perplexed. Avraham Katz-Oz voted in favor, Yossi Sarid against. The early settlement of the Golan after the Six Day War was definitely in line with Labor Party thinking, but when Likud proposed the legal incorporation of the territory by the state of Israel, the leftist strain within the Labor Party took its political toll. The law passed by a majority of 63–21. In political rhyme Foreign Minister Shimon Peres despondently pursued a Jordanian Option to the Palestinian problem in the 1980s, even though the PLO had garnered sweeping authority in the name of the Palestinians earlier in the mid–1970s. Ehud Barak, while tensions and anxieties spread across the region, made a staggering proposal in the 1990s for withdrawal from the Golan Heights; and Yitzhak Rabin came under the fetid fragrance of peace-making with the arch-terrorist Yasser Arafat in 1993. The mainstream leftist outlook was manifestly embodied in the so-called 'centrist' Labor Party which comprised a dangerous coterie of fantasizers reaching for the helm of Israeli power for some years. Peace with Syria and the Palestinians eluded the Left, and Israel was saved from disaster.

Benjamin Netanyahu, elected leader of Likud in 1992, brought a fresh air of realism to the center of political power in Israel. He was young and American–educated, the son a Revisionist Zionist and brother to Yoni who led, but fatally succumbed, in the daring IDF Entebbe hostage rescue operation in 1976. In his first stint as prime minister (1996–99), Netanyahu already encountered inordinate domestic opposition led by the leftist media and the illusionary political establishment. Indeed, he lost in the early successive elections that curtailed his term in office. His declared goal of changing the elites failed dismally. This period already offered a foretaste of the "Deep State" powers which fought the democratic will of the people and its elected Likud leadership.

However, as prime minister once again since 2009, Netanyahu registered impressive successes in six domains, to the chagrin and frustration of the Left:

> ~ Economically, Israel experienced low inflation and low unemployment rates, abundant foreign investment and an excellent international credit status;

~ Ideologically, Israel basically retained the territories of Judea and Samaria despite international pressure, increased the Jewish population with housing construction in settlement communities, and gave political voice to Judea and Samaria/the Golan Heights as integral parts of the country;

~ Diplomatically, Israel extended and strengthened relations in commercial, political, and strategic terms with Asian and Central Asian countries, in Africa, Eastern Europe, and Latin America, while sustaining strong ties with the United States which decided to move its embassy from Tel-Aviv to Jerusalem;

~ Militarily, Israel blocked direct Iranian and Hezbollah proxy threats from Syria while actively destroying arms depots and base sites there;

~ Culturally, Israel began to confront and challenge the "politically-correct" leftist mantras and Ashkenazi prejudices, by demanding loyalty from artists benefiting from state largess, and taking steps to support cultural expressions that had been marginalized and under-represented in the arts;

~ Media, Israel began to diversify information outlets in broadcasting and political commentary, breaking the monolithic leftist domination of the printed and electronic media, and witnessing the appearance of nationalist-oriented journalists.

Netanyahu came to symbolize in his political profile a challenge to the traditional elites in Israel. The leftist elites did not win elections, but their hold on powerful levers of influence in the arts, the judiciary, academia, and the media, was as in the past nonetheless very solid. The elites, the "leftist mafia" in the words of philosopher Moshe Ben-Yosef (Hagar), understood that building a barn and plowing a field are important but only in tandem with establishing a newspaper, opening publishing houses, dominating teachers unions, promoting authors and the arts, investing human resources in the film industry and the theater—because the terrain of ideas and the arena of thought influence the minds of men. The Left strangled voices and views of those other publics and sectors of society denied legitimacy, castigated as unworthy extremists, and debarred from opportunities for advancement.

Netanyahu stood at the crossroads between the people and the elites, and it was the people who gave him the power.

As a result, the elites worked overtime to try and undermine that power, besmirch Netanyahu's integrity, vilify his wife, and accuse him of misdemeanors that, as of 2018, were never verified or proven in a court of law. Character assassination was the weapon used against the Netanyahus. Former General Security Services (GSS/Shabak) chief Carmi Gillon dubbed Netanyahu "an egomaniac who will bring destruction on the state of Israel." Netanyahu was typically maligned as a schemer and plotter, not acknowledged as a politician committed to principles and policies for the welfare of the country. The Left called him a survivor as if he had no higher purpose than holding power. After all, rightists are considered lacking in values and integrity because the Right is, in the stereotypical mangling, full of scoundrels and dim-wits. And yet the Left is hard put to deny the intelligence and experience that Netanyahu possesses and demonstrates in his political rhetoric and diplomatic conduct. The problem is simply that Netanyahu is not a leftist because he is Right. A gross symbolic public sentencing of Netanyahu took the artistic form of a noose around his neck as illustrated in a drawing in 2016 by a student at the Bezalel Art School on the Hebrew University Mount Scopus campus in Jerusalem. The linguistic metaphor contrasted ROPE instead of HOPE, which Netanyahu had killed; so his ritualistic death followed. The artistic community was sinking to the depths of moral petrification. In May 2018, after the Israeli army acting in self-defense killed 62 armed Hamas terrorists in Gaza carrying out violent demonstrations, trying to infiltrate the country and slaughter its Jews, Bezalel students mourned by affixing a memorial wall with the names of the murdered Arabs. Students at Schenkar Fashion College in Tel Aviv, Bezalel's ideological twin, then emulated this display of political treason.

Leftist hope indeed dissolved as Likud won and maintained power from 2009 on. For popular pop-singer Aviv Geffen, whose message was that Israeli youth should not enlist in the army, Likud's 2015 electoral victory was the Nakba (Arabic for "catastrophe") for the so-called Israeli "peace camp."

The Left took to the streets in 2017 in repeated mass demonstrations against Netanyahu's suspected misdemeanors and criminal behavior. Likud was scorned as a party of corrupt politicians. Amnon Lord, writing in *Israel Hayom* on December 15, 2017, spoke of the Left's criminalizing language used against Netanyahu's close associates as "the Balfour [Street] mafia," referring to the location of the Prime Minister's official residence in Jerusalem. By the end of the year, nobody had yet been charged or tried, while in 2018 investigations proceeded with great energy and high public exposure against Netanyahu. He was suspected of bribery charges on a few fronts. Rumors and leaks referred to rather innocuous if not facetious tales of excessive spending on cigars, unpaid bills for an electrician's work, and extravagant spending on take-out food orders. Yet, Saturday night demonstrations protesting the lengthy period of police probes were politically motivated, and the moralistic rhetoric for clean government was visibly exposed in this scurrilous campaign when pro-BDS signs and anti–Zionist slogans were flaunted along with maligning attacks against the prime minister. One demonstrator on Rothschild boulevard in Tel-Aviv carried an image of a guillotine to convey the fate that, he believed, Netanyahu deserved.

But another issue internal to the Right was also critical. While Likud and Netanyahu did favorably well in elections and in forming coalition governments, there is hardly a substantial self-conscious conservative movement in Israel. Over time a number of nationalist/traditional/religious research, educational, artistic, and public institutions were established; but this did not constitute a conservative movement of philosophical substance. The Likud Party as a political entity did not cultivate an organized and coherent cultural agenda. It had succumbed without a fight to the campaign against traditional Jewish culture: it basically lost the culture war it never fought, as illustrated by the exhibitionist and unopposed consensual LGBTQ parades in Tel Aviv and in the holy city of Jerusalem, despite the fact that part of Likud's voting constituencies, though subject to incessant radical propaganda, represented traditional culture regarding sex and marriage, education and religion. Same-sex couples acquired, with Likud consent, public recognition and financial assistance. The Right had adopted the Left's program. Never was Likud interested in challenging the Left on the question of abortion: in Israel it is a permitted and virtually a non-issue. The once differential child allowances allotments that granted families one of whose members had served in the army a greater sum than others was never reinstated by Likud, after the Labor-Left in 1993–94 had decided to unconditionally and universally equalize payments.

Equality became a touchstone of enlightenment and a right undeniable to all citizens, including the Arabs. When Adel Kaadan wanted to build a house in the new Jewish community of Katzir, thus challenging the cultural and historic practice of communities shaped as religiously and ethnically monolithic, the Supreme Court recognized his choice as a citizen to live wherever he chose. The Supreme Court valued equality and human rights as against integral religious/cultural communities. In the Middle East this settlement model was not defamed as apartheid, rather acknowledged as singularly appropriate. Likud was nonetheless averse to taking up the fight of the Jewish residents in Katzir for fear of being demonized as racist. In the judicial revolution launched by Chief Justice Aharon Barak, the prevailing principle was the post-national and post–Zionist ethos of rights for all. The integrity and future of the Jewish state was targeted by the human rights enthusiasts, and Arab provocation was not always understood for the militant tactic it was.

Yet during Netanyahu's tenure as prime minister a popular sensitivity emerged to challenge the Left—not only at the ballot box—but also, and finally, at the nexus of multiple organs of social domination. A conservative counter-culture begged to be born. In Afula, Jewish residents mounted a powerful effort to block Arabs from deceitfully winning rights to build a neighborhood of their own in this Jewish city. It is part of the inter-communal mechanism in Israel and elsewhere that when Arabs move in, non–Arabs feeling uncomfortable move out. So preserving the integrity of a Jewish community seems to demand preventing the entry of Arabs. This is not a sociological law but it can approach the level of a sociological norm.

The Left was screeching and snarling with a vengeance at Likud, the Zionist religious camp, and the settlers, since Netanyahu's 1996 election victory. They couldn't come to terms with the virtue and verdict of democracy and the popular choice. Later, in the 2013 elections, Likud garnered 31 seats, and Labor just 15 (the centrist Yesh Atid party won 19); in 2015, Likud led with 30 to Labor's 24. Central to the swing to the Right was not only Likud outpacing Labor by pluralities, but the consolidation of a rightist bloc that dominated Israeli politics. Alongside Likud were other rightist components as in the 2015 elections: the two Haredi/Ultra–Orthodox parties—Shas and Yahadut HaTorah—were on the Right basically because their voting constituencies were appalled by the Left; and two right-leaning parties led by former Likud stalwarts—

Kulanu headed by Moshe Kahlon, and Yisrael Beitenu headed by Avigdor Lieberman. These parties lined up with Likud in the coalition government in addition to the rightist religious party HaBayit HaYehudi led by Naphtali Bennett. While Likud never came close to garnering half of the Knesset seats, it did cobble together a parliamentary majority to deny the Left the possibility of forming a government. Altogether the coalition partners controlled 66 of the 120 Knesset seats. The contours of this political map could conceivably prevail for many more years to come.

A brief review of election results offers us a clear gauge of the political trends. The Labor Party under its various permutations and nomenclatures experienced a historical decline of far-reaching proportions. From winning 56 Knesset seats in 1969 and 51 in 1973, the party slumped to 44 in 1984 and 1992, then dropped markedly to 26 in 1999, 13 in 2009, rising to 15 in 2013, and improving with 24 in 2015. The far-Left Meretz partner also suffered with a decline from 12 seats in 1992, to 9 in 1996, then 6 in 2013 and just 5 in 2015. There are no other natural party partners to join with Labor in order to form a 60-seat parliamentary majority government. The Arabs are not conventional candidates for this role. This picture contrasts with the situation of Likud which, despite a decline from 43 seats in 1977 to 32 in 1996, and garnering but 30 in 2015, has ideologically compatible partners to form a majority-based coalition government. Likud becomes the axis of a political bloc of parties even when its own electoral performance is not exceptionally impressive, though generally better than the leading center-left party.

However, the Left did not surrender to this political state of affairs. Its dirty rabbit-in-the-hat trick was to warn of the emergence of fascism in Israel. Moshe Negbi, legal commentator conducting a regular radio program, felt himself to be a Paul Revere warning the British were coming. Now the Right was coming, and indeed it had arrived. The Left had no grasp of the zeitgeist. The spirit of the times floated on the air of tradition and religiosity, land and patriotism, individual freedom and capitalism, realism and resolve. What could the socialists and the leftists do to connect with a culture swing that revoked their ideology and disdained their arrogance? The Left resorted to lying about reality, accusing the Right of fomenting a repressive state, denying liberty, crushing freedom. Truth disappeared from their vocabulary and vision. The Left lost whatever they might once have had of integrity and decency, succumbing to a political autism divorced from the real world. They saw demons where none existed except in their wild hallucinations. What they accused the Right of—fascism—was really revelatory of their own inner drive to repulse the rival and drive him out of the political ring. Their frustration and anguish were seemingly boundless.

When Netanyahu wanted to promote a law that defined Israel as a Jewish nation-state or the state of the Jewish people, the Left and their Arab cronies foamed at the mouth. The inherent, essential, and legitimate raison d'être of Israel, and embodied in the language and spirit of the founding declaration from 1948, had become for the wayward post–Zionists a red herring. What was good for Ben-Gurion was now forbidden to Netanyahu. Nonetheless the Knesset passed a first reading of the law on May 1, 2018. Later on July 18, the Knesset passed the final version of the Basic Law: Israel as the Nation-State of the Jewish People by a majority of 62 votes against 55 opposed. Leftists and centrists, post–Zionist Jews and anti–Zionist Arabs, spurned the simple and compelling goal to preserve and enhance the Jewish character of modern Israel.

When Likud Minister of Culture and Sport Miri Regev declared that artists, theater companies, and film-makers, who bashed the state, could not be expected to receive state financial grants for their work, she was strafed with verbal abuse as a commissar of thought-control. One of her targets was the Jaffa Theater where pro–Palestinian sentiments, conveying incitement for terrorism in the poetry of Arab poet Dareen Tatour, beamed from the stage. Miri, basing herself on the law which forbids harmful or disrespectful activities against the state, expected a natural modicum of patriotic spirit, or at a minimum the avoidance of crude anti–Israeli opinions and slurs on the screen and stage. In June 2017, she opposed the highly regarded Arab performer Mira Awad from singing a song by the national Palestinian poet Mahmoud Darwish at a song festival. His legendary hatred of Israel was expressed in a poem he wrote admonishing the Jews—"whose flesh he would eat if he was hungry"—to leave Palestine and die wherever they wish. Regev refused to give legitimacy and exposure to an arch-enemy of the Jewish people and authorize funds for anti-state tirades.

The Left had regularly engaged in arrogant abuse of Likud. An example was singer-entertainer Tikki Dayan who lambasted Likud voters as the "rabble in the food market." Another was Member of Knesset Miki Rosenthal from the (Labor) soi disant Zionist Camp who cynically mocked members of the Likud caucus in May 2017 for their very low

IQs. Former Labor Prime Minister Ehud Barak, addressing the Inter-Disciplinary College at the Herzliya Conference in June 2016, was more vicious yet in charging Likud with having seized power and fomenting fascism. Leftists love democracy, but only when it serves their purpose.

The historic decline of the Left made a thunderous clap in the political heavens. It was full of drama and fury, apocalyptical collapse. They claimed that under Likud Israel would suffer international isolation. War would explode if Israel failed to make peace with the Palestinians. Yes, the Left was unraveling. Rightist Israelis were taunted and disdained as monkeys, as by Hen Barkan, editor of a student rag-sheet *Rosh Patuach*; by Yitzhak Ben-Aharon calling them ignoramuses when they brought Likud to power; and disdained as the lowlifes of the neighborhoods according to Professor Zeev Sternhell of Hebrew University.

The opposite was the case. The rightists got it straight and clear concerning their identity as Jews and proud Israelis; and they had a pristine grasp and understanding of the Arabs as the enemy. The political cards had been dealt differently from what the Left envisioned, and it was unable to adjust to the new hand they were dealt that sent them to the political opposition for many years.

Men, Women, and Others

The extremist branch of the feminist movement is an evolving insurrection to undermine morality, humility, order, and harmony. It is undeniably one of the most sweeping social phenomena in the last hundred years and with vehement rage in the last fifty years. From the politics of the kitchen to the revolution in language, women have made enormous advances. In Israel the public visibility and audibility of women in politics and the media, the arts and academia, the economic market and banking, is ubiquitous and normal. All this is a positive assertion of talent, opportunity, and equity across the board.

Yet rampant liberalism which catalyzed radical feminism extended the war zone far beyond the terrain of gender equality. Feminism traveled sweetly with other happy cults. Pacifism as leftist snobbery was naturally the choice of women, for they loved peace, while men—we know—love war. So the women were to be drawn to leftist politics and choices. Was that not their message to the people? Shulamit Aloni was a trend-setting feminist and pacifist, and others followed. Leftwing Meretz was their natural political home, but it remained a small party, usually ranting and raving against some horrific ill.

Feminism was also a comrade of vegetarianism and its sundry spin-offs. You don't want to slaughter either animals or people. Enter Miki Haimovich, TV presenter, whose claim to fame includes launching a campaign called Meatless Monday. How typical of the feminist crusade and its adjunct causes always telling people how to live their lives.

Beyond feminism lay the murky territory where sexual identity—biologically defined—softened over time by introducing the word gender—socially defined—which became an aspect of personal choice. Tel Aviv, the city of fun, talent, commerce, fashion, and culture, also was home to the extant deviations. People straddling the rainbow prism definitely wanted to live there. After arrogating from God and parents the right to choose one's sex or sexual orientation, a variety of lesbians, homosexuals, and transgenders/transsexuals, assaulted the right of normative society to organize the public space. There arose the challenge to the traditional family—of mother, father and children—with a cauldron of anger against sexual repression along with a gaiety of enthusiasm at the triumph of sexual diversity. The LGBTQ community had taken the high ground to overthrowing the social order whose foundation is the family. It was reported in March 2017 that in Herzliyah, kindergarten and nursery schools would be exposing the children to a mix of gender identities and family combinations. The biological mother-father parental unit was just one of many family options. This war on traditional values was elevated to indoctrination, with mainstream Israeli media serving as the shock troops to assault the walls of normalcy and common sense.

In a television interview in Australia in 2017, MK Merav Michaeli of the Labor Party/Zionist Camp stunned an audience with her radical views. The biological nuclear family engendered by parents, she said, is most dangerous for the children. These parents should not necessarily raise their children, and the state should decide if the parents are worthy of the task. Michaeli, unmarried and childless, could hardly hide her totalitarian philosophy; and added that perhaps children should have more than two parents. This unorthodox incursion into the natural territory of family norms provided a look at the breakdown of Jewish and general values—certainly on the fringes but possibly in the mainstream of leftist thinking in Israel.

Moral confusion marked the era of changing sexual identities and mores. Homosexuality and lesbianism were now publicized and glorified on the streets of Israel, in the media, and in popular celebrations. What was evidently noxious to our grandparents had become normal, no longer baffling, to their grandchildren. A quiet sexual choice could be innocuous, but this had mushroomed into a matter of political warfare and a moral crusade.

One particular public victim of the homosexual campaign to impose its views and condemn anyone who dares challenge this fad was singer Meir Ariel. He criticized this sexual preference, saying in an interview in 1998 that "it's become bon-ton to be a homo." The homo-fascists jeered and cursed him at a rock performance. Their strong point is not tolerance of rival opinions. Ariel died a year later in 1999, but his very special Bob Dylan style music lives on.

This sexual anarchy is historically doomed to fail because, very simply, essentially it enjoys but one-generational longevity. Aside from adoption and surrogate pregnancies, lesbians and homosexuals do not reproduce.

In Israel, these social currents converged with a pugnacious discomfort with the centrality of the army in national culture and life. The Israel Defense Forces (IDF/Tzahal) is really the revolutionary personification of the "new Jew"—strong, virile, and ready to fight. Some saw in the army an incubator for male chauvinism. Truthfully, some senior officers were exposed for sexually exploiting women in uniform. An Israeli male who served in an infantry combat unit is suspected of becoming an oppressor of women. He is seen to be oblivious to female rights and the constructive role of women in society. It follows that the feminist-vegetarian-pacifist and anti-militarist insurrectionary forces oppose large military budgets. They also promote female enlistment in mixed-gender combat units, though women's physical abilities have been proven inferior to those of males. In the past, feminism demanded that female recruits be given entry into the air force as pilots; recently the demand arose for women joining with men in non-segregated tank crews. Could this moral crusade impair military performance?

The radical feminist in Israel and elsewhere is entangled in contradictions. The woman whose body is blessed with the beauty to bring life becomes reluctant to fulfill her own mission. In Israel, the exceptionally radical ones resent the army but demand to penetrate and participate in its ranks. Women agitators demand equality but aspire to rewrite the social code in their image as the superior power figure. Parading pacifism, the campaign has declared war upon anyone and everyone outside of its sectarian borders. It preaches life—but preempts and blocks its manifest message. Promoting feminism and accommodating pornography in the broad cultural domain is a contradiction the radicalized women fail to face. Nudity on the stage of theater, an issue which surfaced in Israel, is a right demanded which otherwise magnifies hedonism and libertinism. Most importantly, its purpose is to bash the traditional sectors in Israeli society. Surely one day the clock of history will turn, and the day will come when this narcissistic rebellion will dissipate and desist. It is one thing to descend into a deviant sexual mode, but quite another to parade this choice in public, with great ostentatiousness to demand government acknowledgment and funding, to claim deviancy as worthy and normalcy, and to furthermore disseminate the message on the radio and television, in the press and literature, and vilify dissension or criticism from any quarter. The negative commandment in the Bible against homosexuality was ignored; the LGBTQ community dictated a positive commandment in the name of liberty, diversity, and pluralism. Those who dared challenge the new dogma in public discourse were slandered. Foucault was definitely correct that in certain situations what can be said and what cannot be said is clearly defined and imposed by the dominant elites.

Some of the most essential dichotomies of life and sex are challenged by a core of seditious warriors. They are unable to differentiate and accept that there is a man and a woman; a normative two-parent family—and this not as a male chauvinist conspiracy against women but as an acknowledgment that the order of life is sacred. Sexual deviancies no longer evoke shame or indignation. It is particularly galling—and this a boisterous theme in Israel—that a couple composed of two men or two women convinces itself that a child of theirs will enjoy a normal emotionally-satisfying upbringing despite the fact that a biological mother or father will be lacking in the child's life. Two fathers cannot compensate for the absence of a mother; two mothers cannot compensate for the absence of a father. Each of the sexes provides the necessary emotional nutrition and role-model necessary for the rearing of a healthy child. The "new family" is a fractured unit resulting from an egocentric decision whose consequences are of no interest to the same-sex couple. This became a non-issue in the public domain in July 2017 when the media mobilized to condemn a court ruling that two men do not have a right to adopt a child. The decision was based on the argument that an adopted child was already emotionally overburdened, and therefore living without the warmth and care of a mother would further disable the child from enjoying a normal childhood. The Likud–led nationalist government, which decidedly lacks a defined conservative agenda, will undoubtedly work to overturn the court ruling. When it comes to aspects of culture, the Right never really challenges the Left at all. In summary, certainly freedom of choice is an essential personal human right to be exercised at will—but with moderation, responsibility, and balance, and in tandem with other values. Some women exuded somewhat excessive dogmatism in what is otherwise a very justified social cause.

The Politics of the Media

Contemporary journalism, wrote Irving Kristol, regards its job as the destruction of all authorities and all institutions. There is a pattern of attack and not just random shots at indiscriminate targets. The media class elite is leftist and somewhat anarchic in orientation. It is uncomfortable with the nation-state ethos of Israel, preferring to conform to international expectations and standards, avoiding distinctions between peoples and cultures. It wants to eliminate discrimination and racism, even though such ills are more imaginary than real social phenomena in Israel. Leftists carry a burden of guilt as manufactured bad conscience. This is what characterizes the *Haaretz* daily newspaper which under the editorship of Gershom Shocken wrote favorably for Jewish intermarriage—a formula not only eliminating Jewish uniqueness but its very peoplehood. His son Amos, loyal to his father's outlook, considered settlements in the territories an anti–Zionist act by a Jewish minority ruling an Arab minority. But that is a false perception of things because the so-called Jewish minority in the territories is part of the overall Jewish majority in Israel. Limiting rights granted the Arab citizen population, as in denying Arabs displaced in the 1948 war from returning to their villages, is not an anti-democratic position but one which understands that democracy presumes that citizens love and defend their country; and the Arabs in Israel do not love or defend their country. This has already been demonstrated by the behavior of the "1948 Arabs" who were astoundingly granted citizenship rights by a country whose existence they opposed from the start—and to this day.

But *Haaretz* maintained its political consistency when, in July 2017, one of the paper's editors, Asaf Ronel, denounced Zionism as apartheid and racism. Another leading newspaper, *Yediot Aharonot,* is only slightly less leftist and only somewhat less sympathetic toward the Palestinians. Prime ministers, like Rabin and Barak, but not Netanyahu, submissively followed the views of *Haaretz* and *Yediot;* thus these two newspapers shared a loathing for Likud leader Benjamin Netanyahu. Journalist Kalman Libskind, writing in *Maariv* in August, 2017, minced no words: from the time Netanyahu was elected in 1996, the media hated him to death.

Israel's overwhelming but not total one-party media, or the media opposition party—for much of it is just that—is as predictable as day follows night. Its dogma is fueled by entrenched leftist bias against the Right and the religious communities. This prejudice became transparent with the beginning of Israeli television broadcasting in 1968. As TV anchor Haim Yavin admitted, the Channel 1 network adopted an antagonistic position to the beginnings of Israeli settlement activity in the newly-conquered/liberated territories, especially in Judea and Samaria. This was probably the kick-start for the ugly wave of anti–Zionism which would wash ashore in Tel Aviv, a particular nationally-detached cultural milieu. Let's leave the Arabs alone and they will leave us alone, Telavivians mused. The clique of broadcasters, reporters, and commentators, shaped political discourse by vilifying settlements and settlers, exposing the infamy of Israeli "occupation," and explaining away Palestinian terrorism and violence as the by-products of collective frustration and economic impoverishment. The Israelis could do no good and the Arabs could do no wrong, in the warped view of the cohorts of the confused and self-incriminating Israeli Israel–bashers. A public survey conducted in 1983, as reported by Moshe Dor in *Maariv,* found that 65 percent of the adult Jewish population believed that the mass media—newspapers, radio, and television—harm national interests. This finding does not strengthen the argument that a free press is a bastion of modern democracy.

It is probably little known abroad that there is state-funded Arabic-language television and radio programming in Israel that covers the gamut of news, entertainment, and more. Of course the Arab population also has full media access to Arabic stations outside of Israel. Hebrew-language TV offers regular and widespread coverage of the Arab sector, Arab opinion, and Palestinian life. To illustrate this, I summarize one evening on Channel 1 dated October 1, 1984 with news items concerning King Hussein of Jordan; East Jerusalem Arabs speaking favorably about the PLO; the suffering endured by Palestinian security prisoners (terrorists!) in a military prison in Nablus; and the strike in the Arab municipal sector and their grievances. Here was a dose of Arab news in Hebrew designed to arouse Jewish sympathy toward Arabs suffering injustices under Israeli rule. About the Jews—their aspirations and problems—not a word. About the settlers there was critical, inaccurate, and demeaning coverage as a rule—they steal Arab land, burn Arab crops, assault Arab youth. Overlooked was the reality that Arabs attack Jews on the roads, uproot their trees and burn their crops, infiltrate and murder Jews in their homes. For fifty years the media both distorted and concealed the true picture in Judea and Samaria with a consistent anti-settler bias.

In the 1980s, the press underwent its own political transformation. The *Maariv* daily moved from the right to the center, *Yediot Aharonot* from the center to the left. *Koteret Rashit* and *Politika* appeared as leftist journals, but then became defunct. The veteran leftist press, *Davar* and *Al-Hamishmar*, ended publication too. *Haaretz* surged to the radical left side of the spectrum, never to regret its heresy.

The favored terminology on news broadcasts was to label the disputed and/or liberated parts of the Land of Israel as the West Bank. This phrase, appropriate perhaps for a financial institution, originated in a distinct political way when the Hashemite Kingdom of Jordan conquered in 1948 and then annexed in 1950 areas west of the Jordan River, from Jenin in the north to Yatta in the south. However, historically—long before the interloper Hashemites who originate from Arabia entered the area—the ancient Israelites/Jews conquered, lived, and flourished. These territories were the core of the biblical land with its Hebrew designation: Judea in the southern area and Samaria in the northern part. The television's purpose in calling the area "West Bank" was to convey its Jordanian connection and imply Israel's illegitimate presence there. The media pounded away at our Jewish national sensibility by employing alien terms for the Hebrew homeland.

The Left's adoption of an anti-settlement and anti-territorial retentionist position served to become the litmus test and precedent for all successive positions adopted on a variety of issues. Radicalism expressed itself in the media's self-defined mission to criticize the government at every turn. It did not see its mandate as merely reporting and informing the public, but rather in very selectively exposing the alleged failures of government and the ills of society that had not been remedied; and so too in ignoring or downsizing irrefutable successes. All this was heavily nuanced to brainwash the public with an anti-nationalist slant. Initially the poison arrows of criticism struck Labor governments, under Eshkol, Meir, and Rabin, and then with ever greater viciousness Likud governments led by Begin and Shamir. When the results of the 1977 general elections were forecast through a voting sample on election day, the facial expression of television presenter Haim Yavin said it all. He was visibly shocked and despondent in reporting that Likud was destined to unexpectedly defeat Labor for the first time in the country's history. Here was the first time that we can say with certitude that the people defeated the media.

From 1977, the entrenchment of leftist thought-control and political prejudice as a fixed feature of the media's message became inexorable. It was so natural a feature that many Israelis, as innocent victims, were hardly aware of it. The weakening of actual leftist political power and popularity drove the Left to an ever higher pitch of howling and bawling. When a given topic is turned into a media and political issue as a clear decision by those dominating the air waves, then you know what the media position will be. It will be consistent and uncompromising, often with a tone of righteous intensity day after day. The media—television, radio, and the printed press—will push its view with the urgency of pontifical infallibility and totalitarian repression. They will sometimes allow a dissenting voice to be thrashed throughout an interview, while deigning liberal balance and fairness on the given issue.

But the people were not fooled. *Monitin* magazine published the results of an opinion poll in 1983 regarding the attitude of Israelis toward the mass media: 65 percent believed the media harm national interests. Israel Medad, representing Ladaat/Israel's Media Watch which monitors the media, reported in October 1999 the fierce opposition of the written press to the Netanyahu government in the months preceding the 1999 elections. No less than 91 percent of the opinion page articles in *Yediot Aharonot* expressed opposition to the Netanyahu government; in *Maariv* the percentage of opposition was 76. In 2017 in particular, Netanyahu was found guilty by the media while investigations of criminal behavior were still being conducted. Netanyahu was lynched on the air waves. He then took a cue from President Donald Trump by scoffing at the Israeli media for twisting facts and reporting fake news.

Chani Luz, a journalist writing in *Hatzofe* in April 2000, reported research results concerning those interviewed on two radio programs, *Inyan Akher* and *Ma Bo'er*. During the period examined the hosts conducted 204 interviews with Knesset members and government ministers from the Ehud Barak Labor–led coalition, and less than 100 from the opposition ranks. More than two-thirds of those interviewed were from the Left. Particular mention is made of those who enjoyed extensive coverage from among whom were the anti–Zionist Arab members of the Knesset—Ahmad Tibi and Azmi Bshaara.

In a study conducted by Abraham Gur in 2008, it was shown that media bias regarding the Oslo Accord and alleged peace process was a proven fact. The number of leftist political participants in television and radio coverage and the time allotted them extended significantly beyond participants from the Right and their allotted time. This was also the case for the Israeli army radio station (*Galatz*). Blatant bias in commentary and analysis of events was proven by this methodological study published by the conservative-nationalist Ariel Center for Policy Research.

In July 2016, the army's radio station under the aegis of the Ministry of Defense reached a new peak in national self-estrangement, and was struck by a type of Stockholm syndrome in broadcasting a program on Mahmoud Darwish. This Palestinian pro-PLO poet was the subject of a serious radiophonic program. The Left was emotionally bonding with the enemy while defending its broadcasting as representing cultural diversity and academic freedom. Here was the enemy within the bowels and entrails of the Israeli security establishment.

Back in 2005, the media as a doctrinaire ideological politburo unanimously supported the "disengagement from the Gaza Strip and northern Samaria" because any and all territorial withdrawals are sweet music to their leftist ears. No major media outlet backed the opponents of withdrawal. The media also stood behind the courts which refused to consider the destruction of the homes of 8,000 Jewish citizens as an infringement of civil rights. The media had a position on this issue which only the blind and deaf would fail to notice. Each news department and political commentary panel endorsed the Sharon government's up-rooting of Israelis who were innocent of any misconduct and were of the highest moral character and national distinction. Journalist Dror Edar wrote ten years after the "disengagement" from Gaza and northern Samaria that Israel still needs pioneers and idealists who love the land. It also needs leaders and media pundits who will understand that fleeing a challenge and confrontation culminates in enemy bellicosity, missile attacks and the abduction of soldiers. The withdrawal also provided the Islamist Hezbollah and Hamas movements the sensation that more war-fare will erode Israel's stamina to persevere. Withdrawal doesn't bring peace, but more warfare, as demonstrated after the 2000 withdrawal from south Lebanon followed by the Second Lebanon War in 2006; and in the case of the withdrawal from all of the Gaza Strip in 2005 in whose aftermath Palestinian aggression compelled Israel to launch major mili-tary operations: Cast Lead in December 2008, Pillar of Defense in November 2012, and Protective Edge in July 2014, all in response to massive Hamas rocket fire at southern Israeli towns and communities within the Green Line borders.

The years of Netanyahu's premiership tenure that began in 2009 provided a number of issues for the media to sign on to with predictable prejudice. Employing appropriate texts, terms, intonation, and moralistic indignation, the media anchor and ancillary personnel joined by care-fully chosen left-leaning studio guests, canonized the singular politically-correct party line:

- ~ profiling President Moshe Katzav as a sex offender before his trial and later opposing his early release from prison;
- ~ protecting Prime Minister Ehud Olmart from public defamation even after he was found guilty of mis-conduct and taking bribes;
- ~ sympathizing with African illegals in the country while refusing to empathize with local Jewish resi-dents in southern Tel Aviv neighborhoods suffering insecurity from this foreign element;
- ~ opposing the Amona settlement in Samaria during a heated national controversy regarding its future;

~ ridiculing Miri Regev, Minister for Culture and Sport, who vigorously confronted leftist tyranny in the arts;

~ belittling PM Netanyahu for his forthright response against Senegal and the Ukraine after passage of United Nations Security Resolution 2334 in December 2016 against Jewish settlements;

~ rebuffing as undemocratic any political or legislative initiatives to contain, curb, and punish clear-cut seditious conduct by Arab members of parliament;

~ advocating mixed male-female military combat units, while dismissing any doubts concerning their appropriateness and effectiveness;

~ defending Arab offenders by concealing their identity as when Arab workers threw rocks from an adjacent building site into a kindergarten in Givatayim full of Jewish children, as the media reported the incident referring to "workers" and ignored their national label;

~ disparaging the Jewish Nation-State Law as discriminatory, if not racist, against the country's non–Jewish minorities.

It's always the same monolithic leftist line. And it's the media which howls about the threat from government interference in the freedom of the media, which itself is a subversive tool for thought-control. Israel would be far more democratic, based on free elections and popular choice, if there were no media apparatchiks snarling and subverting the national will. Here is a novel point in political history: more media, less democracy. The media, especially the three major Israeli television stations, had an agenda which was pursued with steadfast determination all the years. To their relief the nationalist-religious *Arutz 7* radio station was shut down in 2003.

Fortunately, new media outlets like TV channel 20, radio station *Galei Israel*, and also *Radio Yerushalayim*, introduced diversity and political sanity on the airwaves. In the written press the daily *Israel Hayom* and the weekly *Makor Rishon* provided a sympathetic reading of Judaism, Zionism, and Israeli political realism.

The overall unrelenting permanent campaign against Netanyahu was conducted by presenting arbitrary survey findings showing the decline of Likud were elections held at any given point in time—when there was no election in sight, no date and no prognosis for an upcoming election. There was hardly any TV coverage when Netanyahu traveled to West Africa in June 2017 and met with ten state leaders. It was visibly customary for the anti–Netanyahu battle plan to provide but the most minimal media coverage for important visits to Israel by very pro–Israel foreign dignitaries, like Canadian Prime Minister Stephen Harper in 2014. If you liked Netanyahu and admired his political performance, then you were not a friend of the mean-spirited Israeli media. When Indian Prime Minister Narendra Modi visited Israel in July 2017, media coverage was generally more positive. We all watched with pleasure when Netanyahu and Modi greeted one another with a warm hug, and later took a friendly walk in the waters of the Mediterranean Sea. Admittedly India is a favorite site for Israeli youth who travel and hike there in droves year after year.

Media blackout was a favorite way to deny the public a newsworthy item of patriotic sentiment. The example of Yosef Mendelevitch, Israeli Jew and former Soviet Prisoner of Zion until released from an eleven-year sentence in 1981, revealed blatant bias by omission. In December 2017 Mendelvitch was invited to Moscow to receive a Heroism Award in great fanfare and distinction. In Israel the media outlets did not carry the story; Mendelvitch, worthy of honor, while religious and a rightist, did not fit the leftist bill of honor.

The media adepts were unable to mention President Obama and his wife without drooling conspicuously on the screen; nor could they ever mention Donald Trump during the presidential election period in 2016—or after his victory and inauguration—without insinuating a negative opinion of him. One was a blind love affair, the other an endless hate campaign. The media's politics lacked not only balance but also charm and discretion. When President Trump recognized Jerusalem as Israel's capital—a "great moment in Zionist history" said Prime Minister Netanyahu—leftists appeared mournful. The sourpusses are only happy if the Arabs are happy; and Trump did not make them happy. Typically, Ilana Dayan of Channel 2 twice interviewed Barack Obama known for his visceral antipathy to Israel's Likud prime minister.

As noted, opinion polls in Israel consistently showed that most of the population had very little trust in the accuracy of media reporting. This was a statistical finding in the Democracy Institute report for 2016. Normative people were at odds with the media manipulators.

Politics on Israeli television was never far below the surface: even a popular cooking program—*Master Chef*—vibrated with malice toward a skullcap-wearing Samarian settler in October, 2017, even though his participation on the show ought to have been uneventfully normal as one among other contestants. But the mood in the studio was incontestably hostile and spiteful. Niv Ruskin, who moved from anchoring a radio news/interview morning program to be a TV presenter, consistently wore his anti-Right leftist political colors. He would aggressively and rudely interrupt interviewees from the nationalist side while adopting an anti–Likud position. This is the way he treated Amit Haddad, a lawyer representing Sarah Netanyahu, in a brief and rough give-and-take.

Leftists, like Razi Barkai on the army radio station, or Orly Vilnai and Guy Maroz on TV channel 10, never concealed their political preferences. When interviewing a leftist, the conversation was congenial and friendly, and conducted on a first-name basis. If a rightist was interviewed, the tone was generally hostile and the formalities of names was observed. On one occasion in February 2017, Guy Maroz on his morning show hosted a representative from the extreme anti–Zionist B'Tselem organization along with a representative from the nationalist Im Tirtzu group. At one point Maroz turned to the latter guest from Im Tirtzu and said: "I like you even though you are from Im Tirtzu." For Maroz the studio is his, the microphone is his; and declaring his preference will not risk him his job for politicizing his professionalism on the air—maybe even advance him further in his television and public career. As leftist hosts regularly and impolitely interrupted a rightist guest during an interview, it was not surprising that Benjamin Netanyahu publicly complained of the treatment that he endured during Israeli television interviews. The prime minister appropriately cut them to a minimum.

Of particular salience was the pronounced tendency of leftist interviewers to adopt a position when they were presumably expected to pose a question. Likud minister Zeev Elkin, frequently interviewed on television, battled his way to say everything he wanted to say in the face of constant obstructions. It was transparent to a viewer just from watching the anchor's facial expressions if the guest in the studio was a member of the dominant ideological oligarchy, or a wayward stranger who was to be roasted as a hostage or prisoner captive in enemy territory. In an interview that he gave in 2014 in *Makor Rishon*, broadcaster Razi Barkai admitted that the elites in Israel—from the media, the judiciary, academia, and the army—are positioned further left than the average on the political spectrum; meanwhile Israeli society, he admitted, "has moved to the right."

There have been notable personnel additions in the world of the media that give a new resonance of diversity and balance. Major examples included the religious Jews Yair Sherki, Ofer Hadad, Akiva Novick, and Arel Segal—the latter whose army radio program ranked first as the most popular during 2017. No less significant was the delightful appearance as news broadcaster of Shibel Karmi Mansour, a young Druze from Usfiya. A more recent addition was Yishai Shinrav, a young religious Jew living in Revava in Samaria, to host a morning segment on the army station. Avi Ratzon on *Radio Jerusalem*, thoroughly sensible in his commentary, was a breath of fresh air on the air waves. A ray of light began to shine at the end of the long dark leftist tunnel.

The high-handed leftist media thugs do not fail to warn of government intervention that would curtail freedom of expression and opinion—theirs. They eye the Netanyahu government with suspicion and claim for themselves the honorable role of assuring a free media in Israel. But a so-called free media is for them a leftist-dominated media. It would not be an act of repression, but of liberation for the public from a minority tyranny, were the government to trim their political wings. Yet this is exactly what the media fears. Listening to the incessant brainwashing campaigns of Amnon Abramovitz and Raviv Drucker forces us to gasp for free air stifled under a media regime that arrogated the airwaves to promote their hostile views of Israel, Netanyahu, and the nationalist camp. We need government intervention not to stifle the media but to impose the obligation of showing equity and humanity in broadcasting. In 2017 the Likud government voted to close Channel 1 television, and reopen with a more balanced and pluralistic presentation of news and commentary. This could help end eighty years of leftist despotism.

The role of women in television and radio studios emerged with a highly visible and audible profile. In 2016 an impressive 42 percent of reporters, announcers, and presenters in print, radio, and TV were women. There were still a few men scurrying around trying to grab the microphone from the female elite, and some successes were reported. Women virtually came to predominate on the air waves: Yonit Levy, Tamar Ish-Shalom, Gal Gabai, Anat Saragusti, Amalya Dwek, Lucy Aharish, Maya Ziv, Noga Nir Ne'eman, Hila Korach, Sharon Kidon, Dana Weiss, Oshrat Cutler, Rina Matzliah, Dafna Liel, Yael Dan, Estie Perez, Yael Odem, Miri Michaeli, Keren Noybach, Geula Even-Saar, to name many of the starlets. Different was the case of Sivan Rahav Meir, religious in her identity and noticeably congenial in her media/anchor-woman appearances, who carved out a different and non-political persona. She was voted the most popular of all Israeli broadcasters in 2017. Emily Amrousi also added her voice on radio and television for political sanity and Jewish tradition. The prominency of women is unobjectionable, except for the fact that they are exceptionally on the left side of the political spectrum which cannot but compromise their professional, fair, and balanced reporting and commentary. That lethal combination of feminism and leftism conquered the high ground in Israeli society and media, though the sands were perhaps shifting over time.

Anchorwoman Yonit Levy on TV Channel 2 interviewed Prime Minister Netanyahu on April 22, 2010. She virtually demanded that he succumb to President Obama's dictate that all new construction in Jerusalem end. On the same day Orly Vilnai took a metaphoric swipe at Samarian hilltop youth in order to convey empathy with the poor Palestinians. Some of the women commanding the airwaves were never much interested in equality but in raw sock-it-to-him bellicosity.

Other media mutations deserve our attention. An example was the extraordinary political monologue by Assaf Harel on TV channel 10 on February 26, 2017. It was a dirge for the death of the Left. Harel wrapped the corpse in the shrouds of the evil Right. He bemoaned in righteous anger the poverty in Gaza without water, the Israeli theft of Palestinian lands, the shooting at Palestinians, arrests and closures, the virtue of the anti–Zionist Breaking the Silence and B'Tselem organizations, the good work of (so-called) human rights groups . . . dribble on boy. Channel 10 is not publicized as a leftist television network, but as the oracle from on high for enlightening the Israeli people according to unassailable principles and eternal axioms. The Left speaks the truth; but when a rightist opens his mouth, it is at best just his opinion. The late independent-minded poet Aharon Amir castigated the media's ceaseless campaign as filled with whining, despondency, and defeatism. Indeed, the national morale in Israel required a popular slave rebellion against media tyranny that drugged the minds and hearts of decent-minded Israelis.

Against The National Interest: Three Beneficiaries

Among the legendary virtues of Jews is a generosity of spirit to those who in some cases are unworthy of being its fortunate recipients. Helping people whose ideas and behavior undermine the national interest can be, for Israel, an act of foolish pseudo-morality. It is far from moral when you—the giver—will suffer deleterious consequences thereafter.

There are three groups in Israel who do not show interest in the primary concerns of the country, are alienated from the national ethos, refuse to make any solid contribution, and yet enjoy special status in the state whose welfare is of no concern to them. Gratitude is not their habitual virtue.

The Arabs in Israel have advanced since the founding in 1948 in remarkable ways. Briefly: from 150,000 their numbers in 2017 approximated 1.8 million; they have acquired literacy and full educational opportunities, enjoy the array of modern health services, cultivate their collective Arab (–Muslim) identity with state support, and actively participate in the democratic political process. Notwithstanding, Arabs maintain their national-ideological-religious opposition to the right of Israel to exist as a Jewish state. They demand the return of Palestinian refugees with the goal of undermining the Jewish majority demographic reality, and refuse to publicly identify and show allegiance to the flag, anthem, and the struggle of Israel facing constant threat and warfare over the days. Yet despite tensions between Jews and Arabs, and their respective incompatible goals, Israel heaps goodwill and state resources on the Arabs' plate. In 2016, the Netanyahu government decided on a major development plan for the Arab sector to the tune of fifteen billion shekels. This is out of sync with the fact that Arabs vigorously oppose fulfilling military service or even civilian national service. In a survey conducted by the New Wave Research Institute, as reported in *Israel Hayom* on November 24, 2017, only 3 percent of Arab citizens identify as Israelis; 46 percent at the least oppose the existence of a Jewish state; while 85 percent support the return of the 1948 Palestinian refugees to Israel. These malevolent data were sidelined by those commentators who were dazzled by the humbug finding that 73 percent of the Arabs feel a "sense of belonging" to the Jewish state, perhaps in the way a rapist is infatuated with his female victim.

The Africans as migrant laborers in Israel, who snuck across the Sinai border and then demanded refugee status, have partially became part of the tapestry of Israeli society. Tens of thousands of them have moved into the crowded neighborhoods of Tel Aviv, Eilat, Petach Tikva and elsewhere, becoming a scourge to the local population. The purveyors of leftist PC double-speak propaganda defend the Africans as impoverished newcomers to Israel who should enjoy unconditional sympathy and assistance. Many instances of burglary, rape, and murder, have not been sufficient to convince the human rights radicals to choose their own Jewish people above the aliens. Jewish women in southern Tel Aviv complained that the Africans dominate the public domain as theirs, with their loud music, pubs, and businesses, making Israelis feel like strangers in southern Tel Aviv. Israel is a Jewish state, but for the leftists the presence of Africans from Eritrea and Sudan is useful to whittle away at the Zionist vision. The Africans have found work, their children attend schools and kindergartens, and are provided legal advocacy against the immigration authorities whose mission it is to expel the illegals from the country. But expulsion is as infrequent as is snow in summer. The foreigners came from Third World countries to a First World country. But there are laws and borders, and they illegally crossed them. Now there is a physical wall that Prime Minister Netanyahu decided to build to block their entry into the country. Indeed, in 2017 not one illegal African entered the country. With a financial incentive from Israel—$3500 and a plane ticket—some thousands of Sudanese and Eritreans chose to leave Israel. Meanwhile in the southern neighborhoods of Tel Aviv, entire apartment buildings have been taken over by Africans. Elderly Jewish women have been physically assaulted; no Israeli children are in the playgrounds, reported Galit Distel in an exposé on the *nrg* news site on November 12, 2017. Intra–Eritrean violent group clashes on the streets showed the inanity of Israeli policy. The Left charges the Jews with being racist against the Africans, but the Jews living in southern Tel Aviv say they're living in hell. The government decided in early 2018 to arrest infiltrators if they do not decide to leave Israel. Popular opinion was in tune with the government with a two-thirds majority supporting the deportation of the illegal infiltratrors, as reported in a poll cited by *Israel National News* (Feb. 7, 2018). From the point of view of international law, Israel has no obligation to grant illegal migrant workers permanent residence status; and were Israel to do otherwise, the country would be swamped by tens of thousands of more illegals invading the country.

The Haredim/Ultra–Orthodox arrogantly and incorrectly lay claim to their role as preserving the Jewish tradition in modern Israel. It would be more accurate to explain that they have tried to maintain a sentimentalized Galut (Exilic) outlook and way of life, notwithstanding utilizing some modern technological accouterments. Their brand of Judaism is a throwback to an earlier era and place, as they entrench their life as a sectarian community on the margins of Israeli national life. Israeli governments over the years, rather than treating the haredim as the haredim treat the state, chose to pander to this self-serving community, perhaps assuming it would eventually join with the larger society to serve national interests and fill the ranks of the army. However, the haredim choose to stick to their own preferred segregated path, enclosed in their neighborhoods, maintaining their own educational institutions, and nurturing a sub-society with the help of governmental largess. Among themselves, the haredim scoff at what they see as culturally inferior secular Israelis, scorning the ostensibly non-observant Jews as Torah outlaws whose behavior is the cause of Heaven's wrath poured upon Israel through wars and more. All this while the ultra-orthodox sectarians wallow in corruption and criminality—from tax evasion, sexual misdemeanors, to marital Sepharadi–Ashkenazi discrimination. The haredim do not have a good name in the eyes of the Israeli public. Thus, the state's generosity, which is universally equal in Israel through the social welfare apparatus, is totally out of proportion to the lack of reciprocity by the haredim. They do not supply the soldiers and scientists that are essential elements in Israel's national survival; while their exceptional reproduction rate and demographic invasion of many cities and neighborhoods have thrown inter-communal relations into disarray and confrontation. Problems in Arad, Ashdod, Tiberias, and Beit Shemesh, highlight friction between the general public and the ultra-orthodox mob.

Israeli society has followed a path of pluralism and multi-culturalism, not in a way which enriches society but in a way that rigidifies fissures whose long-term impact bodes ill for the country. We await the moment when Israel will cease to be a charitable society and become a full-fledged normal and functioning state enterprise. Her future depends on this.

Meanwhile, the political arena is fractured into partisan parties—the haredi ones in particular—which represent a constituency and not the nation. This would be reasonably tolerable were such parties limited to seats in the legislature—the Knesset—without being partners in coalition governments. The plurality of parties represented in the Knesset due to the proportional representation electoral system, whereby the country acts as one electoral constituency, is good for giving voice to various groups. In short: more views, more chaos, with less national coherency.

The haredi parties which politically lean to the Right have become essential partners with Likud to sustain majority-based rather stable coalition governments. The ultra-orthodox carry the swing-vote: they could at times crown Labor, as in 1992, but they staunchly preferred Likud. Therefore Likud is dependent on them for a right-wing coalition; and this gives the ultra-orthodox the power to squeeze concessions/budgets from Likud whose reign is contingent upon this non–Zionist group.

Anti–Zionism

The discourse of the Left encounters the crisis of the Jewish spirit. The Left audaciously claims that withdrawing from the Land of Israel and territories under Israel's control is an act of high statesmanship. It is even Zionism in full regalia. Three significant withdrawals were recorded: the Oslo–generated pullbacks from 1994–1998 from parts of the Gaza Strip and parts of Judea and Samaria handed a victory to Fatah, the primary faction in the PLO; the 2000 withdrawal from southern Lebanon handed Hezbollah a victory; and the 2005 withdrawal from all of the Gaza Strip (and parts of northern Samaria) gave Hamas in particular a victory. It is astounding that, when Israeli leftism controls the discourse, the media, and the government, nothing outrageous is impossible to market as political wisdom. All the disastrous withdrawals ended in warfare.

Leftist linguistic inversion validated an Orwellian "peace is war" untruth: war against common sense, war against Zionism and Israeli Jews, war against history and its lessons. Oslo launched a war, but the Left adamantly continued to think of Oslo in terms of peace. Thus the converse Orwellian formula was "war is peace" in Palestinian terms. When Israel is no more, there will be peace. The 1,500 murdered Israelis since 1993, from Haifa to Beersheba, especially in Jerusalem and Tel Aviv, were victims of a mindless irresponsible "peace" with the Palestinians, who turned Israel into a public arena of exploding buses, bloodied restaurants, and targeted car attacks on the roads. Confusion in the public dialogue poisoned the mind of innocent citizens. Calling Arabs "local" residents makes barren the native right of Jews to their ancient homeland. Jews are professional agriculturalists, while the Arabs work the land. A television reporter relates that a terrorist from Jenin entered haaretz (the country), limiting that loaded term to pre–1967 Israel without Judea and Samaria. This corruption of traditional concepts is designed to deny Samaria the status of haaretz (the country) and subsume it under the term "territories" as foreign to the Israeli national narrative. The Left hereby redefines the map of our national consciousness and historical memory. The confusion in news items is glaring moreover when it is reported that a certain terrorist cell was uncovered in Judea and Samaria, as if these two areas are one, as if you can simultaneously live in the Galilee and the Negev, or in Florida and Nevada. After fifty years, Judea and Samaria are for many Israelis terra incognita.

Perhaps the most appalling linguistic perversion was when the Labor Party in 2015 renamed its Knesset list "the Zionist Camp." It arrogated the most seminal iconic idea—Zionism—and planted it in a left-wing semi–Zionist party. Generally denigrating settlement construction and flustered by the Nationality Law, the abuse of language parallels the Left's shameless attempt to describe itself as the sane camp (hamachane ha'shafui) in Israeli politics.

In place of the fraudulent culture of peace which has been suffocating intelligent thought and planning, Israel is in need of a culture of war— yes war—to secure its future. This is in accord with the idea that you prepare for war and thus secure the peace.

The anti–Zionism of the Israeli Left and its fellow travelers assumes a variety of forms and discourses. The call for an Israel as a "state of its citizens" necessarily includes anti-Israeli Arabs, and is designed to de-Zionize the Jewish state: first as an idea, then as a political reality. Our only reasonable response available is to tell the truth.

The stench of anti–Judaism like anti–Zionism filled the corridors of power with the Labor victory in 1992. In this spirit Dr. Moshe Granot had opined that studying the Bible—the Jewish Hebrew Bible—corrupts the youth and furnishes them with fascist values. Bible-deniers had surfaced in Israel. For peace-making purposes it was necessary to dilute Jewish identity with its rich storehouse in faith, memory, and literature. Judaism, which posits such fundamentals as God, peoplehood, and land, was considered inimical to peace; so it must be cast to the wind.

Amnon Rubinstein, law professor and politician, bemoaned in *The Zionist Dream Revisited* (Schocken, 1984) the transformation of Zionism's vision of a "secular nation" into a "sacred tribe" with the emergence in the 1970s of a "fundamentalist Judaism." Nationalism replaced humanism (though they are not inimical), and redemption had come in place of peace. Israel, Rubinstein warned, will be a pariah state rather than a normal state. Although his formulations were strident, Rubinstein did identify the cultural dichotomies in Israeli society. But a balance and harmony of the various spiritual and cultural expressions were needed through a combination of tradition and modernity—not a clash of values and visions. This required time and tolerance in the evolving modern Israeli history.

The abandonment of Zionism emerged markedly in the leftist and radicalized Meretz party. When some individual party members favored establishing a Zionist Forum, others rejected the initiative because, for them, Zionism is indeed racism. There both Jewish and Arab members who felt this way, considering that a Zionist affiliation would alienate Palestinian adherents, or potential ones. The idea of a "Jewish" state left its members emotionally cold. Party leader Zahava Gal-On favored canceling the Law of Return which embodies the sacrosanct national right of Jews alone to freely immigrate to Israel. Dr. Tzvia Greenfield, a haredi woman who served briefly as a party Member of Knesset, recalled in an interview in *Makor Rishon* on January 26, 2018, the moment she felt Meretz mutated into a non–Zionist group. This struck her at a party event when most members did not sing the Hatikvah national anthem. Greenfield wrote a book on *The Crash of the Israeli Left* (Yediot Sefarim, 2017) analyzing, among other topics, how the Left had become numb and uncomfortable with the Zionist hope for singular Jewish freedom and sovereignty in the Land.

The Left, Democracy, and Liberalism

The combination of failed policies by the Left with at times indecisive performance by governments on the Right is a baneful feature of Israeli politics. Examples abound of rhetorical rightist ideas that are proposed as policy changes, which yet never come to fruition. Avigdor Lieberman, who heads the secular rightist Israel Beiteinu (Israel is our Home) Party, proposed a very convincing slogan in his election campaigns: "No loyalty, no citizenship." This catch-phrase was directed against the Arabs who enjoy the benefits of citizenship while showing no signs of loyalty or commitment to the Jewish state. Both prior to and following Lieberman's appointment as Minister of Defense in 2016, there was no follow-up legislation or policy reforms to enforce this political idea. His equitable slogan remained hollow. In another rhetorical initiative by the Right, Likud proposed to legislate supervision of the noise level broadcast by the muezzin call to Muslim prayer, especially the early morning blast at 4:00 A.M. Muslims could surely pray freely, but without harassing Jews and others, disrupting their night's sleep. Later Likud, at least for the moment, capitulated to those who argued that the muezzin law would be an infringement of religious liberty and traditional practice.

The last few decades in Israeli politics demonstrated that when the Left declines in its electoral appeal and power, it descends into a terrible rage. If the Left can't rule, then Israel loses its value and importance. Loyalty to Israel ends when the Left begins to disintegrate. A similar set of circumstances appeared in America with the victory of Donald Trump over Hillary Clinton in the 2016 presidential election. The liberals and leftists as virtual anarchists took to the streets and considered the outcome illegitimate. When Likud won its first election in 1977, Labor stalwart Yitzhak Ben Aharon said that the people had made a mistake, implying the illegitimacy of the democratic choice. This is the story of the Left: not, if you can't beat them join them; but if you can't beat them, destroy them. It makes one think that the Left's commitment to democracy is merely circumstantial.

The flip side of Israeli democracy emerges when we inquire whether the political elite wants to rule the people or rather to represent the people. Indirect democracy gives the people the right to choose who will decide national questions in their name: it is the normative form of representative modern democracy wherever democracy, as in Israel, functions. In March 1995 Prime Minister Rabin told a convention of

Reform Rabbis that "what is important is not what the people want. What is important is what is needed for the people." There are times when a Churchill in war can make such a statement for a special historical moment. Israel's prime minister did not seem to know what the people needed when he signed an agreement in 1993 with Yasser Arafat that, rather than bringing peace and security, unleashed waves of Palestinian urban warfare and the bloody murder of hundreds of Israeli citizens.

This explains the inveterate war by the Left against Benjamin Netanyahu. His premiership is anathema to the Left. They have looked in every nook and cranny for signs of corruption, suspicious decisions, excessive personal spending, and arrogant conduct, by which to have him charged, judged, sentenced, and imprisoned. Highlights of rumors, and each with its own story against Netanyahu, relate to moving trucks, staff treatment, personnel appointments, liquor, and submarines. To bring Bibi—Netanyahu's nickname—down, is the Left's political mission. They skirt the democratic process, they nullify the jurisdiction of parliament, and beseech the courts and the police to find him guilty of something, anything. For what is Israel for, and why was it established, if the Left can't rule?

Central to the Left's assault against Likud was raising the specter of a threat to democracy. The Left has not won an election since 1999, but democracy has prevailed and brought the Right to power. Having abandoned an integral vision of a Jewish state as the epitome of Zionist success, and of the Land of Israel as the exclusive homeland of the Jewish people, the Left fell back to become the defender of democracy—which was never endangered except by the Left itself when it held power from 1948 until 1977. It had then fiercely rejected the Right as a legitimate political rival; controlled the media through the Labor-controlled Prime Minister's Office; and used the army as a vehicle of its own party power base. An example of the latter was Ben-Gurion forcing Yigal Allon, from the radical Ahdut Ha-Avoda party, out of the army at the end of the War of Independence. Allon did not fit into the rigorous Mapai ideological fold.

But when out of power, the Left became a clarion voice for the Supreme Court as a pillar of democracy. This point fits the Left's desperate need to undermine Israel's parliamentary democracy by invoking judicial intervention in national and political issues, and controversies.

For the Supreme Court, unelected and elitist, largely Ashkenazi and hewn from a leftist/liberal outlook, was an oligarchical body—appointed by a narrow committee—that did not represent the popular will. When it responded positively to Arab pleas against military decisions regarding security, settlement issues, and land ownership, or to leftist appeals on behalf of illegal African migrant workers, the court revealed its bias. So too when, after the Central Elections Committee barred Arab parties from participating in the 2009 elections because they rejected Israel's national definition as a Jewish state, the Supreme Court overturned the decision. It was an activist court with an arrogant sense of its intellectual superiority and moral standards above those of the elected politicians and their voting constituencies. Minister of Justice Ayelet Shaked from the Bayit HaYehudi Party defied the Supreme Court in a speech in August 2017 on its decision to nullify a government-sponsored law designed to expel illegal African workers, whose numbers approached 40,000 (earlier there were more than 60,000). Shaked charged the court with ignoring Jewish rights while fixated on human rights. Zionism, she pointed out, will not bend before individual rights when the Jewish state has special national tasks—like assuring its Jewish demographic ascendancy. Israel is at war against a multiplicity of Muslim enemies and on many fronts. But the Supreme Court and its leftist camp preferred to direct its efforts against the Jews on the Right. On this subject the Left established the Israel Institute Magazine whose Fall/Winter 2015 issue fulfilled the leftist agenda on the question of "Law and Democracy in Israel." This discourse was code language for the Left to subtly delegitimize the Right and the religious in Israeli politics.

In September, 2017 Chief Justice Miriam Naor refused to participate in a state ceremony celebrating 50 years of Jewish settlement in the liberated areas of Judea and Samaria, the Jordan Valley and the Golan Heights. She considered this a political event, though her decision was a political statement. Of course the pompous leftist judges think they're fooling the public that they are not motivated by their own political agenda. In December 2017, the Supreme Court ordered the Netanyahu government to release and return dead bodies of Hamas terrorists, who were killed when the IDF blew up the "offensive tunnels" constructed under Israeli kibbutzim. Some ephemeral interpretation of the laws of war agitated the frail conscience of the legalists. Israel's political leadership was using this issue to exert pressure on Hamas to release the dead bodies of two Israeli soldiers; the judges were seemingly indifferent to the pain of the parents of the soldiers, while dismissing the policy of Netanyahu toward the terrorist Hamas movement. The un-elected court was usurping power from the elected government of Israel. In the words of Zvi Maor, editor of the *Mida* news site writing in January, 2018, the court had "gone off the rails with regard to its authority."

The Netanyahu government accordingly proposed getting it back on track with a legislative proposal to categorically prescribe parliamentary primacy over the judicial branch. Professor Avraham Diskin, writing in *Israel Hayom* in April 2018, clarified that the Supreme Court practice of nullifying Knesset laws—as three in the years 2013/14/15 regarding the detention of illegal refugee seekers—upsets the balance with the Knesset and is unparalleled in any other democratic state. More ominous is the court's arbitrary practice of voiding the decisions of government: as in annulling the Minister of Interior's order to deny residency status to Hamas political figures in Jerusalem; and in canceling the Minister of Defence's decision to deny entry into Israel of Palestinians from the territories to participate in an alternative and joint memorial ceremony for Israelis and Palestinians as victims of warfare. These are not so much matters of law but opinion; and the court's leftist opinion, manifestly sympathetic to the Arabs, overruled the nationalist position of the Likud–led government.

American author-activist David Horowitz, President of the Freedom Center, explained in his book *Take No Prisoners: The Battle Plan for Defeating the Left* (Regnery Publishing, 2014) that conservatives look at reality and history for lessons in things political. In contrast progressives, like Israeli leftists, live with the delusions of utopianism and self-denial. It was highly unfortunate in this regard that the abstract notion of individual rights—for Arabs and Africans—outweighed in the eyes of the chief justices the national rights of the Jewish people. While Israel has a set of promulgated Basic Laws, it does not have a fully written constitution, as does the United States, which would serve as a single overriding document of governance and fixing the binding relations among the legislature, the executive, and the judiciary. This lacuna leaves the Supreme Court in Israel with extraordinary powers that in practice override those of the other bodies. Parliament is only nominally supreme in Israel's parliamentary democracy.

Of telling significance was the power wielded by the president of the Supreme Court Aharon Barak during his tenure in the years 1995–2006. He advanced the activist revolution of judicial intervention in political decisions taken by the elected government. Radical Arab electoral lists, which as noted were disqualified by a multi-party parliamentary committee, were reinstated by the high court and permitted to participate in elections despite their anti–Jewish State platform. In 2005 Barak's bias was glaring as he blocked the appointment of Professor Ruth Gavison to the court by pointing out that she "has an agenda"—obviously not Aharon Barak's. Gavison indeed, we believe, was against a secular state, supported a secular-religious covenant, while opposing court activism. Barak feared a more democratic and pluralistic coloration to the Supreme Court. He preferred a monolithic body that he could dominate without rivals and dissension. Rule by the court is oligarchy, maybe even judicial despotism; rule by the people is democracy.

When Prime Minister Netanyahu proposed legislating executive primacy over the judicial branch, the court moguls gasped in horror. Esther Hayut, chief justice of the Supreme Court, declared in a speech in mid–April 2018, that democracy is the bulwark for the solidarity of the citizens; and while there is validity in this idea, the essential glue of unity in Israel is grounded in Jewish–Zionist solidarity. The most profound essence and ethos of Israel is the Jewish people and their collective bond. For Hayut, perhaps looking for world approval for the court's defense of human rights and liberties—as for hostile Arabs and alien Africans, her "significant others" live in the West, not Israel. One wonders how important is the Jewish public, its needs, fears, and wellbeing, in the eyes of the judicial mandarins in Jerusalem. Their judicial decisions often suggest that the people count for little.

How it happened that the authentic classical liberalism of John Stuart Mill metastasized into liberal tyranny and thought-control is an intriguing historical question. The idea that a man could sit in his house and engage in whatever personal actions, but without harming another human being, was the basic bedrock of a liberal philosophy. Yet liberalism has metamorphosed in Israel into a very illiberal ideology serving the country's anti-liberal antagonists and enemies.

Two major paths emerged in the domains of culture, society, and politics, in Israel's modern history.

One path led to unbridled individualism, narcissism, moral anarchy, and political relativism. Everything was allowed because nothing was forbidden. Instances of pornography, rape, and violence spread. Israeli society somewhat lost its collective compass, and the bonds that brought people together were stretched, though not severed. Patriotism was frowned upon in certain Israeli cultural circles.

A second path of liberalism in Israel is a more intricate phenomenon to lend itself to a precise explanation. The liberals became totalitarians in dictating what to think, how to feel, what to say and not to say, and how to relate to the Arab "Other." The oppressive agencies told us: that Arafat was a partner for peace; that it was unfortunate that negotiations in the 1990s had not culminated in an agreement whose centerpiece would have been returning the Golan Heights to Syrian rule; that Elor Azarya, a soldier who was charged with killing a wounded terrorist in Hebron in 2016, was guilty of a serious offense; that Sara Netanyahu, who perhaps used small funds from the public treasury for the care of her ailing father, was deserving of being tarred and feathered in the public square; that Obama was a great American president and a great friend of Israel, notwithstanding his disgraceful treatment of Netanyahu and his warm feelings toward Islamic extremism; and that no one but no one with any minimum intelligence would have preferred Donald Trump to Hillary Clinton as a U.S. president. The tyranny of the Left was a major part of the political landscape. These positions were liberal by a soft-hearted definition because they reflected values of peace, forgiveness, and human life. The problem is that they were not examined in the context of policy consequences.

Moreover, liberalism can lead to nihilism and reality-denying as when Israelis on the Left are unwilling to call Arab citizens a potential fifth column and an ever-present foe of the Jewish state. After all, on Israel's Independence Day in May, 2018, Arabs in the north of the country near Atlit paraded Palestinian flags and marched in commemoration of their 1948 Nakba (catastrophe)—while chanting in Arabic that "This is our land. We'll continue our struggle at any price." This event was not an expression of the freedom of opinion and assembly, but an act of sedition and rebellion.

The oxymoronic tension within the term the Zionist Left was generally overlooked in public discussion. The liberal nomenclature had already told us that opening up a high-tech company is an act of Zionism, that providing charity to the poor is an act of Zionism, and that conceding the land of Israel is also an act of Zionism. The corruption of language meant that words and truth had parted company.

Leftist tyranny was at home in the halls of the universities. The universal, open, and pluralistic ethos seemingly vanished—if it had ever existed—from Israeli academia. One tale among many relates to the days after the assassination of PM Yitzhak Rabin in 1995 and the assault upon the religious Zionist Bar-Ilan University because the apparent assassin, a student there, was a religious Zionist. The public defamation of Bar-Ilan led to leftist intellectuals demanding the university's closure. One effect of this repressive Soviet–style atmosphere was the purge of noted military historian Dr. Uri Milstein from the faculty. When his colleague, the nationalist patriot Professor Hillel Weiss, was asked by Milstein why he had not protested, Weiss answered: "I was scared to lose my position."

Academic thuggery had led the late Professor Robert Wistrich of Hebrew University to say that someone who supports the state of Israel cannot expect to enjoy a dazzling career in Israeli academia. Post–Zionism became the leitmotif in the Arts and Humanities faculties. A prominent locale for this ideological deviation was Ben-Gurion University in Beersheba, but there were others. Appropriately, faculty at Ben-Gurion University proudly showed their political colors when they granted a prize to the anti–Zionist NGO Breaking the Silence organization, which concocts charges against soldiers and their treatment of Arabs in the territories. Active abroad, the organization sullies the name of Israel and wins acclaim by the enemies of the Jewish state.

Erez Tadmor, a primary figure in the nationalist Im Tirtzu group, wrote an important book called *Right Voters, Left Rules* (Sella-Meir, 2017), which dissected, analyzed, and cataloged the Left's near-monopolistic domination and exploitation of the levers of power and influence. At the polls, Israel was a democracy; after the elections and regardless of the results, the Left continued to man and manipulate through political-style nepotism the arenas of thought, education, and theater; communications and media; law and justice; the senior state bureaucratic staff; the cultural and artistic discourse; and the broad extra-parliamentary domain. The Supreme Court was a leftist bunker, the electronic media and much of the written press an assault squad, the universities a command center, the State Attorney's Office the inquisitorial board. All the smug and sooty radical saboteurs ganged up on the Jewish state, reveling in criminalizing soldiers and demonizing settlers, fabricating victimized Arabs, sensitizing to Palestinian law-breakers. People from the Right and the religious Zionist camp would uncomfortably distance themselves publicly from so-called extreme rightist views, or just kept quiet and succumb to being third-class citizens in a leftist state. I don't know how the career of television interviewer Haim Etgar was affected when in 2016 he revealed that he moved from the Left to the Right. The popular media personality Avri Gilad was proud to declare his commitment to Zionism which as a self-disclosure does not seem to have harmed his career. Times are changing, it seems. It appeared that to be a positive Israeli in this transformative era placed you on the political Right of the spectrum.

The Left has exercised, to use the term employed by Gramsci, hegemony over Israeli society, culture, and politics, by imposing a system of beliefs on people. The Left did not allow the Right to define itself, to bring itself into existence, to give itself its defining features. The Right was to be a mere creation of leftist imagination. The Right was whatever the Left said: racist, colonialist, fascist, discriminatory, primitive. From Ben-Gurion's crude dismissal of Begin, to Peres and Barak and Herzog scandalously defaming Netanyahu, we see that the Left strove for a political universe devoid of the Right. When the rabid Left booed Minister of Culture Miri Regev at every public event, we learn that not only do they have no manners nor show respect for the government, but they believe that the Right has no right to speak. Not in the Knesset, not in a TV studio interview, not at a dignified cultural festival. And then there was Professor Ariel Hershfeld who admitted, when he served as the artistic director of the International Poets Festival in Jerusalem in 2006, that he didn't invite poetess Hava Pinchas-Cohen because he had a problem with "her political position." Hershfeld considered immoral her position on settlements and other subjects, so he disqualified her professional creativity and achievements. Here we have an example of the political church that the Left in Israel built and religiously attended in the corridors of their minds. We shall further develop this subject later on.

The Left Loves to Hate

Marxism set the doctrinal and emotional tone for ideological hatred of the enemy. The enemy was the capitalist propertied class; socialism, more moderate, also charged the working-class vanguard with the task of hating the wealthy. In Israel's formative pre-state period, there were leftist ideologues like the Marxist Zionist Ber Borochov whose first commitment was to class solidarity and not national solidarity. That meant that a Jewish worker considered an Arab worker his brother-in-arms against a Jewish capitalist. Socialist internationalism defined Israel's Labor Party connections and camaraderie with Palme, Mitterand, Brandt, Kreisky, and other kindred European ideological spirits. This delusionary thinking could not easily be squared with Israeli interests. After all, these European socialist leaders ran to hug Yasser Arafat in the 1970s and recognize the murderous Palestine Liberation Organization as a national liberation movement.

The Israeli Left targeted political forces on the Right side of the spectrum. It inherited its antipathy to the Right, or what might be perceived as the Right, from an early Zionist childhood. One of its first targets was the underground NILI spy network centered in Zichron Yaakov that, in the twilight of Turkish rule in Palestine in the years of World War One, established secret contact with British authorities in the region. This was a dramatic and daring move which proved to be the optimal political choice. The British indeed conquered Palestine and then promised to facilitate the establishment of a national home for the Jewish people. But the dominant leadership in the emerging new Zionist yishuv, socialists in character from the beginning of the twentieth-century and the Second Aliya, who disdained the mannerisms and culture of the agricultural private-propertied moshavot, adamantly opposed the pro–British and partisan maneuver. They legitimately feared a vindictive Ottoman-Turk response. Nevertheless, the nationalist NILI group, demeaned as bourgeoisie non-socialist, was vindicated in the end. This did not in any way dilute the socialists' hatred of the Aharonson family and NILI which was defamed and its members ostracized. A hundred years later the cinders of hatred have not been extinguished. Ehud Ben-Ezer, who manages an active internet site, continues to write about the exploits of NILI to try and secure for it a place of honor and heroism in the annals of Zionist history.

We have the agonizing confession by NILI member Yosef Lishansky who proclaimed that he never betrayed the homeland, meaning he did not reveal any information about NILI operations. He grieved the hatred by a fellow–Jew as stronger than any other hatred. In December 1917 the Turks, who had already exterminated about one million Armenians, put Lishansky to death. There were reports of rejoicing among some in the Hebrew communities in the country.

Ideological hounding and physically attacking the nationalist-rightist groups continued through the years of the British Mandate. Distinct from the Left, the activist Brit Habiryonim and Brit Hahashmonaim set their sights on instructing Hebrew youth to build a militant Torah state. Haganah Beit, which emerged later as Etzel or Irgun in the latter part of the 1930s, was dismissed as marginal and stigmatized as breaking the ranks of Jewish unity. It advocated a vigorous policy against Arab violence, while the staid Jewish Agency/Mapai approach was defined as restraint (havlaga). In the run-up to declaring the state in 1948, Ben-Gurion isolated Menachem Begin and the Irgun patriots from the councils of decision-making and leadership. Moreover, following the highly controversial battle at Deir Yassin just weeks before the declaration of the state, Ben-Gurion chose to condemn the role of the Irgun and went so far as offering an apology to King Abdallah of Jordan.

Without in any way ignoring or diminishing his extraordinary contribution in the founding and leadership of the Jewish state, Ben-Gurion was a rough-and-tough politician. It was conventional for Ben-Gurion, heading Mapai and serving as prime minister, to declare that all Jewish parties were eligible for participation in coalition governments except Herut, the party version of the Revisionist movement and the political successor to the pre-state Irgun. Begin was in the Knesset but never a member of a Ben-Gurion-led government. Yet, in the traumatic days preceding the outbreak of the June 1967 war, when Israel's fate was hanging in the balance, Menachem Begin was invited into the government by Labor Prime Minister Levi Eshkol; this while Begin actually proposed that Ben-Gurion be approached to take over the reins of government in the pre-war crisis days.

Ben-Gurion was pedantic and ruthless in shaping the Israeli national memory in a way to banish the contribution and role of Etzel and Lehi in leading to the founding of the state. Udi Lebel, a sociologist from Ariel University, detailed in *The Road to the Pantheon* (Carmel, 2007) how the Mapai leadership delegitimized the Revisionists and equated them with Nazis and fascists. Following the establishment of Israel, the fallen among the so-called dissident groups were denied recognition, their names were excluded from memorial ceremonies and sites, and living members were denied National Insurance payments for soldiers and pre-state fighters. Ben-Gurion as prime minister went so far as to deny the transfer and burial of Zeev Jabotinsky's remains from the United States where he died in 1940 to the free state of Israel. Only when Levi Eshkol became prime minister was Jabotinsky reinterred in 1964 on Mount Herzl in Jerusalem.

In the following decades the names changed but the mean-spirited and hate-filled motivation of the Left remained the same. The Labor Party, even more its adjunct satellite ideological squads and cultural elites, all trained their sites in the 1970s on the Gush Emunim religious–Zionist settler movement. Author Amos Oz virulently portrayed the group of idealistic patriots as "obtuse and cruel [who] emerged from a dark corner of Judaism . . . guilty of crimes against humanity." The mainstream public was instructed to vilify Rabbi Meir Kahane and his Kach Party as racist. And over the course of time, every party from Likud and further to the Right was scorned by the leftist dogmatists of enlightenment and democracy whose rays of light and sweetness didn't shine on the protagonists from the Right.

Hatred is a most potent emotion—Machiavelli wrote about this—and the Left exploited it against its political and ideological opponents. Open debate between competing political visions was not how things were done in Israel. If debate was open and free, then the Right might convince the public that it and not the Left is a far more sensible and credible political camp. The Left did not only hate the Right; it essentially hated the people. This is the big secret it tried to obscure. Leftist condescension toward the Israelis colored its otherwise vaunted love for the people. It is axiomatic in Marxism and other totalitarian ideologies to believe that the people must be led and guided because it does not have the developed self-consciousness to know what is its own good. For this God gave us the totalitarian Left.

Leftists, adept at character assassination, conventionally denigrate political rivals, as in the practice to heap contempt upon rightists: MK Betzalel Smotrich from the HaBayit HaYehudi Party was demonized as a racist; and Likud Druze Minister of Communications Ayoub Kara was defamed as incompetent. The inability of the Left to conduct a reasonable discussion about ideological principles and political performance is one of the most convincing pieces of evidence that their primary goal is to delegitimize and crush opponents, rather than engage in a civil dialogue. This generally reflects upon the distinct possibility that, alongside the Left's first-class ego, they are enfeebled intellectually by second-class minds.

Palestinian Terrorism

Palestinian nationalism, though it hardly merits such a distinctive definition, was born as a terrorist movement. This is the background from the 1920s for the century-old war by murder, massacre, and ambush against Jewish civilians in their homes, on the roads, in the forests, and in shopping malls. Zionism was born with a vision of construction; the Palestinian campaign is riveted to a delight in destruction of anything Jewish or Israeli. There is no end of the war in sight, nor can there be considering the very special circumstances in its historical and religious origins.

After the appalling and bloody Palestinian terrorist intifadas that erupted in 1987 and 2000, the lone single terrorist intifada struck Israel with savagery and carnage beginning in 2016. In January, an Arab citizen from the village of Arara murdered two Jews in cold blood in a Tel-Aviv restaurant; in June, two Arabs from Yatta in the southern West Bank murdered four Jews in a Tel-Aviv restaurant. Citizens or not, these Palestinians were driven by the same Islamic doctrine to kill Jews "in the path of Allah" and His holy war.

On January 8, 2017, an Arab driving a large truck maliciously slammed into and ran over a group of soldiers who were on an educational tour in southern Jerusalem at the East Talpiot promenade site. In this fatal attack four young soldiers were murdered and thirteen injured. The terror attack ended when a civilian shot the Arab driver, with a few soldiers also shooting to neutralize the terrorist. In this attack against Israelis, another sea of sorrow engulfed the families of the unfortunate victims.

A culture of violence is one mark of the Arab tribe and the Muslim believers in fighting against Jews (and others). In the 1929 pogrom that was a massacre of Jews in Hebron, Arab neighbors-turned-murderers mutilated their bodies in the most vicious way. In the War of Independence, Arabs who killed Jews in the fighting typically mutilated their bodies in a spasm of wild frenzy. Leftist author Yoram Kaniuk, having fought for his people's survival in battles near Jerusalem in the war, mentioned this atrocity in his book *1948* (Yediot Aharonot, 2010).

Israel's response to some savage attack is measured and responsible, resonating self-control in the jungle of warfare. No death penalty is administered, no one is expelled. This response is inadequate, unsatisfactory, carrying no powerful punch to convey deterrence to prevent future atrocities by Arabs, or impose sufficient pain to punish the Arab terrorists. Israel adheres to a police manual strategy: arresting the culprit, assuring his legal defense, convicting him as a criminal, jailing him, yet with attendant privileges like reading materials, family visits, and even opportunities for academic studies.

Israel's context of warfare against terrorism is in reality fraught with the semantics of a religious war by Islamic jihad. The Arab Muslims are not criminals but warriors. Better it would be to expel the Arab and his family rather than imprison him. You need to show that Arab terrorism will produce Arab depopulation from Palestine; and this is the way to deter future terrorists and contain threats to the Jewish population and Israeli public.

Only expulsion can meet the standards of justice and reflect a proper Jewish national reaction to the horrors of Islamic warfare. If you really care, then you would never tolerate the recurrence of Palestinian terrorism, but rather do everything necessary to end it. And it can be ended when the perpetrator will know beforehand that he has signed the expulsion order for his father, mother, grandmother, grandfather, brothers and sisters, sons and daughters, at the moment that he assaults a Jew or an Israeli. Before the sun sets, the entire family has disappeared from Israel, never to set foot again on the sacred soil of this land. For the terrorist murderer himself, capital punishment would certainly be the appropriate step for Israel to take to assure justice and deterrence. But nothing can outdo banishment as the ultimate Palestinian loss.

The Arab–Muslim neighbor next door to the terrorist will thereafter bring the guillotine down close to his son's neck to warn him that his youthful desire for virgins and paradise will send his father to a living hell—uprooted, impoverished, dislocated. This is a formula for an effecttive policy that must be tested and validated.

Israel between East and West

For most of Israel's recent history the country was eager to identify with the West as a strategic, economic, and cultural reference point. Israel wanted to imitate the progressive, liberal, and advanced West which had, nonetheless, been the home of virulent antisemitism, with Europe the locus of Nazism and the Holocaust. But as author Moshe Ben Yosef understood, it was the holocaust of Christian humanism that died in Auschwitz. Thus Zionism relying on the European conscience and morality was not a prudent choice, as history recorded. At times Europe armed the Arabs but boycotted Israel, was obsequious toward the Muslims in promoting peace conditions for the Palestinian–Israeli conflict that threatened the survival of Israel—calling upon her to withdraw from all the territories and agree to a PLO–Palestinian state. The Europeans, trying to absolve themselves of their guilt for Nazism and Fascism, projected unto Israel guilt for occupying Palestinian lands. Were Israel to abjectly submit to the purity and stringency of European dicta about democracy, equality, and humanism; and likewise tremble at European charges of Israeli racism, apartheid, and occupation; all that could together assure that Europe would deal the Jews another holocaust orchestrated with its Muslim allies. It appears that unfinished business is something that still stirs Europe's hopes to play a world role again. Exceptional to this survey was the generosity of spirit that animated the United States to assist Israel on a variety of military and political fronts.

It took some time for Israeli foreign policy to veer toward the East (and Africa) and cultivate ties with Asia, the continent on which Israel herself is situated. Having been vomited out by Europe, it made perfect sense for the Jews to turn toward India, China, Japan, South Korea, and other countries where there was no history of anti–Semitism. Ties between Israel and Asian states in the economic and military domains tightened and relationships soared toward the end of the twentieth-century, and since.

Decades of Western opprobrium of Israel's "occupation" was not the kind of issue which would incite Asian rancor. India has been perennially bogged down with the question of Kashmir and Pakistan's competing claim. Chinese occupation of Tibet has been widely ignored but not by the Tibetan victims. Japan relentlessly claims that Russia occupies some of her islands. Israel's much denigrated "occupation" of the West Bank is merely an inversion of historical Muslim occupation of the Land of Israel.

The Asian peoples were, unlike the European peoples, less pedantic about whether or not Israel adopted the Western version of democracy and egalitarianism; and living in the real world of life and not the imaginary world of ideals, Asians looked at Israel as a partner and not as a punching bag. Israel now had the opportunity to set itself free from the chains with which the West had shackled her. This was an opportunity for national liberation which required a healthy sense of native Jewish identity in the East. After all, the people of Israel are from the East and to which they returned home. Utopias did not make the rounds in the East. Rather a calm and confident sense of identity and rootedness were and are the mark of Asia. It is in this environment that Israel can discover herself, and her friends.

Zionist thinker Martin Buber was particularly sensitive to the Oriental origins and character of the Jewish soul. He considered, as did Ahad Ha'am, that Westernization had sapped the strength of the Jews in Europe, and Zionism required more than just political renewal. Diaspora life had left the Jews in a cultural coma whose remedy would come through the renaissance of the Jews in their ancient homeland. A spiritual renaissance fit the broader Asian landscape and it was there, and not in the West, that afforded the Jews the conditions to rediscover the deeper melodies of their natal origins. This prescription was a fitting script for the patriotic and spiritually oriented Israelis on the political Right.

Chapter Two

History and Culture of Israeli Politics

The hegemony of the Left in Israeli politics featured prominently in the initial period of Zionist history. From its early days, socialism and nationalism were bound together in the revival of Jewish peoplehood on the road to statehood. Marx and Lenin provided an ideological framework and impetus for Jewish socialism in the Land of Israel. Three major components of the socialist creed galvanized the Zionist engine: class struggle, the proletarian dictatorship, and a vision of utopian justice and equality. Along with Gramsci, Marx and Lenin called for a vanguard party in the name of the working class to confront and smash the capitalist bourgeois order. This elite vehicle would mobilize the masses for revolutionary struggle, using pitchforks, knives, and guns, also workers strikes and propagandistic agitation to undermine the status quo, on the road to establishing the rule of the proletariat and the peasants. No reformist or pseudo-bourgeoisie morality would stand in the path of the revolutionary transformation in history from exploitation and oppression to liberation and freedom.

In the Beginning there was Socialism

Socialism, perhaps with a resonance of Jewish roots in a morally rich culture, posits the collective over the individual, and the state above society. Its elite leadership draws upon the assumption that people lack the mental faculties to know what ought to be done and how society should be organized. Like Saint Simon, who believed that the administration of things would replace the government of men; and August Comte who argued that if you cannot disagree in mathematics, then why would you disagree in ethics and social science? A closed mind and a resolute conviction would shape thinking and action.

Nietzsche, who found fault with the idea of equality as a leveling oppression against great people, saw the roots of socialism in Christianity. It represented the revolt of the weak and assured the elimination of strong human virtues. According to Igor Shafarevich, socialism signified the denial of god because now men would control the world in total. The Israeli case certainly fit the equation that identified socialism with secularism, an erosion of Judaism on the scale of personal and national ideas. History would later prove that the drying up of the spiritual wells would eventually lead to the bankruptcy of socialism and the decay of socialist parties in Israel. The spirit always needs refreshing and this can be found in individuality, family, property, culture, and religion. Ultimately people must choose life and not ideas. One very central idea for the kibbutz communal collective was the very radical notion that children would not live with their parents, nor would parents raise their children. This was the task of the doctrinaire ideological educators in the name of strict socialist discipline.

Marxism and its socialist offshoots were virtually at war with Judaism. Jewish socialists charged in a Hebrew proclamation in 1876 that Jews were responsible for pogroms and anti–Semitism directed against the community. Marx himself notoriously did not only hate Jews, though he was a Jew by birth, but he hated God. A culture of totalitarianism and atheism was essential in building the ideological platform for socialism in the Zionist project. A release of tremendous human energy featured prominently in this period.

The socialist idealists who came to the Land of Israel in the early twentieth-century had imbibed from the writings and spirit of a revolutionary tide that was sweeping ashore in Europe and Russia. The Zionists felt an ideological kinship with the struggle of workers elsewhere and grafted internationalist solidarity to the trunk of Jewish nationalism. This duality gave birth to questions of loyalty and coherence in Zionist thinking and would demand clarification as to whether Jews were first members of a revolutionary international class, or of a revolutionary national enterprise. Ben-Gurion, tottering on this fundamental question, would by the 1920s choose the nation before the class.

A secularist ethos characterized much of the Jewish national revival in the historic homeland. Torah Law and rabbinic authority were considered marginal and inessential in building a radically new Jewish pioneering society, full of dynamism and collective purpose. Traditional Judaism was considered by many a burden and a distraction.

A constellation of socialist institutions and instruments of control spread across the new Yishuv community before the founding of Israel. Mapai, established in 1929, served as the quintessential socialist party and came to dominate the political arena until the establishment of the state in 1948, and thereafter until 1977. Mapai stood at the apex of the hegemonic interconnected network. It was the political summit of socialist enterprises: Bank Hapoalim in finance, the daily *Davar* newspaper, the Sifriat Poalim publishing house, the Tnuva agricultural agency, the Solel Boneh construction company, the Histadrut workers union, the Kupat Holim (Sick Fund), the Hagana para-military organization, while controlling the Jewish Agency and the World Zionist Organization. Peter Medding analyzed how the party was identified with the "emerging state" which it dominated from 1935. The Labor movement's power bordered on a near-totalitarian control and repression of competing parties. The Revisionist Movement led by Zeev Jabotinsky was vilified as a fascist deviant, and the Irgun nationalist militia that Menachem Begin led from 1942 was, as intimated earlier, defamed as an aberration from the responsible rule by Mapai in national Zionist politics, and vis-à-vis the British Mandate in Palestine.

It is reasonable to consider in this context Foucault's notion that power must hate and suppress truth. When the role of Betar/Revisionists was eliminated from the historical narrative of the Warsaw Ghetto Uprising in 1943, leaving the glory solely in the brave hands of the socialist-leftist camp, we learned how the role of rewriting history is designed to advance the present and future political status of one side alone.

The domestic enemies of socialism in its classic formulation are family, religion, and property. Although capitalism definitely represents freedom, socialism claimed that freedom is achieved when totalitarian rule from above imposes its structure of domination over individuals. When the individual loses the sense of himself and is submerged in the collectivity, it is then that socialism considers that man has been liberated from egoism as he merges with all mankind. This twisted reasoning, whereby a person must be alienated from himself, identifies freedom with despotism in the socialist turning of truths on their head. For at root socialism represents slavery and not freedom.

The governments led by Prime Minister Ben-Gurion shaped the social and geographic map. East European/Russian Ashkenazim stood at the political summit of power with sparse representation for Oriental/Sephardi Jews. The horrific suspicion that childless European–origin Ashkenazi couples, maybe in Israel and America, abducted through official channels Yemenite babies illustrated the possible extent of radical human engineering manipulations of the Jewish population. In the 1950s, with no prior notice and no preparation, the centralized settlement policy acted deviously to transport North African olim (immigrants) to distant and desolate parts of the Negev desert area to establish new towns—like Dimona, Sderot, and Yeruham. Although there was good reason in this settlement scheme for national development and the dispersion of the population, the mode of its execution was bereft of human sensitivity. State planning and socialist utopianism were standard mechanisms in the collectivist-designed Israeli society.

An additional word about socialism as an economic and social philosophy is necessary. While providing welfare policies for the good of the people in health and educational services, the governing doctrine produced high tax rates, high inflation, and high prices—especially in housing. Tax evasion and a Black Market economy were widespread; Israel was strapped with the burden of requiring foreign aid; and the country was not seen as attractive for foreign investors. An especially ubiquitous hurdle to overcome was the extensive state bureaucracy which choked efficiency and liberty in the nexus between the government and the people. When Likud came to power under Begin, and more so under Netanyahu as Finance Minister and later as prime minister, the government lowered tax rates, inflation fell, and foreign investment boomed. Socialism was a virtually failed economic project, and by the beginning of the twenty-first century the word itself disappeared from public discussion. Free enterprise became the keynote for Israel's economic growth.

That said, a controlling mind-set and governmental apparatus of leftist origins continues to burden the conduct of life in Israel. The Histadrut Empire has much collapsed but it metastasized, at least symbolically, into a legacy of laws and regulations, fines and punishments, penetrating all corners of society. Large interventionist government is everywhere. Israelis feel instinctively that the state owes them every-thing and will take care of them; and the state assumes that responsi-bility in a commendably positive way. This is socialism with a smile. The Ministry of Education decides the curriculum in schools for the entire country, affirmative action is fixed to advance minorities in the public service sector; rabbis decide which marriage is legally permissible and recognized; checking the mechanical functioning of your private car is a mandatory and expensive test on an annual basis; private citizens and the legal authorities are forever disseminating rumors of sex or tax crimes allegedly committed by public personalities whose investigation often ends with no accusations or solid findings—but the career and lives of people are destroyed, as happened with MK Yinon Magal and Minister Silvan Shalom. The Likud Right—a kind of cultural appendage of the Left—never dismantled the system; yet steps in the right liberal-izing direction have been taken.

Socialism is an idea and loving humanity is a chant. It exploited people's passions and was deeply embedded in egoism—what's yours is mine—in the way that sadism claims that you have a right to that which belongs to others. In effect, because human and property rights are tangential and virtually illegitimate in the mindset of socialism, we can perhaps understand how it happens that Israel as a state had the auda-city, unparalleled in history, to violate Jewish private properties and destroy Zionist settlement communities in Yamit in 1982, Gush Katif in 2005, and in other places and times. Ariel Sharon, whose mode of political behavior was quintessentially Mapai–style though he was a leader of Likud, was the primary agent for the crimes against Israeli citizens in 1982 and 2005. The socialist mindset, as analyzed by Paul Johnson and Robert Loewenberg, is a web of narcissism and idealism in which the unbridled authority of government decides that private peo-ple do not have a moral right to their identities or possessions.

Another and more glaring aberration was the pro–Soviet orientation by Mapam and Ahdut Ha-avoda in the 1940s and 1950s, despite the staggering butchery carried out by Joseph Stalin. The Zionists saw in Moscow an additional or alternative communist capital to socialist Jerusalem, or Haifa. Russia as the "second homeland" for some Israelis produced Jewish spies or informers for the Soviet Union, among whom apparently was Moshe Sneh the leader of the Israel Communist Party who in the early 1960s provided the Soviet ambassador in Israel information on the country's nuclear program. Children in HaShomer HaTzair kibbutzim would for many years celebrate the 1917 October Russian Communist Revolution. Journalist Amnon Lord, who after Oslo crossed over from the political Left to the Right, himself experienced this socialist/nihilist ceremony as a young boy. The eradication of a Jewish identity was the objective and the ultimate moral flaw in socialist circles. Behind the attraction to the Soviet Union was the ingrained alienation from the United States and visceral hatred of Western imperialism. Israel was part of the wrong global camp, it might be said, when she adjusted her foreign policy in line with that of the United States.

In the post Six Day War era, the Left took upon itself to guide and teach, defend and propagate, on behalf of the Palestinians in the territories. In losing their national compass the Left became a partner to the Palestinian campaign against Israel. This anti–Zionist deviation produced collaboration and confluence between the Left and the Palestinians, culminating with the Oslo Accords—Arab MKs supporting Rabin's government—which gave the PLO weapons and territory and left the Jews bloodied in the streets of Jerusalem, Tel Aviv, Haifa, and other Israeli cities. Zeev Jabotinsky had a clear vision when he propounded the idea of Khad Ness (single flag)—without socialism but just nationalism for the rebirth and health of the Jewish people in their homeland.

Politics is Everything

Politics was routinized and totalized in the Israeli social reality. Political scientists Dan Horowitz and Moshe Lissak identified the centrality of the political component in Israeli society which in their judgment outweighed the democratic one. There was no constitution to limit the powers of government, while Israeli society was established from the top down by the historical elites who ruled into the 1970s.

The structure of power was comprehensive and monolithic in its political orientation. In the statist economy, the banks and large economic institutions were essentially controlled by the government, or belonged to the state. Media outlets, certainly radio and television, served the purposes of Prime Minister Ben-Gurion and leftist policy purposes. The army, like the police and intelligence services, was politicized from the start with senior appointments going to officers that were networking with the political elite in power. The intellectual motif in academia usually reflected leftism, even more extreme than that of Mapai–led governments. The arts, including music and theater, as with Hanoch Levin's grotesque presentation of Israelis after the 1967 war in Bathtub Queen (*Malkat Ambatya*), belonged to the leftist in-crowd. This became yet more pronounced in the 1970s and thereafter.

The Supreme Court was politicized when left-leaning Chief Justice Aharon Barak and his chosen successor in 2006 Dorit Beinish unilaterally determined that everything is justiciable. The court intervened in government decisions relating to security and military matters, as when it ordered the army not to destroy a home in the Gaza Strip from which the Palestinians shot repeatedly at Israelis traveling on the nearby road. Non-citizen Arab enemies enjoyed property rights that superseded the right of Jews to security and life. In another court decision, a military commander was reprimanded that the route of the security fence built to block terrorist infiltration did not accommodate the Arab villagers at B'ilin, and therefore the route would have to be altered. Menachem Begin had majestically declared that "there were judges in Jerusalem"— perhaps political judges—and the Arabs exploited this situation.

The winds of the Left were also blowing from the Office of the Prosecution with Talia Sasson dealing with the question of the legality— in her opinion the illegality—of settlements. The government's legal adviser Michael Ben Yair in 1996 began a criminal investigation of Minister of Justice Yaakov Ne'eman who Ben Yair called "a fascist." Ne'eman was later exonerated in trial. Many public figures, politicians, and government ministers, almost all of whom from the Right, were victims of the politicization of the judicial apparatus: generals of great standing like Rafael Eitan (Raful) and Avigdor Kahalani were investigated and publicly defamed, but never convicted. This leftist political witch-hunt in persecuting the Right behind the foil of legality wrote volumes on the venomous anti-democratic anti-liberal animus motivating the Left in its war against the nationalist camp.

The Labor Party under Golda Meir, Yitzhak Rabin, and Shimon Peres, was suffering from a Zionist decline, unable to respond positively to the challenge of settling Judea and Samaria. The May 1977 elections provided a moment of democratic enthusiasm, a popular citizen rebellion, with the restoration of a proud Zionist sensibility among the Israeli people. But as Moshe Ben Yosef wrote, the Mapai stalwarts knew how to rule, but Likud was only beginning and haltingly to master the art.

Professor Yonatan Shapiro summarized the first decades in Israel's modern history when there was no healthy democratic political competition. The Labor Party modality in the conduct of politics and economics passed from being a pseudo-science and became a religion. While melodies of socialism and Zionism rang proudly in the public domain, Labor's conduct of government was not only inspired by Marx but evoked as well the deviousness of Machiavelli. In the Israeli political vernacular, the party name Mapai—an acronym for the Hebrew words The Land of Israel Workers Party—gave birth to the popular neologism *Mapainik*. This identified someone who artfully manipulated political situations by subterfuge, at times breaking the rules, for achieving ends that served the party's success and rule. A term of opprobrium—Mapainik—acquired status for the slick and slimy politico. Most everything was permissible; and whatever might cause political damage to the party would be buried and hidden from public view.

Two examples exemplify Mapai ways and gains. Its political machine established and managed the Military Government imposed upon the Arabs in the country from 1949–1966, and all the while the Arabs, subjected to stiff controls and regulations, voted for Mapai and its Arab lists in general elections. The Yom Kippur War of 1973 took place under a failed Mapai leadership, yet in the election soon thereafter the party incredibly was still able to come out ahead of its Likud competitor.

The extraordinary renaissance in Jewish history embodied in the state of Israel unleashed such pride and joy that the inconveniences and deficiencies under Labor rule were ignored or forgiven. The state inaugurated rituals whose powerful message was unifying and meaningful. Such was the case with the two-minute total silence and stand-still when the sirens sounded across the land to signal the beginning of Remembrance Day for the fallen soldiers of the IDF. This moment of popular regimentation and control of memory was a way to manipulate grief. The Israeli people exceedingly identified with this idea, while the state under Labor assured its elevated and untouchable rule in the mythology of politics and war.

Now that we have suggested that democracy can be a ruse, and the political establishment morally hollow in some way, we can better appreciate that the 1992 Basic Law of the Dignity of Man and his Liberty fixed a fundamental principle, or perhaps floated a slogan void of meaning. The democracy/dictatorship coupling has sensitized us to the nimble ambiguity of terms and forms. The idea that the 1992 Law empowered Israelis with more liberties and honor than they previously enjoyed is a highly dubious point. The detention of Israeli citizens without charges or legal representation, moreover under administrative orders and without a trial, is well-known: it has been police practice against Jewish settlement youth in Judea and Samaria before the Basic Law and after. Right-wing activists have been in particular victims of police brutality, governmental abuse, and defamation. When the Israeli Supreme Court adjudicated the case of the Amona settlement in 2017, it issued an order to dismantle the site and expel its residents in the name of presumptive legal property rights that Arabs claimed. The court trampled on any sense of equity and humanity. Just as law is not necessarily equated with justice, so democracy does not automatically square with liberty. The state is designed to serve society, however it may also crush it in the name of tendentious ideals. It was Kenneth Minogue who wrote that "fools are paramount in politics, and there is nothing which they are unable to destroy."

In the period of the Oslo Accord the twin goals of peace and democracy, very plastic and malleable, forged the assault weapons of the Left against the Right. Political tactics of obfuscation and distraction worked with devastating effect to advance the Labor Party's program under Rabin and Peres. The Oslo swindle was plotted in darkness and born in sin, abundant with Israeli hubris and misunderstandings. All this was recently detailed by Avi Shilon in *The Left Wing's Sorrow* (Dvir, 2017) that focuses on the role of Deputy Foreign Minister Yossi Beilin, concerning the collapse of the peace camp. Prime Minister Rabin effectively bribed and manipulated members of Knesset to assure their support in what was a crucial and close vote in which, on September 23, 1993, only 61 members, just one more than half in the legislature, approved the accord. Labor Party MK Yuli Tamir actually admitted that the agreement "was not conceived in a democratic fashion." This transparent conniving could only evolve from ideological fanaticism to plant an intoxicating utopia on earth. Along the way Rabin shattered the rules of democratic politics on a weighty national issue which required special majority support. Peace was a god for atheists more than a statesmanlike goal for politicians.

Democracy was a good thing when it served the benefit of Labor and the Left, but very defective when the Right came out ahead. In July 2000, the Knesset elected Moshe Katsav of the Likud Party and not Labor stalwart Shimon Peres to be the president of Israel. This upset victory aroused the ire and frustration of the Left. Labor Party Knesset speaker Shevah Weiss suggested "that the vote was merely incidental" and did not reflect a substantial political shift. Katsav's 63–57 win was, pro-Labor pundits wrote, the result of political machinations as if politics was the land of the pure. Labor MK Colette Avital explained that ethnic (Oriental/Sephardic) considerations had a role in the electoral results. Democracy is a fine system, but only when your side wins.

All in all, Israel's democracy is exceptionally representative of the diversity of political views in the country. The proportional representation electoral system allows marginal or minority views to gain representation in the Knesset, as lacking concentrated constituency support in any locality does not prevent a party from winning sufficient votes nationally to pass the electoral threshold. It has been common for approximately ten or so parties to gain parliamentary representation. While this situation can be costly to the effort in generating national unity and political consensus, yet many otherwise small groups can play a role in party politics.

But if there was any threat to the fabric of democracy, the Left made sure to warn of the danger the Right posed for the stability of the system. The Left stereotyped extra-parliamentary nationalist groups like Gush Emunim and Zu Artzeinu, certainly Kach, as enemies of the state, charging that they did not accord legitimacy to the elected democratic institutions. But few if any groups were dedicated to the state and their love of the land more than those three vanguard patriotic movements. Their civil protests never crossed the line to sedition and broadly remained within the framework of the law.

The poet Goethe identified chauvinism in the early nineteenth-century as darkening the moral and intellectual skies in Germany. His view was universalist and humanist without any nationalist prejudice even for his own people. But in modern Israel, where nationalism provides the cultural stamp of Jewish identity, the skies shine with the light of renewal and renaissance. Zionism is not a triumphalist-supremacist ideology, rather a doctrine for survival, homecoming, and normalcy in the ancient biblical homeland. Its measure is modest and its tone enhanced by the soft light blue-and-white sea-and-sky national colors.

Democracy and the Arabs

The democratic equation that juxtaposes rights with obligations breaks down in the case of the Arab citizens of Israel. Since 1948, the Arabs have remained indifferent and hostile, pugnacious and militant, in their attitude toward the Jewish state. They were granted citizenship, they vote and are elected to the Knesset, they enjoy a state-funded Arabic school system, they retain full religious freedom, they have radio and television broadcasting in their mother tongue, they have access to higher education, acquire prestigious positions as doctors and professors; yet complain and protest, defame the state, despise Zionism, and castigate Israel as discriminatory and racist. Never was so much given to so many who deserve and appreciate so little. For all of their nagging and whining, Arabs compose 16.5 percent of the university student population, slightly less than their total proportion in the country. A fourth of the doctors in the Rambam Hospital in Haifa are Arabs. In the country as a whole, Arabs constitute 38 percent of the pharmacists and 20 percent of the nurses. This is an impressive profile of an educated and professional Arab sector that services the medical field. But it touches on individual talent and personal advance, not on collective dedication or loyalty to the state.

In 2017 a delegation of Arab dentists from Israel attended a medical course in Bogota, and when each foreign delegation sang their country's national anthem, the "Israelis" refused to sing HaTikvah. They chose to sing an Arab anthem instead. For them, the Jewish state of Israel is not their state; so why, it could be asked, should they be treated as normative Israelis when they reject Israel's normative Jewish character? They don't have to be Israelis, they don't have to sing HaTikvah. Good riddance!

Democracy, that strange and sophisticated concoction, is good for the Arabs. When it became fashionable to call Israel a "Jewish and democratic state," this was a key step forward to calling her a Jewish and "Other" state. For pre-state Zionism, the Arabs were adversaries and enemies; in Israel, the Arabs became fellow-citizens. The impact of this notoriously ludicrous transformation has baffled the Jews ever since. It follows that it was nominally unobjectionable that the exceptionally assertive Arab leadership issued the Democratic Constitution in 2007, which defined Israel as a bilingual and multi-cultural state, traveling the road to becoming a fully bi-national state for Jews and Arabs: two peoples in one state. Not any longer a Jewish state with an Arab minority. Democracy was a fitting ideal with which to expunge the Zionist core from Israel.

The Arabs in Israel adopted the democratic slogan of Israel as "a state of all its citizens." This egalitarian definition for a civic polity was introduced by Azmi Bsharra, Arab intellectual and author, and promoted in defiance of Israel as a Jewish national state. The manipulative fraudulence behind this slogan was exposed when Bsharra, a Member of Knesset who was suspected of engaging in espionage for Hezbollah, the Lebanese Shiite terrorist and Iranian proxy militia, fled Israel in 2007 for fear of being arrested. This seditious citizen was not interested in transforming Israel into a secular democracy, but in launching its political annihilation.

Admittedly, Israel is necessarily a Jewish state based on the hegemony of one group over all others. It is the nation-state of an organic, historical, particular people (as are the nation-states of Japan, Russia, and Ireland). Non–Jews in the Jewish state can choose to accommodate the reality and participate appropriately, while enjoying the benefits of life and citizenship in Israel; or they can vent their venom against Israel and ideologically marginalize themselves by choice. The Druze chose the first path, the Arabs the second. The demagogues screaming "apartheid" against Israel could not deafen us to the incremental changes in Israeli society, which made it a far more inclusive polity for non–Jews over the decades.

But most Arab citizens, indeed 67 percent in a survey released by the Israel Democracy Institute in late 2017, were adamant in continuing to reject the definition of Israel as the Jewish nation-state. That finding was sufficient for a majority of Jewish respondents—58 percent—to call for revoking citizenship from those Arabs. The gap between Jews and Arabs had not been closed despite a shared citizenship in the state of Israel.

Good citizenship demands active participation for the welfare of the state. Aristotle pointed out that while each individual has his personal interests in mind, as a citizen he is committed for the safety of the state as such. This calls for military service which the Arabs have overwhelmingly refused to perform. Israel exists despite the Arabs, and her democracy stretches as far as vigilance allows. In the Knesset Arab members rant and rave against the state and the army, and give voice not only to local grievances but serve as a sounding-board for national Palestinian demands against Israel. Indeed their entire perspective on all issues is Palestinian, never Israeli whatsoever. They never have a good word to say about Israel. Examples of Arab treachery against the state were provided by members of Knesset from the Joint Arab List: Hanin Zoabi was on board the Gaza–bound pro–Palestinian Mavi Marmara ship in 2010, scorning the Israeli commandos who confronted the band of Israel–haters as "murderers;" and Basil Ghattas was found guilty of smuggling cellphones and SIM cards to Palestinian terrorists he visited in an Israeli security prison, that led to his being sentenced to two-year imprisonment. Arab MK Ahmed Tibi was present at the United Nations on November 29, 2017, for the International Day of Solidarity with the Palestinian People; he wasn't about to celebrate that date when, in 1947, the UN resolved that a Jewish state and an Arab state should be established in Palestine. He bewailed the absence of the Arab state while bemoaning the Jewish state in which he was a citizen and parliamentarian no less. The fact of Arab citizens of Israel cajoling with the Palestinian enemy quashed any legitimacy to their place in the country or in the Knesset. Tens of Arabs in Israel were uncovered as expressing their support for ISIS and a few actually left to join their ranks in Syria. Upon their return, Israeli authorities arrested, sentenced, and incarcerated these traitors.

An Arab village in Wadi Ara or the Galilee is conventionally a somewhat sleepy idyllic locale for good folks going about their daily lives. But if something untoward occurs, like police coming to arrest a criminal offender, then a torrent of militant Islamic Palestinian fervor erupts. The mob runs rabid through the streets. This eventuality is always just below the surface of things.

As Arabs, as Palestinians, and as Muslims, these citizens of Israel did not cultivate a proud feeling of solidarity or show a patriotic spirit. Israel was not guilty for being what she was, and the Arabs were not in a way guilty for being what they are. They carry the historical scar of losing land, home, and honor in 1948. The memory and humiliation sting until today. Waiting for the moment for revenge has not weakened their resolve. As such, the democratic regime, despite its fairness and inclusiveness, was unable to bridge the gap that separated Jews from Arabs. Will common sense—just simple common sense—triumph one day to draw a lesson from this situation? Recall that George Orwell wrote that "the heresy of heresies is common sense."

Here is a microcosmic example of Israeli political nonsense. Makbula Nassar, a pro–Palestinian, anti–Zionist Arab woman in Israel, got a job in the Drivers Safety Authority within the Ministry of Transportation. It was later discovered that her personal and political biography included membership in the Association for the Internally Displaced Arabs in Israel. This group promotes the return of both the 1948 refugees and the displaced residents from Israel's War of Independence. Israel as a Jewish state would be undermined were steps taken in the spirit of the association. Ironic that Makbula had a job from the state whose very existence she opposed.

The Arabs on both sides of the Green Line have judicial cronies in Jewish Jerusalem. This is verified when suspected security felons petition the High Court to have their detention reduced and prison sentences delayed or shortened—and this happens; or when the court issues a restraining order to prevent the destruction of illegal construction in Arab villages, in contrast to court intervention ordering the government to destroy Jewish housing suspected of illegal procedures (as occurred in Beit-El, Amona, and Netiv Ha-Avot). In Israel it is possible for a non-citizen—an Arab from the territories—to petition the court in Jerusalem to intervene on his behalf against the elected government of Israel. Even an individual who has no standing with an issue enjoys the freedom to demand redress for an alleged injustice from the court, though he himself is not even directly affected at all by the matter.

And there is another farcical example of Israel's democracy regarding Arab "out of the box" behavior. Arab MKs, who are legally obliged to work within the framework of our political system, provide an example of impertinence, if not of political subversion. They turned to the European Union in 2017 to complain and protest to a foreign body of their being victims of discrimination in Israel. This is flagrantly unacceptable conduct for citizens who serve in the sovereign national parliament as democractically-elected representatives.

The rise of Israel in 1948 was at the expense of the Palestinians: the Jewish triumph was the Arab Nakba (catastrophe). For the Palestinians, the occupation began in 1948 and not 1967. This remains the essence of the national Palestinian consciousness and historic frame of reference. Sakhnin and Arabe in the Galilee (since 1948), as Kalkilya and Dahariya in the West Bank (since 1967), are all victims of occupation and repression according to the Palestinian narrative. Many decades of living within Israel, both for the "internal" Palestinians from 1948 as for the other Palestinians from 1967, have not eroded their cohesive identity as Arabs who lost their patrimony, for which they continue their struggle until today. The scathing example of Arab students at Haifa University in 1999, as in earlier years and since, entails militant demonstrations on campus, raising the PLO flag, chanting "In Blood and Fire We Will Redeem Palestine," and physically attacking Jewish nationalist students and policemen. This event transforms a university into an arena for Palestinian insurrection within and against the Jewish state. The Leftist Forum, in which the post–Zionist historian Professor Ilan Pappe plays an important role, regards Israel as an apartheid state; thus the Forum is a natural ally of the Arab campaign on campus to erode the Jewish and Zionist character of Haifa University. Professor Sammy Smooha, teaching sociology at the same university, conducted an opinion survey of the Arab sector in 2017 to find that only 44 percent agree that Israel should have a Jewish majority. Smooha has written that Israel is an ethnic democracy, thus acknowledging that the place of Arabs in Jewish Israel, certainly the very militant among them, is an anomaly.

A 1994 film called *Istiqlal* (Independence) produced by Jews with state funding presented the steadfast constancy of Arab citizens' revulsion from Israel. The theme deals with the irrelevance of Israel's Independence Day for Arabs and how it resounds with their loss and tragedy. The Arabs feel about the Israeli flag what a Jew would feel about a Nazi flag. The Arab citizen is first a Palestinian, not an Arab Israeli. This admitted, there are many Arabs who have for practical and personal purposes accommodated Israel, living and working comfortably alongside the Jews in the country.

Politically Correct balderdash had its day in silly Zionist musings. Both Jabotinsky and Ben-Gurion addressed serious questions about the Arabs. David Ben-Gurion declared in a paradoxical riddle that it is unthinkable that in a Jewish state an Arab could not become president; or at least be prime minister if a Jew was president, said Jabotinsky. When Ben-Gurion made his statement at a Mapai meeting on December 3, 1947, the idea of a Jewish state had already been proposed by the United Nations in the Partition Resolution just a few days earlier on November 29. Jabotinsky, who died in 1940, announced his liberal commitment when the Arabs were a clear majority of the country's population. Sweet nothings were at times part of the rhetoric Zionists employed; perhaps they even believed what they said.

Yoram Hazony cited in his book *The Jewish State: The Struggle for Israel's Soul* (Basic Books, 2000) lists of Israeli mediators and peace-makers. Authors/intellectuals/professors the likes of Avi Shlaim, Tom Segev, Menachem Brickner, Avishai Margalit, even Eliezer Schweid, proposed adding an Arab symbol to the Israeli flag in order to accommodate Arab sensitivities and universalize the flag's meaning. These Jews trivialized the Arab adversary's faith and beliefs, and those of the Jews as well. An Islamic crescent beside the Star of David would not be sufficient to erase for the Arabs the humiliation of Israel's establishment and their catastrophic loss. Philosopher Martin Buber had opposed the creation of a Jewish state prior to its founding; Professor Asa Kasher opposed the Law of Return. But Ben-Gurion had called Buber and his ilk "national apostates."

Any honest observer of the Israeli situation will recognize the incongruity of a mass of Arabs living in Israel whose existence is anathema to them. Let each side retain its identity, worship its faith, and cherish its memories—and separate one from the other, once and for all. There are countries with a binational or pluralistic ethnic character that enjoy the culture and circumstances for co-existence and power-sharing in a political environment of tolerance and civility. Israel is not such a country and the circumstances of the Jewish–Arab imbroglio do not support true peace and mutual accommodation. Let us not be foolish; let us be realistic.

The Arab leadership generally and the Islamic Movement leaders, like Sheikh Raed Salah, openly show solidarity with Hamas and incite their followers against Israel for allegedly endangering the Aqsa Mosque on the Temple Mount in Jerusalem. Salah has for many years advanced the Arab narrative that the flag of Islam should be hoisted above all lands—including Palestine—that were once under Muslim rule. He has insisted that the Arabs of Israel are victims of discrimination and oppression, and that they must struggle against the insidious cultural process of "Israelization." Strengthening Islamic faith and prayer, and a religious consciousness that Islam in Israel is targeted by the Zionist forces, created an atmosphere of hostility against the state in Arab villages. In mid–July 2017 three Arabs from Umm al-Fahm wielding semi-automatic weapons on the Temple Mount murdered two Israeli policemen. The terrorists were summarily killed and their funeral in Umm al-Fahm, attended by many thousands of rabid Arab youth flying Palestinian flags, gushed with revulsion for Israel. One of the mothers of the Arab murderers distributed candy at the funeral to celebrate her son's courageous deed for saving Al Aqsa from Jewish pollution.

The Palestinians in their self-definition consider themselves Arabs in Israel, but not Israelis. Their Knesset representatives are just "deputies" but not Israeli deputies. The Palestinian discourse forbids any semblance of accommodating Israel's legitimate existence. Israel is the enemy and not the homeland: the homeland is Palestine. The Arab inhabitants are Palestinians. The Israelis are foreign interlopers—indeed for Arab MK Zoabi, in a speech in Dallas in 2017, "the Jews are not a nationality;" indeed Zionism should end and the Palestinian refugees should return back to their villages and homes from before 1948. Israeli democracy was for Zoabi and her comrades a political tool to destroy the Jewish state and turn it into "a democratic secular state." This was a theme that Arafat and other Palestinians had long ago proposed. Democracy was a blessing for the Arabs in Israel: they could freely undermine Israel from within by enjoying the rights of citizens and parliamentarians. The components of the entrenched Palestinian narrative offer no room for true rapprochement between Jews and Arabs. Therefore, the Arab enemy should leave. In history Czechs and Germans could not live together; so too Poles and Germans; like Algerians and French; Zambians and Europeans; Muslims and Hindus in Pakistan; Armenians and Azeris in Azerbaijan. Jews and Arabs in ancient Arabia did not live together as the Muslims expelled al-Yahud. The Arabs could emigrate from Israel, or the Jews could expel them.

Leftist, progressive, and liberal, indoctrination failed to beguile normal Jews. The Guttman Institute for Applied Social Research reported in June 1990 that popular support for transfer of Arabs from Judea, Samaria, and Gaza was a majority opinion among Israelis. Among Likud, rightist, and religious voters, some 75 percent favored a policy that would "cause the Arabs to leave." Israeli youth to the tune of 67 percent supported this position. Three small parties that favored transfer were Kach, HaTehiya, and Moledet, though none of them exist today. But support for transferring or expelling Arabs on both sides of the Green Line from the country continues to enjoy broad support. Polling from

2014 and 2015 conducted by the Pew Research Center found that nearly half of the Jewish respondents favor expelling Arabs from (pre–1967) Israel. Close to 80 percent believe that Jews should receive preferential treatment over non–Jews. While the latter is a compelling statistic, so too the finding that non–Jewish Israelis who willingly stand with the Jews and serve in the military—like the Druze community—should no less than Jews enjoy preferential treatment. Those who give should get; this is not to discriminate against anyone because the path to service and loyalty is open to all. Let us add that over 90 percent of Arab voters in general elections, as in 2015, cast ballots for an Arab electoral list that is anti–Zionist and pro–Palestinian in orientation. Simply put: Arab sympathies and loyalties do not lie with Israel.

This was paraded with political vulgarity in the streets of open and tolerant Tel Aviv on August 11, 2018. Ostensibly protesting the Nation-State Law by demanding justice and equality, 30,000 Arab citizens waved the Palestinian flag and shouted in the name of martyrdom and redemption to liberate Palestine from Israel. By comparison, in an earlier rally against the law, Druze citizens waved the Israeli flag alongside their own communal one.

Even in seemingly non-political matters, the Arabs are a troubling source of crime and major felonies in the country. Statistics released by the Police authorities as reported on November 1, 2017 in *Israel Hayom* newspaper found that the approximate 20 percent Arab proportion of the total population were the cause of 57 percent of murder cases, 59 percent for arson, 45 percent for theft, and 26 percent of drug trafficking crimes. Similar statistics were recorded for 2016. Arab theft of farm animals and damage to agricultural equipment have been widespread and unresolved crimes. This in no way deters Arabs from promoting their narrative of victimology, though in fact Israel's affirmative action pro–Arab policy benefits them far beyond their numbers. This is the case through National Insurance payments, subventions to local government, and turning a blind eye to their unreported incomes. Journalist Akiva Bigman wrote a detailed investigative report on these matters on the *Mida* internet site on November 11, 2014.

I have been consistent in my assessment over the decades that the fundamental incompatibility between the Jews and the Arabs and their respective identities, faiths, and interests in the Land, cannot be overcome. I presented my findings and conclusions on this matter in my book

Israel and the Territories (Turtledove, 1978) and in a subsequent work *Toward a New Israel: The Jewish State and the Arab Question* (AMS, 1992). Neither my analysis nor the reality changed since then. After all we have been through, the Jewish people are not about to succumb to the prejudices and preferences of others, who propose post-national, globalist, and multi-ethnic political views—be they friends or foes.

But as for the pipe dream of Jewish–Arab peace or true Israeli–Palestinian reconciliation, it behooves us to recall the rhythmic Arab proverb: el-adu ma besiir hbiib ila lama yesiir el-himar tabib (the enemy will not become a lover until the donkey becomes a doctor). This is bad news for all the peace-makers and utopian idealists.

Political Vocabulary

In the competition between Right and Left in defining the terminology of political discourse, the Left with their Arab allies have been excessively successful. Nakba (the Palestinian tragedy of 1948) and the right of return (Haq el-Awda) for Palestinian refugees; Zionism as Racism and Israeli Apartheid; Settlements as obstacles to peace and the Occupa-tion—these politically loaded words organize emotions, direct percep-tions, and dictate political positions. Israel and the world have been inundated by Arab terminology marked by a Palestinian discourse. This was the perverse result of the Left's war against Zionism.

The conventional use of the word "democracy" is an indelible victory for the Left. The Left arrogates to itself the right to speak in the name of the people, while the Right is considered to speak in the name of marginal groups outside of the national consensus and whose interests and outlooks conflict with those of the people. Terms like oligarchy and tycoons are used in Israel with the intent to vilify the economic Right and the pilfering capitalists. So too the Left identifies its ideological opponents with crass terms—fanatic, messianic, and extreme. Yitzhak Rabin earned the title of statesman in 1993 when he conceded to the PLO areas of the Land of Israel; and Benjamin Netanyahu in 2009 earned public and media acclaim when he declared his readiness to agree to a Palestinian state. Manipulation of language was absolutely divorced from sound political judgment.

When Netanyahu defeated Shimon Peres in the direct election for prime minister in 1996, Peres offered the explanation that "the Jews de-feated the Israelis." Netanyahu spoke the idiom for a traditional, conservative, nationalist constituency; Peres for a more secular, liberal, and politically concessionary voting population. This dichotomy did not mean Netanyahu's Jews were not Israelis, or that Peres' Israelis were not Jews. It was a question of emphasis, nuance, and identity politics.

Ben-Gurion's terminology in referring to Menachem Begin, the leader of Herut (precursor of Likud), was no less than appalling. In an explosive outburst in a letter he wrote in 1963 to author Haim Gouri, as published by Amnon Lord, Ben-Gurion called Begin "a Hitlerian type" who wants to destroy all the Arabs; and that if he ever comes to power he will dismiss the military command and bring in hoodlums to run the army. Begin was elected in 1977, offered the senior civil service staff to remain in their positions, later offering the Arabs in the territories full autonomy. Ben-Gurion's blind hatred of Begin and the Right was born of ideological stagnation over many generations. Indeed, Ben-Gurion threw a hitlerian epithet at Jabotinsky in the 1930s, calling him Vladimir [his Russian personal name] Hitler!

The Politically Correct imposition of the sole legitimate mode of speech has been particularly evident regarding the Arabs in Israel. Any untoward reference of Arabs immediately raises the specter of racism. It is common that Jews prefer to live in Jewish neighborhoods and if they express their opposition to living alongside Arab neighbors, they are denigrated as racists and extreme nationalists. That Arab villages are extraterritorial enclaves within the Jewish state, where Jews hardly enter and would not live in, is not considered a consequence of Arab racism against Jews. Opinion polls have shown that a majority of Jews believe that Arabs should not be members of the Knesset, because they do not show loyalty to the state and its ethos; this while the Arabs are spared any criticism or defamation for their separatist position. The political vocabulary is weighted against the Right—the nationalists, the patriots, and the religious.

The Arabs in the West Bank sustained their own interpretation of peace different from the Israeli leftists gathered in the fold of the Labor Party and Meretz. The Jewish romanticists would speak of "one land, two peoples" as a stroke of symmetry and equality between historic enemies in one country. In the eyes of Arafat and his fellow Muslim jihadists, there is no Jewish people but only a Jewish religious community; truth be told, the so-called Palestinians are hardly more than "Arabs of

Palestine." And the Arab sense of peace is equated ultimately and necessarily with nothing less than the annihilation of Israel.

The melodious political nonsense of "the two-state solution" should not fool anyone. The Palestinians were never committed to the idea of a Palestinian state alongside Israel. When Edward Said wrote in *The Question of Palestine* (Vintage, 1979) that he favored a Palestinian state, he was honest enough to add that not to have all of Palestine will be a "haunting loss." The Palestinian state idea was the mush and muddle of the Left. Palestinians would now and then throw a political curve ball in the direction of the vacuous slogan, but it was caught only by the dazed Jewish catcher. The Palestinians wanted a revolution and not a state; the liberation of Palestine and not peace with Israel. But the two-state idea would linger on for many years, its calming resonance echoing in diplomatic statements and peace-making quarters. What a waste of time and language! Even Netanyahu embraced the idea in order to ward off the international community.

One particularly blatant corruption of language concerned the terminology used for the fate of settlers whose settlements were destroyed by government decision. Israeli citizens were "evacuated" from their homes and communities, when in fact they were "expelled." People in the Yamit Enclave in 1982 and in Gush Katif in 2005 did not choose to leave. People are evacuated when they are in danger, as when a blazing fire threatens them, and the authorities save the endangered folks and evacuate them to safety. The Israeli settlers were indeed endangered by their own government. They didn't flee from a fire, they were expelled by the state. The laundering of words was designed to portray the government as doing something on behalf of the settlers, and thereby desensitize us to the outrage of a state expelling its good citizens for no compelling reason or fault of their own.

The political vocabulary of the Left never really spoke to the people or for the people. It haughtily spoke with an idealistic and utopian panache that left the people out of the political picture. When government minister Yossi Sarid said in the mid–1990s that "the Oslo Accords were not to blame [for Palestinian terrorism] but the reality was to blame," you could hear the voice of an inspired though angry oracle who would not admit error in judgment and could not come to terms with the political situation, or acknowledge moral responsibility. And when Shimon Peres berated the Right by asking "What is your alternative" [to withdrawal], his arrogance could not sanction a reconsideration of policy after the bloodshed that Oslo unleashed on the streets of Israel. Rabin had also commiserated pitifully that if Israel doesn't stick with the PLO/Fatah on the Oslo track, then Israel would be left with Hamas. The prime minister had difficulty connecting the dots, that Fatah and Hamas differed only in tactics, not in their shared long-term strategic vision.

The abuse of language was marked with the Left incessantly remonstrating on behalf of a political process and the need for political progress on the Israeli–Palestinian track. Movement toward so-called peace was necessary to avoid stagnation, to unhitch the status quo, and begin talks with Palestinian Authority Chairman Mahmoud Abbas after he succeeded Arafat in 2004. If not, tension would escalate and violence would erupt. This was the constant warning and dire forecast emanating from Labor, Meretz, and Peace Now. The Left's call for an Israeli political initiative was code-language for Israeli withdrawal.

The framework of political thought on Oslo was that of moral equivalence: that the Israelis and the Palestinians each had equal rights to freedom and statehood. It was this language which paved the way to exonerate the Palestinians for violating the agreement—not collecting illegal weapons, not ceasing vicious anti–Israeli propaganda, and not ceasing their terrorist rampage against Jews. On the Fatah Facebook page from October 31, 2016, the PLO faction glorified a police officer-turned-terrorist who shot and wounded three Israeli soldiers.

Yet the Left was never wrong and Israel was always guilty. The leftist blunder, if it was ever admitted to, was ironically its Oslo political wrongdoing in 1993 that brought the Right to power in 1996. Isaac Newton's third law of physics pointed out that an action produces a reaction. This is a scientific fact and also a political one. The Left took decisions in the name of and against the opinion of a majority of Israelis; and the people responded against Labor and for Likud. The seesaw of democracy, in Israel as elsewhere, eventually turns in the opposite but right direction.

The Cultural Transformation in Politics

Demographic and cultural changes have altered the political map in Israel and led to the decline of the hegemonic Ashkenazi/European-origin elite power structure. This is a process that began in the 1970s, produced the Likud victory in 1977, and sustained Likud domination of the political arena into the second decade of the twenty-first century. In combination with this development was the growing strength of ultra-orthodox parties who generally participated in coalition governments with Likud and therefore consummated an alliance between the Right and the religious Zionists with Haredi non–Zionists, against Labor and the Left. The emergence of a political Center as an axis on the political map was an elusive challenge that began in 1977 with the appearance of the Da'sh Party, resurfacing in 2013 with Yair Lapid heading the Yesh Atid party.

A majority right-wing electorate emerged in Israel to shape the contours of politics for the upcoming generations. In 1983 Daniel Elazar, president of the Jerusalem Center for Public Affairs, referred to "Israel's New Majority." This new majority was essentially composed of three constituencies in shaping public opinion; changing public discourse would take more time:

> ~ The Sephardi/Oriental/Eastern/North African Jews: leaning clearly in favor of Judaic tradition and identity, religious faith, bound to the Land of Israel and loyal to the state of Israel;
> ~ The Russian/former Soviet Union Jews: patriotic sentiments, tough on security issues, and liberal in economic matters;
> ~ The religious Zionist Jews: ideological believers in the historic and prophetic redemptive process, Torah–committed to the Land of Israel, resolute on security-territorial issues.

These voting blocs could assure—as they have for most of the elections in the last few decades—the rule of the Right. This is no conspiratorial scheme, rather an understanding of demographic trends and the alignment of opinion that favors territorial retention and settlement construction. The Israelis are political hardliners, suspicious of the Arabs, and patriotic in the pinch. The leftist media have been trying to brainwash the people for decades, but election results suggest this has been a failed and vain attempt to indoctrinate proud and vibrant Israelis. Three successive election successes by Netanyahu and Likud, in 2009, 2013, and 2015, illustrated "the power of the people." The democratic game is ultimately played out at the ballot box and not in the television studio.

The decadence of the Left or far-Left, and its dragging Labor into the morass, is really a case-study of privileged class bias gone awry. The wealthy and financially strong middle-class was overwhelmingly Ashkenazi, and it suffered from a malignant arrogance against mainstream lower-class/economically deprived and regionally peripheral/ Likud voters. Israeli youth's turn toward nationalist sentiments was also anathema to the Left. Class has always been an awkward and deceptive factor in national voting patterns; but it is undeniable that the popular rebellion had about it a nuance of class politics.

The three voting blocs of Sephardim, Russians, and the religious, gave birth to sectoral and ethnic parties that otherwise could be seen as fracturing national unity. The Shas party spoke for Sephardim and Yahadut HaTorah for the Ashkenazi haredim; Israel Be-Aliya and Israel Beitainu appealed to Russians and former Soviet Union residents; Mafdal (National Religious Party) and Habayit HaYehudi for the religious. Other small party initiatives failed to pass the electoral threshold and remained out of the Knesset; or entered the Knesset—examples are Tami, HaTehiya, and Moledet—but fell by the wayside thereafter. The Knesset has always been a fractious and rambunctious debating forum.

But a larger question still loomed on the political horizon. The people had fixed a prominent rightist-nationalist imprint on the fabric of Israeli politics, and a conservative cultural sensibility for tradition and country resonated deeply in the soul of the Jewish nation. As R. Emmett Tyrrell Jr. clarified about America, so for Israel the conservatives do not really like to intensely engage in politics. For them, society should run and roll on its inner rhythm as organic capitalism does with the natural exchange of goods and services, and best if government is small and non-intrusive. The Right did not contend effectively to remove the leftist/secular elites from positions and institutions of pervasive influence in the social and cultural, judicial, media, and academic, domains. The Right governed, but the Left continues—for now—to rule. Only time would tell whether democracy would win out in Israel, which also carried within it the subtext of whether Judaism and Zionism would win out. The Right proudly carried the national tradition in its heart and in policy-making, and this gave it the advantage to authentically represent the people's yearnings and identity. Modernity, Westernization, and secularism had not extracted tradition from the Jewish spirit of the Israelis.

We shall review and examine this issue and related subjects in the following chapters.

Chapter Three

THE ISRAELI RIGHT

Settlers and Politicians

The program and the praxis of the Israeli Right after the 1967 Six Day War appeared to take a page from the history of the Zionist Left. Once proud and committed to practical Zionism and the settlement enterprise, the Left had built the country before 1948 and thereafter, establishing agricultural kibbutzim and moshavim in the north and south of the country, building new towns like Arad and Karmiel, in a stirring manifestation of ideological tenacity and national purpose. The Right was ridiculed as speaking and not doing, making declarations for unreasonable political goals rather than laying the foundation for the Jewish National Home on the ground. Menachem Begin indeed was a superb orator, while David Ben-Gurion at the age of 67 went to live in the isolated community Sde Boker in the Negev desert.

After the elections of May 1977, Prime Minister Begin soon visited Kedumim, the first settlement in the heart of the Samarian mountains founded in late 1975. Referring to the biblical site Elon Moreh (Shechem/Nablus), Begin enthusiastically proclaimed that there will be many more Elonei Moreh. Using the plural form of the word, his vision came true in the succeeding years. By 2016 the Local Samarian Council alone represented 35 settlements and 35,000 inhabitants.

So it was the Right that raised the flag of Zionism on high, clung to the Land of Israel, and promoted Jewish settlement. Likud stole the ideological thunder from the Left, and the reaction of the Left was to denigrate the very spirit, energy, and daring, that it itself had sustained in earlier decades. What was acceptable for the leftist geese was unacceptable for the rightest gander.

While the Labor Party had consented and provided basic resources for the beginning of settlement construction in the Golan Heights and the Jordan Valley, the religious nationalists became the major popular force to mobilize Jews to return as a people to the core of the land in Judea and Samaria. The founding of Gush Emunim in 1974 as an agent for organizing and propelling settlement was the touchstone of the new nationalist era. Israel's celebrated satirist Ephraim Kishon wrote his seminal praise of those idealistic youth in an article in *Maariv* on May 4, 1976, titled "The Israel Prize for Gush Emunim," whose love of the homeland would become legendary and politically explosive in challenging Labor under Rabin and Peres, and even Likud prime ministers thereafter. The settlement map would change the politics of Israel and set up a barrier to the possibility of a Palestinian state. There seemed to be a direct correspondence between the expansion of Jewish settlement and Likud's hold on power. The approximate 400,000 Israelis in 2015 living across the Green Line in over 150 towns and communities was a human reality in tandem with the political reality of repeated Likud victories under Benjamin Netanyahu. Yet notwithstanding, over the years the settler community and its public supporters repeatedly encountered governments limiting and opposing and even threatening to uproot established settlements. It was Likud under Menachem Begin that destroyed the northern Sinai Yamit salient villages in 1982 in the context of the Israeli–Egyptian peace treaty; and Likud–elected Ariel Sharon did likewise, and for no compelling political reason, in the northern Negev Gush Katif bloc in 2005. Earlier in 1998, under Netanyahu, Likud destroyed four Jewish communities in Samaria for Oslo–related political nonsense; and then Amona in 2017 for ostensibly legal reasons. Even when the Right was in power the settlement enterprise, which had been the historical vehicle for the rise of the Likud, was in mortal danger, threatened by friends and foes alike.

It had been in an atmosphere of Palestinian terrorism that a Jewish Underground was surreptitiously formed in 1980 by twenty-seven young men, overwhelmingly residents in Judea and Samaria. It was the murder of six young Jews in Hebron on May 2 that year that consolidated the group which set out to exact retribution. The concerted response took place on June 2, with the bombing and maiming of three West Bank mayors, in Ramallah, El-Bireh, and Nablus. In 1984 all 27 members of the underground were uncovered, arrested, tried, and given prison sentences. The Jewish Underground was born in frustration at the deteriorating security situation in Judea and Samaria. The members took action. They were overwhelmingly denounced by the general and religious community as violent law-breakers who violated state authority. The entire episode evoked debate and controversy, but the settlement enterprise continued to expand, and the members of the underground were rehabilitated in the public eye years later.

The political spinoff from the dynamic settlement enterprise accelerated in the face of leftist derision and opposition. Demonstrations and large gatherings, even hunger strikes, were part of the arsenal of the settlers' struggle to pressure successive governments to further advance construction in Judea and Samaria. When ten core settlement groups unilaterally set up new community outposts in the autumn of 1977, this dramatic initiative was designed to compel a wavering Likud government led by Menachem Begin to acknowledge the grass roots momentum; and when a mass pro-settlement demonstration took place in Tel Aviv in July 2000, it was for the purpose of pressuring the Labor government of Ehud Barak not to yield land to the Palestinians.

Successes and defeats marked the record of the settlement movement since 1967. Despite domestic and international condemnation, great demographic strides were made. The town of Maale Adumim with its 40,000 residents, just a few miles east of Jerusalem, represented a strategic gain for territorial retention. President George W. Bush, in recognizing in 2004 the political reality of settlement blocs, granted Israel a major policy boost. Yet, as noted, great disappointment and sadness struck when the Israeli–Egyptian agreement of 1979 included complete withdrawal from the Sinai Peninsula and the dismantlement of Israeli communities; and so too when the Cairo Agreement of 1994 and Oslo 2 in 1995 led to withdrawal from parts of Judea and Samaria, specifically seven cities—Jenin, Nablus/Shechem, Tulkarem, Kalkilya, Ramallah, Bethlehem and (most of) Hebron—which came under Palestinian rule. Nevertheless, fifty years after the June 1967 War the ledger was conclusively positive. There was no Zionist justification or political compensation for a delusionary peace.

Voices on the Right

Rightists-nationalists have an inherent and historical feeling that they are victims of discrimination and exclusion in Israel, and that their voices are silenced. They operated from weakness and their influence was minor. However, they evinced faith in their cause and energy in their resolve, despite being muffled and censored by the illiberal Left.

One early right-nationalist initiative came from the Movement for Greater Israel (mistranslated from the Hebrew Eretz-Israel Ha-Shleima) that was formed in July 1967. It promoted Jewish settlement and retention of the territories captured in the Six Day War. Its founders were a mixture of Labor Zionists and Revisionists, distinguished writers and poets like Natan Alterman, Aharon Amir, Haim Gouri, Eliezer Livneh, Moshe Shamir, Zev Vilnay, Uri Zvi Greenberg—who for the sake of the Zionist revolution was ready "to turn his pen into a hammer;" also Nobel Laureate Shmuel Yosef Agnon, Zvi Shiloah, Israel Eldad, and others from the security/military fields. They brought exceptional talent and authority to the campaign for Eretz-Israel. Politically the group dissolved, yet as individuals each left his mark.

Here, then, is a detailed though necessarily incomplete roster of the "good guys" on the Right who campaigned, demonstrated, and wrote on behalf of a strong Jewish state, Israeli rule in Judea and Samaria, Jewish settlement—and against a Palestinian state, territorial withdrawal, dismantlement of settlements, and dividing the capital of Jerusalem.

Recording those individuals and organizations that stood with the Jewish state is a moral and historical obligation for future generations. It is a matter of pride in their dedication to heritage and country. While some of the people listed have passed away and their memory be blessed, others are still active on the right side of Israeli affairs.

~ **On Jerusalem**
~ The Movement of the Temple Mount Faithful founded by Gershon Solomon promoted the right of Jews to pray on the Temple Mount in Jerusalem and advance toward the construction of the Third Temple; Rabbi Israel Ariel founded the Temple Institute; Ateret Cohanim, a yeshiva Jewish academy engaged in Torah study, also active in real estate purchases to "redeem" land in East Jerusalem with funding from Irving Moskowitz; Yibane Ha-Mikdash (The Movement for Building the Temple) founded by Rabbi Yosef Elboim; Chaim Silberstein, Director of Keep Jerusalem [Im Eshkachech Yerushalayim], for the unity of

Jerusalem; Yosef Dayan and Baruch Ben Yosef advocated the restoration of a biblical Monarchy; Arie Hess, active on behalf of the Greater Jerusalem Council. The Ministry of Housing apparently supported property purchases in East Jerusalem with a government budget.

~ **On Settlements and against Oslo**

~ Novelist-cum-politician Moshe Shamir, once affiliated with the Labor movement, called for focusing on a national ideal, and was pained by the withdrawal from Sinai (1979–82); MK Elyakim Haetzni from Hebron/Kiryat Arba and MK Arieh Eldad from Kfar Adumim; Author Ora Shem-Ur who advocated the transfer of Arabs from Eretz-Israel; Israel Medad of the Begin Heritage Center, Steven Plaut from Haifa University, and Hillel Weiss from Bar-Ilan University; author-attorney Howard Grief, journalist Caroline Glick, settler-author Hanan Porat, teacher-author Hagi Ben Artzi, blogger/tour guide Shalom Pollack; intellectuals Shabtai Ben Dov, Yehuda Etzion, and Ohad Kamin; journalists Eliezer Whartman, Moshe Kohn, Sarah Honig, Yechiel Leiter; journalists-cum-public figures Hagai Segal, Uri Elitzur, and Uri Orbach; Shmuel Katz and David Bar Ilan; journalist Eliyahu Amikam; professors David Bukay, Moshe Sharon, and Raphael Israeli; professors Benjamin Akzin and Arieh Zaritsky; Lehi–author Ezra ElNakam Yachin; writers Sha'i Ben Tekoah and Yishai Fleisher; authors Meir Uziel, Michael Widlanski, and Yosef Nedava; journalist Amnon Lord; Ted Belman who established the *Israpundit* blog; author Aharon Megged berating Israel's intelligentsia for identifying with the enemy that was "committed to our annihilation;" author Hillel Halkin railing against post–Zionism; Efraim Karsh editor of *Israel Studies*; songwriter and singer Naomi Shemer of "Jerusalem of Gold" fame, whose lyrics included the words "that the market square in the Old City is empty" when Jews were not there (though Arabs were), and dared to write that the

Arabs prefer their murders "hot and steaming, not sterile like the Nazis;" author Naomi Frenkel who moved to Kiryat Arba in Hebron, and rejected the psychology of the ghetto which exuded alienation from the Land of Israel across the 1967 lines; university nationalist student clubs like Aviv; the Struggle Staff [Mateh Hamaavak] and the Committee Against the [Palestinian] Autonomy Plan and Oslo; My Truth founded by Avihai Shorshan to protect state lands from Arab poachers; and Jeremy Dery active on the pro–Israel hasbara/information front.

~ **Activist Nationalist Figures**
~ Leading pioneering settlers in Judea and Samaria: Danielle Weiss, Pinhas Wallerstein, Menachem Felix, and Benny Katzover; The Women in Green founded by Nadia Matar and Yehudit Katzover, promoting Israeli sovereignty in Judea and Samaria; Zo Artzeini founded by Moshe Feiglin, leading a popular campaign of street protests against the Oslo Accords; Moshe Zar was active in land purchases and settlement in Samaria; Eli Yogev and Henri Daskal to revitalize Zionism and unite the Right; Noam Arnon spokesman for the Hebron Jewish community; tour guide Aharon Pick; Moshe Leshem and Shlomo Baum heading the Committee for the Golan; Nachliel Office for Yesha [Hebrew acronym for Judea, Samaria, Gaza] founded by Mordechai Sones; activists Yael Amishav Medved, Shoshana Hilkiyahu, and Marsha Feinstein; Zeev Hever ("Zambish") a leader in settlement activity; Yaakov Katz (Ketzele) at Beit-El; Mattot Arim led by Susie Dim for political activism; Michael Ben-Ari and Baruch Marzel active on issues pertaining to Jewish settlement, an integral Jewish state, and against the Left and its anti–Zionist agenda.

~ **Rabbis on the Land of Israel and Israel as a Jewish state**

~ Rabbi Tzvi Yehuda Kook head of the Mercaz HaRav Yeshiva, and rabbis Mordechai Eliyahu and his son Shmuel Eliyahu; Rabbi Dov Lior and Rabbi Eliezer Waldman; Rabbi Moshe Levinger who spearheaded the return to Hebron in 1968; rabbis Meir Kahane, Benny Elon, and David Bar Haim; rabbis Yitzhak Ginzberg, Zalman Melamed and his son Eliezer Melamed.

~ **Organizations Advancing Jewish and Israeli Interests**

~ The Eretz Israel Academy in Kedumim (Samaria) founded by Zvi Slonim; The Council for Jewish Settlement in Judea, Samaria, and Gaza founded by Israel Harel; Midreshet Tagar of Etzel veterans; Midreshet Atzag [Uri Zvi Greenberg] founded by Geula Cohen; Elisha—Citizens for Judea, Samaria and Gaza, founded by Alex Kans, protesting PLO political activities in Jerusalem; Maoz—Zionist Nationalist Movement led by Golda Yellin, for Jewish immigration (aliya) from Soviet Russia and against Oslo; The Center for Jewish Activism; The Ariel Center for Policy Research founded by Arieh Stav; Mekimi to advance Jewish Leadership; Jordan Is Palestine Committee; The Jerusalem Institute for Western Defense founded by Yohanan Ramati; Manhigut Yehudit [Jewish Leadership] led by Moti (Mordechai) Karpel; Moledet (Homeland) founded by Rehavam Zeevi, for voluntary Arab emigration; the Zionist Writers Group headed by Balfour Hakak; the Center for Jewish Political Thought and the Israel Torah Foundation founded by Yoel Lerner; the Nansen Institute headed by Rabbi Chaim Simons who proposed Arab population transfer; Hai Vekayam founded by Yehuda Etzion for spiritual renewal and Jewish leadership; The Center for Jewish Activism at Har Bracha in Samaria; The Association of Professors for a Strong Israel led over the years, by among others, Asa Lifschitz, Yosef

Rabbani, Ron Breiner, and Mordechai (Moti) Kedar; The Engagement Movement [Hitchabrut] founded by Zvi MiSinai to engage "Arabs" who are of Jewish descent; Israel Sheli (My Israel) founded by Ayelet Shaked and Naphtali Bennett; The Organization for Human Rights [of Jews] in Judea, Samaria, and Gaza founded by Orit Struck; The Center for Near East Policy Research founded by David Bedein, investigating the misconduct of UNRWA; Palestinian Media Watch founded by Itamar Marcus monitoring the PLO Palestinian Authority; The Jewish Covenant Alliance founded by Aaron Braunstein; Michael Ben-Horin headed Medinat Yehuda for Jewish sovereignty over all Judea and Samaria based on Torah law; Terror Victims Association led by Meir Indor; Shalom LeDorot of Rabbi Yoel Schwartz and Oded Kitov to strengthen Judaism in Israel; Klal Israel for Jewish government and law; HaShomer HeHadash founded by Yoel Zilberman to protect Jewish lands and farms from Arab theft and damage in the Galilee and Negev; My Truth founded by Matan Katzman to defend IDF soldiers from smear campaigns, and Our Soldiers Speak providing a public platform for IDF officers speaking abroad; the legal organization Shurat HaDin (Israel Law Center) headed by lawyer Nitzana Darshan-Leitner exposing the funding of terrorism; The College for Jewish Statesmanship founded by Amit Halevy and Asaf Malach; Honenu founded by Shmuel Medad (Zangi) providing free legal aid for Jews; The Jerusalem Summit; The Israel Land Fund headed by Arieh King; Im Tirtzu [If You Will It] established by Ronen Shoval to promote nationalist Zionist causes; Israel Policy Center founded by Yitzhak Klein; the Institute for Zionist Strategies founded by Israel Harel to cultivate the Jewish character of Israel; Martin Sherman, founder of the Israel Institute for Strategic Studies; Dore Gold as president of the Jerusalem Center for Public Affairs recognized the need to detoxify Palestinian schools from years of incitement; The Menahem Begin Heritage Center;

The Foundation for Constitutional Democracy founded by Professor Paul Eidelberg; My Israel; Danny Ayalon who founded the Truth About Israel site; Kohelet Policy Forum; the Israel Allies Foundation founded by MK Yuri Stern and headed by Josh Reinstein to establish ties with pro–Israel parliamentarians around the world; Reservists on Duty headed by Amit Deri, with Israeli soldiers and citizens—like Dema Taya (Muslim woman), Muhammad Kabiya (Bedouin), Ram Asad (Druze), and Jonathan Elkhoury (Christian)—publicly defending the reputation of the IDF abroad; *World Israel News* site; the Jerusalem Institute for Strategic Studies; a belated arrival to the distinguished national club was the Begin-Sadat (BESA) Center at Bar-Ilan University; and Ad Kan—Youth for Israel, to expose extreme Jewish leftist, pro–Palestinian, and anti–Israel activities.

~ **Media and Publications**
~ *Nekuda*, a magazine for the settlement movement founded by Israel Harel; *Counterpoint* newspaper; *HaYarden - Eretz Israel Weekly* newspaper founded by Aharon Ben Ami; *Messer* newspaper; *Nativ* journal founded and edited by Arieh Stav; *Ha-Umma Quarterly*; Aleph Yod; Lekhatkhila - Manhigut Yehudit edited by Mordechai (Moti) Karpel; *Arutz Sheva* [Israel National News] radio station and internet site established by Shulamit Melamed; Middle East Media and Research Institute (MEMRI) directed by Yigal Carmon; *Makor Rishon* weekly newspaper edited by Hagai Segal; *HaShiloah* journal founded and edited by Yoav Sorek; Clarion Project founded by Rabbi Raphael Shore; *Latma* satirical TV program founded by Caroline Glick; Ladaat/Israel's Media Watch; *Israel Hayom* daily; IMRA—Independent Media Review and Analysis by Aaron Lerner; the *Mida* electronic commentary site founded by Ran Baratz; *Maraah* magazine site founded by Daphna Netanyahu; *The Land of Israel Network*; *Israel Video Network* providing news and commen-

        tary; and Eretz-Israel Shelanu as a media infor-
mation source.

~   Worthy of mention are Bassam Eid and Khaled Abu
Toameh, two exceptionally courageous Arab defen-
ders of media accuracy, advocating Israel's public
reputation as a liberal democracy, while exposing
the rogue features of the Palestinian Authority.
Living in Israel, they have defended Israel in public
forums abroad.

~   This is only a partial list of the good guys. Some of
the individuals are no longer alive, and a number of
their outfits ended their work. But they represented
honest reporting, nationalist views, and a welcome
antidote to leftist bias in the media.

Popular Opinion

A surge of nationalist spirit accompanied and supported the patriotic settlement movement. It evolved during years when Jews struck roots in the mountains and valleys of Judea and Samaria, the Jordan Valley, the Golan Heights, and the Yamit and Katif zones in and near the Gaza Strip. Meanwhile, Palestinian terrorism—by rocks, knives, vehicles, gunfire, and bombs—assaulted Israelis throughout the country. Arabs in "little Israel" demonstrated against the government, Arabs in the territories murdered Jews.

In the summer of 1985 the Israeli daily *Maariv* published the results of a poll showing two-thirds of the general public favored the immediate release of all the men in the Jewish Underground, who had been arrested a year earlier. This illustrated how divorced the ruling class was from the sensitivities of the average Israeli man and woman.

An opinion poll in 1987 discovered that forty percent of Israeli Jewish youth supported Jewish "terror" organizations that would take revenge on Arab terrorism. A survey of high school students conducted in 1990 at the Hebrew University by Professor Kalman Binyamini revealed that despite a reported leftist orientation toward conflict-resolution with the Palestinians regarding the future of the territories, respondents yet by an eighty percent margin favored the idea of Arabs leaving the Land of Israel; and in this spirit seventy-two percent did not trust the loyalty of the Arab citizens in Israel.

A more integral and personal attachment to Judaism in faith and observance contributed to a more resolute and often anti–Arab opinion. This connection between religion and politics was researched by Professor Yochanan Peres and published in 1992 in *Sociological Papers (volume 1)*, showing that the ultra-orthodox and the religious in Israel had significantly more rigorous and stringent views regarding Arabs than did the secular Jewish population. The first two sectors registered higher than the secular group in agreeing with the idea that Arabs not be eligible to sit in the Knesset, and that only Jews should enjoy national rights in the Land of Israel. A more markedly Jewish state was one in which the role and rights of the Arabs would be limited and marginal to the national enterprise.

Another survey conducted by Dr. Devorah Carmil from Haifa University in 1997 found that among youth from the ages 16–18, 74 percent preferred that only Jews live in Israel, while 61 percent of the respondents opposed equal rights for the Arabs. The very presence of Arabs in the Knesset was considered by 73 percent as a threat to Israeli security.

The Israel Institute for Democracy reported findings in 2015 according to which 37 percent of Jewish survey respondents favored the radical position of encouraging Arab emigration from among Israeli citizens. Forty-two percent believed that the Arabs did not accept the very existence of the state and desire its destruction. That a majority of the Arab citizens declared they were a part of the Palestinian people was undoubtedly a critical component in shaping Jewish opinion toward them. Meaning: if you are not with us, then you are against us. That same survey reported that 60 percent of the Jews favored canceling the right of the Arabs to vote. In 2016, against the political background of a profound and ongoing Jewish–Arab ideological and political rift, a survey conducted by *Israel Hayom* daily newspaper reported that 59 percent of high school Jewish youth identified themselves as rightists, only 13 percent as leftists. Eighty-two percent believed there was no possibility of reaching a political settlement with the Palestinians.

A constellation of factors, that included Jewish national identity and Zionist ideology, shaped a generally hawkish political public opinion among youth and lower-age groups in particular. Domestic Arab hostility to Israel and unrelenting Palestinian terrorism hardened Israeli resolve, as the Jews articulated a lack of trust in Arab citizens, favored bolstering the Jewish state, and expressed support for Jewish settlements in the territories. Likud and other nationalist and religious parties were the political repositories for these views. Corresponding with Likud–led governments under Yitzhak Shamir (prime minister in 1983–84 and 1986–92) and Benjamin Netanyahu (prime minister in 1996–99, then since 2009) was the rightist emphasis in public opinion. A research survey conducted in 2010 by Dr. Udi Lebel found that 52 percent of the Israeli public considered Jewish settlement in Judea and Samaria a security belt for the state and an act of Zionism.

At the other end of the spectrum, the Israeli Left ultimately discarded its ideological apparel and adopted the Palestinian war against Israel as its own. It took sides in the conflict, and it wasn't the Israeli one. This is where the decline of the Left displayed its supreme treason against Zionism. Leftist MKs and public personalities would almost ritualistically visit Arafat and later Mahmoud Abbas at Palestinian Authority head-quarters in Ramallah, but avoid visiting Jewish residents nearby at the Psagot and Ofra communities.

In this connection we wonder whether the major threat to Israel came from the Arabs or from the Jewish Left. Without leftist solidarity with the Arabs, their threat to Israel would diminish considerably. A united Israeli stance against the Palestinians would have demonstrated the futility of the Palestinian war. We will later return to this interesting theme.

We mentioned Ben-Gurion and Begin at the beginning of this chapter. They were both deeply proud Jews and emotionally connected to Eretz-Israel, the homeland whose very name exercised an enchanting spell on Jews throughout history. Naomi Shemer, songwriter and singer, was present (as I was) at the dramatic Gush Emunim trek to Sebastia in 1975 that broke the self-imposed Israeli prohibition of Jews settling in Samaria. In a famous song she wrote and brought to the Sebastia Zionist "happening," Naomi evoked the image of a Jew who was sleepwalking in a dreamlike mental state, saying: "the Land of Israel belongs to the [Jewish] people of Israel." Leftist journalist Nahum Barnea considered Shemer a loss to the "sane Israel" camp having chosen, in his words, "the vulgar [nationalist] rejectionist" camp instead. The Left punished Naomi Shemer, boycotted her music and demeaned her talent, while claiming that they believe in freedom of speech—but only, we well know, for their political kind. Shemer held her ground of dignity and her political views, though at times withheld expressing them for fear of leftist reprisals. Two popular singers, Arik Lavi and Dudi Elharar, both were aware of leftist hostility to their nationalist pro-settlement views.

Songwriter and singer Ariel Zilber was punished by the ruling music community for his known right-wing political views. In 2014, initially to be awarded the ACUM recognition for lifetime achievements in music, the prize was subsequently downgraded to an award for his musical accomplishments. The disgraceful ceremony for this event was broadcast for all Zilber fans to see.

Glila Ron-Feder-Amit, the noteworthy author of popular books for youth and the general public, sported a nationalist outlook which may not have damaged her career; though she was hardly interviewed in the media.

***

The impressive experience of the conservative movement in America beginning in the 1960s to engage in the war of ideas against the liberal Left, and mobilize resources for battle, was not adequately replicated in Israel. Think tanks, media outlets, literary publications, seminars and briefings, were part of the panoply of right-wing policy institutions and methods in the United States to get the message out. Conservative foundations funded newsletters, policy journals, websites, television and radio broadcasting networks, and right-of-center magazines, with the goal of defining the public issues and shaping the national agenda.

In the last few decades in Israel, there were admittedly signs of public vitality and significant developments in the rightist camp. Yet one of the major reasons for the failure of the Right to mount a strong opposition to leftist domination in the arena of ideas was not the lack of talent but the failure of the nationalist political class—primarily Likud—to acknowledge, elevate, promote, and fund the efforts that emerged from below. It seems that the dominant rightist party is only slowly learning its lesson.

Few on the Right publicly and directly challenged the leftist agenda on culture and society. Value-related questions were under the repressive and ruthless rule of one camp. When Rabbi Yigal Levinstein, heading the pre-army academy in Eli in Samaria, dared in 2016 to talk about the homosexuality deviance that the IDF was accommodating, if not promoting, a storm of protest burst forth. After all, the Left cultural avant-garde had assured that every Israeli movie had to have a homo in it. The Rabbi showed courage to open a debate with the sanctimonious leftist game-plan which had become part of the IDF cultural ethos. It was time to return to Bible, biology, and traditional family values, to assure the integrity of the IDF and Israel herself as a self-respecting Jewish society.

Another most courageous, unflinching, and articulate rightist to confront the Left was Likud Minister of Culture and Sport Miri Regev, as when in 2017 she protested nudity in the theater which artists considered art and not pornography. Miri spoke in the name of civility, culture, and Jewish values. The radical libertarian Left spoke in the name of freedom of artistic expression which in this case was an insult to decent men and women. The minister also confronted with a threat to cut state funding those producers including Arab ones that exploited theater for pro–Palestinian propaganda, as in the Akko (Acre) Fringe Theater Festival. The Left's tolerance of everything, except Zionism, settlements, and the land, was the hallmark of a culture in decay. The Al-Midan (Arabic) Theater in Haifa, which operated as the national Palestinian theater, found that it lost state funding when it presented a play in 2016 on the Arab Israeli terrorist Walid Daka who was a member of a cell that had murdered Moshe Tamam, an Israeli soldier back in 1984. Al-Midan was a theatrical agent for staging political warfare against Israel.

Miri Regev was committed to revise the cultural agenda, promoting arts in the geographic periphery and elevating Sephardi–Oriental artists to the forefront. The Left was outraged and its language and behavior became vile. Film critic Gadi Orshar compared Regev to Goebbels and the leftist gang yelled at Miri at every public occasion. The entrenched cultural apparatchiks unsurprisingly showed little sign of culture. Actor Lior Ashkenazi (a Sephardi name!) refused to meet with Miri Regev at the Monaco Film Festival in 2016.

A typical example of leftist oppression was the refusal of the Israel Film Fund and the Rabinovitz Fund to provide support for movie director Ro'i Horenstein who was working on a film that would present the courage of air force pilots in the Six Day War. He was rejected when he asked for financial support for the ongoing project. Only for political but not professional reasons was Horenstein refused. War is destructive, said the controllers of funds, and the film was not reflecting the complexity of the subject. Towns in the outlying periphery in the north and south of the country, and communities beyond the Green Line, were boycotted by the movie funders. Tel-Aviv was the center of the arts and leftism was its paramount motif. No movie in which Arabs in Israel might say that their life in Israel was satisfactory was ever shown to the public. The Arab victimization theme was the only narrative that Israelis would hear and see, as decided upon by the politico nomenklatura. Documentary films on Israel and produced by Israelis present the country as bad, discriminatory, heartless, and racist. This was the finding by Yigal Hecht in his film *Beiti* (My Home). The excellent film *Ruach Aheret* (A Different Spirit) produced by Menorah Hazani, relating with sensitivity the life of her father Benny Katzover as an early pioneer in Kiryat Arba and Elon Moreh, was funded by private contributions. Yet a change was in the air with a breeze promising new rhythms of cultural melodies.

Chapter Four

JEWISH RIGHTISTS ABROAD

The Zionist movement from its origins was a global Jewish undertaking. The truly modern character, organization, financial resources, and impetus were intimately connected with world Jewry. Not surprisingly, the debate and division between the Left and the Right, or the hawks and the doves, within Israel was replicated abroad in the Jewish diaspora. This became exceptionally apparent from the 1970s when questions of peace and territories rose to the summit of Israel's political and diplomatic agenda, and Jews in the world responded accordingly. The traditional ideological fissure between Zionist youth movements, like the nationalist Betar and the socialist HaShomer HaTzair, provoked controversy among Jews. Multiple issues concerning the Gush Emunim settlement movement from 1974, the war in Lebanon in 1982, the Intifada from 1987, and the Oslo Accord in 1993; thereafter the assassination of Yitzhak Rabin in 1995, the election of Benjamin Netanyahu in 1996, the election of Ehud Barak in 1999, the disengagement from the Gaza Strip and northern Samaria in 2005, and the Second Lebanese War in 2006; all provided, with Israel's military operations in Gaza in 2010, 2012, and 2014, subjects for Jews abroad to express their views and the differences among them.

The politically conscious, active and involved, Jews in the United States and Canada, the United Kingdom and France, and elsewhere, felt deeply connected and emotionally charged to enter into the ring of intra–Israeli/Jewish political hassling. On the one hand, the controversial question of "double loyalty" was skirted and ignored as Jews, like other free people, were not inhibited or leery from publicly adopting positions regarding Israel, though they did not live there. And on the other hand, the question of non-citizens of Israel trying to sway public opinion regarding Israel and perhaps in Israel did not become a problematic matter to the extent that, as Jews, their voices would be heard but not necessarily heeded. The bonds of inclusive Jewish national solidarity provided legitimacy for Jews everywhere to relate actively to the politics of Israel which, when all is said and done, and thanks to the Law of Return, is the homeland for all Jews in the world. At any moment, Jews can pick up and come to Israel and acquire citizenship upon their very arrival.

Commitment and Action

The nationalist pro–Israel advocacy groups focused on supporting the Land of Israel, territorial retention, and the building of settlements. They rejected the PLO and Palestinian national claims west of the Jordan River, suspected "peace" initiatives U.S.–sponsored or otherwise, and opposed the "peace" process as disingenuous and a threat to Israel's integrity and existence. A sense of urgency was conveyed by Israel's supporters in their writings and actions, as at demonstrations on university campuses and in cities abroad. The dedication shown in hasbara information and public forums undertaken on behalf of the nationalist position was probably more impressive than any measure of success in influencing general public opinion in the world or impacting upon policy in Israel. The pro–Israel lobby in Washington had a reputation for carrying political weight in establishment circles.

~ **Organizations** (on the Right, affiliated with the Right, or not on the Left)

~ AFSI (Americans for a Safe Israel) founded by Herb Zweibon was based in New York and established branches throughout America, adopting a resolute ideological stance for territorial retention; *OUTPOST* was its feature publication with Rael-Jean Isaac a leading writer along with Joseph Puder and Bernard Smith; Julian White served as president of the Los Angeles AFSI chapter, and Sol Modell was a prolific writer; Unity Coalition for Israel (UCI) founded by Esther Levens brought together 200 separate Jewish and Christian organizations and advocated Israel's territorial integrity; The Canadian Institute for Jewish Research (CIJR), established by Professor Fred Krantz in Montreal, was both an intellectual forum and an activist group that sided with Israeli nationalist positions; The ZOA (Zionist Organization of America) under President Morton Klein engaged in active campaigns to promote the Israeli Right position, arguing that U.S. aid should be denied the PLO; CAMERA (Committee for Accuracy in Middle East Reporting in America), which fought the anti–Israel media bias, was founded by Charles Jacobs and Winifred Meiselman, and whose prominent Boston Chapter was headed by Andrea Levin; Bertram Korn Jr. directed the Philadelphia CAMERA chapter, and there were branches throughout America; Geoffrey Clarfield in Toronto worked through his Mozuud outfit; BIPAC—Britain/Israel Public Affairs Committee with Jane Moonman as director; The Rebel Media headed by Ezra Levant in Canada; Americans for Undivided Israel was funded by George Topas in New Jersey; JINSA—Jewish Institute for National Security Affairs in Washington; The Freeman Center for Strategic Studies directed by Bernard Shapiro located in Houston advocated the positions of the YESHA Council of Jewish settlements in Judea, Samaria and Gaza; The TAGAR [Revisionist/Betar] student activist movement of Montreal and The Student Coalition for a Just Peace in the Middle East also in Montreal; Winston Mideast Analysis and Commentary founded by Emanuel Winston in Chicago, that regularly exposed and opposed in the 1990s the Labor Party's willingness to accept a Palestinian state and to grant the PLO an official presence in Jerusalem; the Jordan Is Palestine committees from America, Australia, and the United Kingdom headed internationally by David Singer, proposed that Palestinian nationhood be located east of the Jordan River in the framework of the Hashemite Kingdom; FLAME: Facts and Logic About the Middle East under President Gerardo Joffe in San Francisco advocated Israeli territorial retention and opposed concessions to the PLO; WOJAC (World Organization of Jews from Arab Countries) founded by Professor Maurice Romani represented Jews as victims of Arab persecution and expulsion; The International Association of Jewish Lawyers and Jurists (American Section) under President Justice Jerome Hornblass; the Hasbara Fellowships Canada in Toronto; United Nations Watch (UNW) in Geneva headed by Hillel Neuer fights against the monstrous United Nations assaults against the state of Israel; the Jewish Policy Center in Washington; the Washington–based Endowment for Middle East Truth headed by Sarah Stern; Scholars for Peace in the Middle East; World Values Network, fighting BDS anti–Semitism, was established by Rabbi Shmuley Boteach; and the Coalition for Jewish Values directed by Rabbi Yaakov Menken and Rabbi Pesach Lerner.

~ **Writers and Activists**
~ Professors Edward Alexander , as in his book *Jews Against Themselves* (Transaction, 2015), defended in buoyant language the Jewish state from its detractors and haters, as did Ruth Wisse backing Israel from vituperative assaults by Jews in partic-ular; David Littman and Gisèle (Bat Ye'or) his wife, based in Geneva, exposed Islam's culture of hate toward Jews and Israel; Dan Nimrod in Montreal, whose voluminous writings appeared under the label of Dawn Publishing and The Canadian Jewish Herald, attacked the Jewish Left in his book *Peace Now: Blueprint for National Suicide* (Dawn, 1984) and ardently defended Israel's nationalist position; Aviel Leitner was editor of the *Judean Lawyer Student Newspaper* in New York; Leonard Horwin in Los Angeles was sympathetic to Likud and corre-sponded extensively in advocating the rightist Israeli position that included opposing a Palestinian state; media personality Dennis Prager; Edward Sturm in New York wrote about the strategic necessity of the mountains of Judea and Samaria remaining under Israeli control; the activist Hadassah "Dasi" Marcus, Manfred Lehmann, and Rabbi Avi Weiss all from New York; Michel Gurfinkiel in Paris; Joan Levin in

Arizona; Professor Louis René Beres on Israeli strategic needs; Irving Taitel from Chicago, philanthropist and speaker supported Gush Emunim; journalist Melanie Phillips in London (and Jerusalem) and activist Barbara Oberman; Mark Langfan from New York who designed a topographical model to show the folly of territorial withdrawal; Professor Robert Loewenberg delineating Israel's strategic requirements and opposing any withdrawal; Pamela Geller who considered that most of Israel's media is jewicidal; Joel Carmichael editor of *Midstream*; Sidney Goodman in England on Israel's rights to the Land; Jerome (Jerry) Gordon editor of the New English Review; writer Michael Zimmerman of Chicago; publicist Eli Hertz who blogs at Myths and Facts; Martin Blecher writing from Sweden; journalist Fiamma Nirenstein in Rome (and Jerusalem); and the initiative by Middle East Forum president Daniel Pipes in launching the Israel Victory Project in 2016.

All gave of their time and talents to defend Israel, her national interests and the Land.

The Diaspora–Israel Nexus

In many instances, the rightist Jews abroad were linked to politicians and parties in Israel. Contacts were cultivated, some had personal dimensions, and all carried ideological significance. Contacts and correspondence, often direct and sometimes amorphous, existed with Likud, HaTehiya, and the NRP (National Religious Party) in Israel. Some of the Jews resided in Israel for a number of years, others visited frequently. The diaspora contingent assisted Israelis in arranging speaking engagements in the United States, and I personally was a beneficiary of this. The example of Herut veteran Shmuel Katz in virtually launching AFSI is an exceptional case of joint efforts. The Jews abroad felt they were contributing to Israel's struggle.

Zionism was no longer a small dynamic enterprise of the few sustained and supported by a large far-flung and powerful Jewish diaspora. From 650,000 Israelis in 1948, they numbered more than six and a third million in 2018. Israeli Jews alone constituted close to one half of all the

Jews in the world. Israel had become in its revolutionary demographic growth and political development the beating heart of the Jewish world in all respects—spiritual and otherwise. For a self-identified Zionist Jew—or any nominal Jew—to remain outside of the homeland was to be detached from the vitality and centrality of the contemporary Jewish drama. Israel was the playing field where Jewish action took place.

The conclusion drawn is that, without powerful organs of influence and expression, the activists and writers on the Right maintained their moral integrity on behalf of Israel even when their voices could not easily be heard in Jerusalem. This does not in a way deny their role in teaching diaspora Jews and gentiles about Israel, while advocating for her rights and explaining her condition. They tried to counter the mass media and political assaults on Israel. They wrote letters to newspapers, distributed political declarations, organized lectures, canvassed Washington politicians, and demonstrated in public their support for Israel's interests and rights. This was an educational program of great importance to sustain Jewish commitment to the Jewish people and portray the justice of Israel's case. The Arab–Israeli conflict in the Middle East is projected in universities in New York and California, Montreal and Toronto, and Jews must be made aware of Israel's war for survival which is, by implication, the war for the survival of all of the House of Israel.

Chapter Five

Non–Jewish Rightists in Israel

and Abroad

~ I begin this chapter by repeating a point I mentioned in the Preface: one doesn't have to be on the
political Right to support Israel, and many who do
favor Israel would not define themselves as
rightists. It is only for convenience, symmetry, and
simplicity, and considering the Israeli context, that I
nonetheless use the term—rightist—and my apolo-
gies to those who may resent this.

The biblical (gentile) prophet Bilaam foresaw that the Jewish people is
destined "to dwell alone." Yet it nonetheless has been the beneficiary of
non–Jewish favor and support. The ancient Israelites had friends, like
Yitro (Jethro) the Midian priest, and the ancient Jewish exiles enjoyed
the encouragement of the Persian King Cyrus to return back to the
Hebrew homeland. In modern times the Jews were again to return to the
Land of Israel, and Herzl's prophetic call resounded in 1897 that "in five
or fifty years" the Jewish state will be (re-)established. Backing Herzl and
believing in his mission was William Hechler, an English Protestant
chaplain, enthusiastically believing in divine providence guiding historical affairs. British Prime Minister Lloyd George and Foreign Minister
James Balfour were among the leading Christian gentile political figures
who, during the period of the First World War and thereafter, provided
international recognition for the Zionist enterprise. John Patterson
commanded and admired the Zion Mule Corps Jewish soldiers who
fought alongside British soldiers in the Great War. The San Remo con-

ference in 1920 and the League of Nations Mandate for Palestine in 1922 testified that the non–Jewish world believed in the justice of the Jewish Return. Orde Wingate, a British military officer, advised and trained the Zionists to accelerate and intensify their military operations against Arab marauders and murderers in the 1930s. The non–Jewish world diplomatically mobilized in 1947 as the United Nations recommended the establishment of a Jewish State in the Land of Israel. America was in the forefront recognizing the reborn Jewish state of Israel in 1948.

The state of Israel has been admired and assisted from inestimable numbers of governments, organizations, and individuals. Czech politicians provided Israel with military hardware in 1948, and French politicians in the 1950s were instrumental in furthering Israel's nuclear program. Prominent national leaders like José Maria Azar in Spain, Stephen Harper in Canada, and Silvio Berlusconi of Italy, were prominent international leaders openly pro–Israel in their views and policies. There were many senior American officials who publicly expressed support for Israel and appreciation for Israel's contribution to U.S. interests—Secretary of State General Alexander Haig Jr., and American ambassadors to the United Nations—Daniel Patrick Moynihan, Jean Kirkpatrick, John Bolton, and most recently Nikki Haley; also exceptionally supportive of Israel was diplomat Alan Keyes and politician Allen West. Small peoples and minorities in the Middle East cooperated and collaborated with the Jewish state—among them Kurds, Lebanese (Maronites), and Druze; others like North African Berbers empathized with Israel. Not all of the exploits of friends and allies became public knowledge. It is reasonable to assume that Israeli intelligence gathering and clandestine security operations enjoyed the assistance of gentiles, as intimated in books written on the Mossad.

Christian Zionists

Many friends of Israel were Christians who strongly believed that the Return of the Jewish People to their homeland was a sign and a step toward fulfilling a Christian evangelical messianic vision. These individuals, many of whom would identify as Christian Zionists, saw no contradiction between their Christian faith and enthusiastic commitment to Israel. In fact, these two features were bound together in a religious doctrine that surfaced and strengthened over the years. Many Christians were returning to their Jewish biblical and spiritual roots and identifying that Jesus was, after all, a Jew. One exceptionally prominent pro–Israel Christian activist was Mike Evans who founded the Friends of Zion Museum in Jerusalem; while another noteworthy adherent to the ranks of pro–Israel organizations is the Zion Christian Church of South Africa led by Bishop Dr. Barnabas Lekganyane.

Christian religious activism included expressing political opinions on Middle Eastern affairs, invariably adopting a pro–Israel stance against the Palestinians and the PLO. Traditional Muslim hostility and persecution of Christians in the Middle East also accounted for siding with the Jews.

The seminal biblical source which was at the foundation of Christian solidarity with the Jewish People touches on God blessing Abraham in the Book of Genesis, chapter 12, verse 3: "I will bless those who bless you, and whoever curses you I will curse." It is this divine promise that has been a beacon of light for Christians wanting to receive a blessing for themselves by their blessing the people of Israel.

~ **Israel**
~ Christian Friends of Israel – Jerusalem directed by Ray Sanders; The International Christian Embassy of Jerusalem with branches around the world was founded in 1980 by Jan Willem van der Hoeven and led by David Parsons, convening an annual Feast of Tabernacles Celebration and joining in the Jerusalem parade, with Christian participation from as far away as Zimbabwe, Indonesia, and Papua New Guinea, and advocating that countries move their embassy from Tel Aviv to Jerusalem; Bridges for Peace directed by Clarence Wagner and Rebecca Brimmer; Christian believer Herman Besner came from Germany to settle in Israel, a lover of the Bible who declared that the Land of Israel belongs to the Jewish people; Dr. Petra Heldt the director of the Ecumenical Council in Jerusalem and scholar Malcolm Lowe; Patrick Goodenough broadcasting for the *CNS* network; HaYovel evangelical ministry founded by Tommy Waller bringing volunteers to work in the vineyards of Psagot and Har Bracha in Samaria.

~ **Abroad—Internationally**

~ Support for a right-wing Israeli position became an essential part of the conservative Christian Right ethos in the United States, especially in the south. Evangelical churches and pastors, but also other Christian leaders and groups, adopted a pro–Zionist stance in support of Judea and Samaria. They emboldened Israeli governments to resist pressure to withdraw from the post–1967 lines. Millions of dollars were contributed to provide aid and services to Israel. It was considered God's will that the biblical Land of Israel and a united Jerusalem remain eternally within the borders of the state of Israel.

~ On January 27, 1992, *The Washington Times* carried an item that 33 Christian leaders in America urged President Bush to act on a $10 billion loan guarantee to help settle Soviet Jews in Israel. Because Israeli Prime Minister Yitzhak Shamir rejected Bush's demand that funds not be used to enable new immigrants from residing in Judea and Samaria, the president refused to provide the guarantees. For the Christians, Judea and Samaria were kosher country as part of the biblical Land of Israel.

Here is a list of some of the individuals and organizations supporting the Israeli Right and its positions:

~ CIPAC (the Christians Israel Public Action Campaign) headed by Richard Hellman, working in Washington and with chapters across America on behalf of Israel; Stand With Israel founded by Ralph Reed of the Republican Party in Georgia, mobilizing churches for Israel; Tom Trento, the intrepid director of The United West site in Florida; Reverend Jerry Vines of the Southern Baptist Convention; the California Christian Committee for Israel; zealous Christians like Reverend Pat Robertson who headed the *CBN* (*Christian Broadcasting Network*) and Reverend Jerry Falwell who, during the annual national leadership convention of the Moral Majority Movement in

Jerusalem in November 1983, declared Israel the liberator of Lebanon in the 1982 war and said Israel should never surrender Judea–Samaria; Kare Kristiansen who resigned from the 1994 Norwegian Nobel Committee because Arafat was awarded the peace prize; author Conor Cruise O'Brien who understood that at the heart of Zionism is an inherent link between religion and nationality; Pastor John Hagee and his Ministries of San Antonio consistently supporting Israel's right to the Land while heading the Christians United For Israel (CUFI) organization with its sweeping international presence; Dexter Van Zile, Christian media analyst at Boston–based CAMERA; Evangelical Christians like Dr. John Walvoord president of the Dallas Theological Seminary and Pastor Randy Sager, certainly Billy Graham, Franklin Graham, Mike Huckabee, Gordon Robertson, and Paula White; Serbian bishop Jovan Culibrk; the Christian Mideast Conference in California; Ed McAteer organized an annual prayer breakfast in support of Israel; the millions-strong United With Israel organization; Christopher Ruddy, founder and publisher of *NEWSMAX* magazine; author Christopher Barder; Sheikh Abdul Hadi Palazzi and journalist Giulio Meotti in Italy; Erich Sontag in Germany; Professor and Muslim reformer Salim Mansur in Ontario and the courageous Charles Yacoub in Quebec; Joseph Farah, president of *WorldNetDaily* and Cal Thomas; naturalized Americans Brigitte Gabriel—who calls herself a "passionate Zionist"—originally from Lebanon, Nonie Darwish from Egypt, Ayaan Hirsi Ali from Somalia, Wafa Sultan from Syria, and Irshad Manji from Uganda; the courageous Dutch politician Geert Wilders and his countryman Pee Koelewijn, a Christian Zionist leader; the Mekoya movement founded by Ikoro Tashima in Japan with love for Bible and Israel; British professor and author Denis MacEoin; American professors of Lebanese origin Walid Phares, Franck Salameh, and Robert Rabil; Professor of International Law Robert Barnidge Jr.;

Jamie Glazov of Frontpage.com and his intrepid *Glazov Gang* show; Jay Leno, American TV talk show host and Glenn Beck media personality; Frank Gaffney heading the Center for Security Policy in Washington; British army colonel Richard Kemp; Sandra Solomon and Chloe Valdory, among pro–Israel speakers, political activists, and philo–Zionists; journalist Faith Goldy in Canada; and the launching of the Christian Media Summit in Jerusalem attended in October 2017 by pro–Israel journalists from 30 countries.

~ A joint inter-faith pro–Israel organization is Jews and Christians United With Israel (UWI) that was established in 2006 and recently, in 2018, promoted a petition that gathered close to a million signatures from 170 countries in support of a united Jerusalem as Israel's capital. Fighting media bias and the BDS movement, UWI is on the battlefield of ideas in a global struggle for Israel.

A Comment

The renowned San Francisco longshoreman-philosopher Eric Hoffer uttered his somber but significant 1968 prophesy which carries more dramatic significance today than at the time. Even when Israel was strong and conveyed an image of determination, Hoffer insightfully understood that the long history of the Jewish people was more instructive than a passing moment. "I have a premonition," he said, "that will not leave me: as it goes with Israel so it will go with all of us. Should Israel perish the holocaust will be upon us. Israel must live!" Hoffer linked the fate of Israel with the fate of the world, certainly the Western world based on liberty and tolerance. He saw after the 1967 Six Day War that Israel's military victory could not in itself assure its permanent survival. Forces of hatred loomed on the horizon. In the Middle East, Iran with others would assume the Muslim leadership of the war to exterminate Israel and its people. Now, with the ghastly violence and demographic and religious expansion of Islam into the West, the link between Israel and the world has become manifest to all but the blind and the deniers. Israel is now on the front lines of a war whose battlefield extends throughout the Western world and beyond. Hoffer sensed the future before it arrived.

We have identified the righteous among the nations who have chosen to see Israel in the light of prophecy, morality, and justice. Standing with the Jews in these precarious and threatening days conveys light in the darkness that permeates our world and lives. In the war of civilization and liberty against barbarism, Israel indeed is a part of and the symbol of a global drama. Eric Hoffer had the exceptional wisdom to see and foresee the meaning of things in this era of history.

Chapter Six

THE ISRAELI LEFT

It is hard to pinpoint when the Leftist crack-up began. Perhaps already in 1948 when the Mapai leadership failed to liberate the heart of the homeland in the War of Independence and left Judea and Samaria and Old Jerusalem—in foreign hands; then in 1949 accommodated itself to a map of Israel without Shiloh and Hebron. Maybe in 1967 when, after a tremendous military victory against Arab armies, Israel was baffled what to do with the liberated lands. Perhaps the crack-up struck in 1973, when traumatized by the Arab military assault, there were those as on the far-Left who believed "the state is finished," as reported by Amnon Lord in his book *The Israeli Left: From Socialism to Nihilism* (Tammuz, 1988). Maybe the crack-up surfaced in 1977 when the nationalist Likud party carried off a mini-revolutionary electoral triumph against the Labor Party. Or maybe in 1981 when the previous Likud victory was replicated. Perhaps the crack-up exploded wide open with the shameful and incredulous recognition of the Palestine Liberation Organization and the signing of the Oslo Accord in 1993, and its successive agreements and tragic consequences. In the process the Labor Party moved to the far left and suffered public rejection. People raised their eyebrows and scratched their heads, wondering what had come over the party that built the modern state of Israel.

The contemporary political hallmark of the Left is support for the Arab war against Israel. Of course they may deny this, but they always side with the Palestinians and denounce the Right. Peace with the PLO, despite its 1964 covenant axiom to "liberate Palestine" and its 1974 "phases plan" to destroy Israel in stages, became the banner of leftist aspirations. It replaced socialism, the welfare state, human rights, or international brotherhood. Netanyahu was once recorded whispering into the ear of the kabbalist Rabbi Yitzhak Kadouri, wondering whether the leftists were really Jewish in feeling, thinking, and action. It would be a little too insulting to call them Hebrew–speaking gentiles; after all the leftists are bona fide Jews.

The Left equates power with immorality because power will be used against the less powerful and the weak; therefore it is a bad thing. To impose your will through power—force or violence—is to cause pain or damage to the other. The Left sanctifies non-power most especially when they are out of power. Author David Grossman, Israel Prize laureate, wrote in *The Yellow Wind* (Penguin, 1988) that he traveled through the West Bank to understand "how an entire nation like mine, an enlightened nation by all accounts, is able to train itself to live as a conqueror without making its own life wretched." Considering the profound Islamic hatred of Jews, the incessant Arab war against Israelis and iron-clad rejection of the Jewish state, the terrorism, rocket-fire, border incursions—it becomes a glaring truth that being a conqueror is a far better choice than being butchered to death by Muslim savages.

I once asked a leftist in a public exchange of views: if he faced the question of whether he would be a conqueror or be conquered, what would he choose. Agitated by my question, he refused to answer. He would no doubt want to say that he doesn't want to be a conqueror, but presumably the sanity cells still reverberating in his mind send a signal that he really doesn't want to be conquered—and certainly not by Arabs! I defined his choice in either/or terms; he balked. He doesn't want to upset the Arabs by being a conqueror/ruler/occupier; but perhaps this is preferable even for a leftist than being conquered/ruled/occupied by Muslims. Reveling in my leftist's awkwardness, I posed another question. If you were forced to expel a group, would you choose to expel Jews or Arabs from their homes? He again remained silent and disheartened. He certainly would not want to expel Arabs; if he was honest, he would admit that he would prefer to expel Jews. That is a dismal self-disclosure for all to hear. This is a bit too humiliating to admit in public, even for a leftist.

The Left is also uncomfortable with principles and not only with power. When the leftists are confronted by people with principles from the Right—committed to tradition and family, the Land of Israel and state of Israel—they condemn rigid views and fundamentalist patriotism. Leftist rage bursts out upon rightists who love the land and go out to settle it despite all the inconveniences, dangers, and defamers. This was the experience endured by the idealist Gush pioneers from the 1970s. Prime Minister Rabin spoke of this valiant movement as "a cancer in the tissue of Israel's democratic society." Gush Emunim set out, to use the classic Zionist terminology, "to redeem the land" on the barren hills of Samaria. They didn't go to seize power, subvert the government, or invade the Knesset in Jerusalem.

***

When Israel began to build its military power, contend effectively with Arab enemies, and flex its muscles on the Palestinians, the Left, or some on the Left, felt uncomfortable and embarrassed. Israeli satirist Ephraim Kishon wrote a book *So Sorry We Won!* (Maariv/MaArv, 1968) after the Six Day War triumph, well knowing that the world likes Jews as victims and not as victors. But the Israeli Left was itself squeamish at the pounding we administered to Arab armies. Liberal guilt invaded the false Jewish consciousness. Professor Alice Shalvi, feminist and leftist, considered the 1967 victory "very bad for us." She felt it had a debilitating effect on Israel's moral character. Losing the war would in all probability have had an even greater debilitating effect on Israel's physical existence.

The real danger of the Left, wrote Zvi Shiloah in his book *Leftism in Israel* (Yaron Golan, 1991), was its intellectual hegemony in Israeli society. They held positions where thought, words, and culture abound. They shape your mind, they dictate your feelings. The ideal of peace after 1967 could be achieved, leftists mused, if Israel abandons the liberated territories.

But to leave the geographical heart of Eretz-Israel is to leave thousands of years of Jewish history. Questions of identity and pride intermingled with political issues. When novelist Yoram Kaniuk favored canceling the Law of Return which gives every Jew the right to immigrate to Israel and acquire citizenship, he was foregoing the Jewish people in the name, perhaps, of a non–Israeli nation. For while there are Israelis, there is no Israeli nation as such. Kaniuk himself officially renounced his belonging to the Jewish "religion." In this alienated spirit half of radical leftist HaShomer HaTzair kibbutz youth declared around 1990, that they are Jewish only because they were born Jewish, not due to rigorous

Jewish identity and education. One of the principles of their leftist movement was the brotherhood of nations; it had a more powerful influence than the call of Zionism itself. In the days after Israel's independence, HaShomer HaTzair called for the return of 150,000 Palestinian refugees, a move that would have endangered the safety of Jews facing an enlarged, aggressive, internal, enemy population. Ben-Gurion refused to accede to this idea, and because of it the far Left utterly despised him. "Zionism [Jewish nationalism] is Racism" snarled the United Nations in 1975, and the Left was undecided whether to agree or not.

If you think about it, an Israeli Leftist is a virtual political oxymoron. How can a Jew in Israel, living in a state of war every second of his and the state's life, be so delusional to rely on the fatuous perspective of leftism—appeasing a savage enemy; ignoring the vulnerability of the June 4, 1967 borders; betraying the national patrimony; and throwing common sense to the wind? This leftist crack-up was born of infantilism and penitence. Fanaticism for peace was their prize ambition. Fortunately for Israel, the Arabs—especially the Palestinians and the Syrians—stymied the leftists' rush into the bowels of oblivion.

From its ideological love of Stalin to its rapturous enthrallment with Arafat, the Left strode the path of bewilderment, treason, and anti–Zionism. This is a shameful tale of betrayal and worship of mass murderers of Jews, and others. The Left flattered evil leaders while seeking inspiration and drawing hope from them. In 2014, 250 leftists from academic, cultural, and political circles joined forces to call for a Jewish–Arab front to oppose Israel's colonization [settlement] policy in the so-called Palestinian territories, and her exclusivist policy that denied Arab citizens full rights and participation. Among the signers of the protest were play-writer Yehoshua Sobol; former Knesset speaker Avrum Burg—who authored a book that declared Israel should not be a Jewish state and that its Law of Return should be radically altered; Professor Orit Kedar of Hebrew University, and Professor Niv Gordon of Ben Gurion University in Beersheba. Judging by the 2015 election results, with Netanyahu and Likud remaining in power, the Israeli public was not convinced that Israel was the cesspool of depravity and wickedness in the Middle East. There were apparently far more worthy candidates for that dubious title.

Gush Katif, 2005

On the sand dunes of the Mediterranean coast, south of Ashkelon in the Gaza Strip, Israel had established a town, Neve Dekalim, and 17 thriving communities. Gush Katif, as the settlement zone was called, became noteworthy for its agricultural products which became a household word in Israel, and lucrative exports to the markets of Europe. With courage and faith, the Zionist and primarily religious residents withstood Palestinian mortar bombs and rocket fire, stabbings and shootings, to hold their ground, and push on with pioneering determination. Then in 2005, after its Yamit zone settlement predecessor had been destroyed by an Israeli decision in 1982, the Katif zone was on the chopping block.

In the tense days prior to the Israeli expulsion of Israeli inhabitants in August 2005 from the Jewish enclave of Gush Katif, the Left regarded the Zionist religious community as beyond the political ken of Jewish brotherhood. The fact that the government was destroying the lives, homes, and livelihood of over 8,000 hard-working Jewish Israeli citizens was not seen as a travesty of justice and morality. Except for Justice Edmond Levy, 10 judges on the Supreme Court sanctioned the expulsion operation. The policy goal was to separate Jews from Arabs and thus reduce tensions and conflict, though no Israeli–Palestinian agreement was reached between the two sides. The government of Ariel Sharon that decided on the unilateral withdrawal was seen as above all criticism that otherwise might restrain such a brutal policy. The judicial system and left-wing establishment—the media elites—ignored weighty suspicions of criminal felonies committed by Sharon and his son Gilad in the "Greek island affair"—involving bribery by Likud member David Appel—in order that he stay in power and implement the withdrawal from Gaza. For the Left, withdrawal was a delirious potion; crime was incidental and forgivable. But that was not all that was full of odious corruption.

As the mutineer leader of Likud and prime minister, Ariel ("Arik") Sharon trampled on democratic principles when he and his slavish followers bolted from the party, defamed its true loyalists, and formed a new party called Kadima. This occurred after an internal Likud referendum showed that a 60:40 margin opposed Sharon's "disengagement" plan. He broke his promise to honor the decision of his own party, and left Likud. As events were later to demonstrate, the withdrawal from all of the Gaza Strip did not bring the peace and security that Sharon promised, but an intensification of Israeli–Palestinian conflict and bloodshed. Following the army's expulsion of the Jews and the demolition of their homes, the Palestinians set fire to the synagogues.

At the time, Doron Rosenblum writing in *Haaretz* identified the enemy on the Right: "Anyone who behaves like an enemy, walks like an enemy and makes the sound of an enemy, at least let him not complain about being treated like an enemy." Dan Margalit writing in *Maariv* argued in favor of placing quotas on the number of religious Jews allowed to serve as officers in the IDF. Matti Golan in *The Jerusalem Post* stated "that religion and democracy simply do not go together" and then suggested that the Zionist religious population, because of its ideological mindset, is inherently anti-democratic. In the course of the weeks preceding withdrawal and expulsion, euphemized as the "disengagement" from the Gaza Strip, elements of the religious community protested yet succumbed to the authority of the government and the integrity of the state. The so-called enemy on the Right in 2005 rose to the higher ethos declared by Menachem Begin—"just not civil war" among Jews; this warning was from earlier days when Ben-Gurion's minions shelled the Revisionist/Etzel/Irgun Altalena ship off the coast of Tel Aviv in June 1948. Ami Zamir, a Likud member and a former Irgun fighter in the 1940s, recalled that Ariel Sharon had been active and personally carried out violent assaults against members of the Irgun. Sharon showed signs of being a political chameleon throughout his long and rather illustrious public and military career.

The legal establishment from the High Court through the State Attorney General and the Legal Advisor to the Prime Minister had been politicized by leftist penetration over many decades. Gush Katif youth who actively protested the expulsion saw their civil rights abused and trampled upon. Young children were arrested and detained. Judges were pro-active in facilitating the government to carry out its policy with a minimum of public opposition and popular commotion. The sacred legal principle of the right to private property was ignored.

Popular singers who showed solidarity with Gush Katif paid a professional price. Ariel Zilber and Nimrod Lev went against the mainstream of their musical circles. Music stores removed Zilber's discs from the shelves. Both singers were banned from the airwaves.

The Left and Rabin had promised security with the 1994 Oslo–inspired partial Israeli withdrawal from Gaza City and its environs. Sharon then promised security with the complete Jewish withdrawal from the Strip in 2005. Sharon's promises were as hollow as Rabin's. The disengagement from the entire Gaza Strip led, as noted, to an exacerbation of Palestinian rocket and mortar strikes against the Israeli population. Gush Katif was gone, so the next proximate target was the northern Negev. In response to incessant Arab attacks, Israel launched military operations in 2008/9, 2012, and 2014. The Palestinians took control of all of the Gaza Strip, dreaming of conquering nothing less than all of Israel as their objective.

The Left had earlier ridiculed the Likud's scare stories and warnings as to the dire consequences of a unilateral withdrawal. As Sarah Honig wrote in *The Jerusalem Post* in July 2006, Likud foresaw what would transpire. Sharon's disengagement from Gaza was a monumental security blunder.

Many of the political decision-makers and fellow travelers, likewise senior police officers and army commanders, came to grief and fell from grace following their role in the expulsion of Jews from Gush Katif. We mention the names of Ariel Sharon, Ehud Olmert, Moshe Katzav; Moshe Karadi, Uri Bar Lev, and Niso Shaham; no less the IDF Chief of Staff Dan Halutz.

The Left and the Palestinians: Attacking the Right

It was during the Likud–Labor National Unity government led then by Yitzhak Shamir that Foreign Minister Shimon Peres met with Arafat in 1986 and violated the Prevention of Terrorism Act. He was not held accountable or investigated because the willingness of certain Israelis to recognize the PLO superseded any other principle or consideration. Earlier, as prime minister, Peres, and his underlings had been exploring secret links with the PLO through European and Egyptian mediators with an eye to legitimizing the PLO for peace-making purposes. Yitzhak Shamir, then Israel's Likud foreign minister, was kept in the dark; Peres, the "indefatigable schemer" so-labeled by Yitzhak Rabin, was a loose political cannon. One Israeli who didn't intend to deceive at all was journalist Amos Kenan who in 1985 wrote that he had been meeting with members of the PLO, and that he would continue to do so in violation of the law.

Different from the experience of Peres who successfully circumvented the law with impunity was the case of Abe Nathan, known for his offshore radio station *The Voice of Peace*. He visited Arafat in Tunis in 1988, and a court in Ramla later sentenced him to six years in jail for breaking the anti-terrorism law; he later sat for only six months. But Shimon Peres, shielded by a media blanket, was above the law and the normative political and judicial rules.

Typically, in June 1994, it was revealed that Peres had concealed promises he had made to Arafat regarding the free functioning of Palestinian institutions in "East Jerusalem." Arabs in that part of the city knew that living under Israeli rule in what they call the "occupation" was far more tolerable and beneficial than they had initially anticipated. In 1987 the Jerusalem City Council decided to provide cheaper municipal facilities to children in Jerusalem—but only to the Arab children in the eastern side of the capital. Nevertheless, Arab schools in East Jerusalem refused to fly an Israeli flag. At the time, the Education Minister was Laborite Yitzhak Navon.

Leftist attacks against the Right went beyond the despicable. In an article in *Haaretz* in 1987, leftist MK Dedi Zucker told a Palestinian audience at the Orient House Hotel in East Jerusalem that "the [Jewish] settlers live off [Palestinian] blood . . . they drink it . . ." Zucker drew upon the anti–Semitic blood libel of Jews murdering non–Jews. Poet Yitzhak Leor charged the religious pioneers with "baking the blood of Palestinian youths into their Passover unleavened bread matzot." We don't need gentile anti–Semites when we have Jewish ones.

Gilad Atzmon, musician and activist who renounced his Israeli citizenship after immigrating to England, adopted another explicit anti–Semitic stereotype in charging the Jews with trying to rule over the entire world. It is said that he calls himself a "Hebrew–speaking Palestinian."

Leftist animus against the nationalist camp aimed specifically at the broader settler enterprise in the territories. Journalist Yaron London, in an article in *Yediot Aharonot* in February 1992, referred to the pioneers as colonizers who stole land from the Palestinians. On his daily evening news and commentary TV emission, London would consistently refer to the "occupied territories," using the nasty and negative anti–Israeli terminology.

At a Peace Now rally in Tel Aviv in June 1989, Israeli author Amos Oz referred to Gush Emunim as "a small sect ... messianic and cruel, a Jewish Hezbollah;" and in an article in *Yediot Aharonot* on June 8, 1989, as reported by Arieh Stav in his "Notes on the Dialectics of Israeli Anti-semitism", Oz pummeled the pioneers as "a bunch of armed gangsters, criminals against humanity ... pogromists ... from the cellars of bestiality and defilement." These idealistic young Israeli patriots were redeeming their homeland, overwhelmingly legally and peacefully, despite sweeping rumors and reports of Jewish youth vandalizing and stealing Arab property. Oz lacked a sense of proportion, not to mention civility. The few instances when hilltop youth took action against Arabs came in response to Arab violence and murder of Jews, extensive destruction of agricultural lands, and provocations and attacks on the roads.

Oz, unable to understand the intent of Arafat's thugs and murderers, derided Israel's fear of a tiny Palestinian state in Shechem (Nablus) and Hebron as delirious. Having written in his book *In the Land of Israel* in 1984 that "Nationalism itself is, in my eyes, the curse of mankind," did Oz consider so-called Palestinian nationalism, and not only Jewish nationalism, a curse? His commitment to the Palestinians was nonetheless firm. He and his diehard fanatics would prevent the transfer of Arabs out of the land "even if we have to lie down under the wheels of the trucks. Even if we have to blow up the bridges" [across the Jordan River]. Such theatrical dedication unto death was the mark of a man seeking a sacred cause—not his own.

Throughout the 1980s, radical and hate-filled leftists were explicit about the inevitability of civil war between the state, the Left, and the army on one side, and the Right and the settlers on the other. It was a life-and-death struggle over the spirit and power in Israel. Novelist A.B. Yehoshua foresaw this violence in an article he penned in 1983 in *Maariv*, as did journalist Ran Edelist writing in *Hadashot* in 1988. It was not the democratic game that would decide who is in power and in the name of what program and values, but violence. The Left had a history of violence in their own historic legacy, against both Jews and Arabs it should be noted. For the Left, the intra–Jewish war was the essence of the situation; the Arabs bothered the Left far less. On the settlement enterprise, Meretz MK Yossi Sarid in 2002 provided his own erratic medical diagnosis calling it a cancerous growth.

The leftist alliance with the Palestinians evolved and intensified in direct relation to the Left's frustration with the Right's domination of the political arena. Asi Dayan, son of the legendary Moshe Dayan, wrote in *HaOlam Hazeh* in 1979 that in the upcoming Jewish civil war the Arabs would join with the Left to carry out pogroms in Israel. The radical Gideon Spiro, who considered that Palestinians killing settlers is not an act of murder, wrote in *Kol Ha'ir* that his ultimate fantasy is to marry an Arab woman and raise a family with her. Leah Rabin was quoted as saying, after Arafat kissed the Rabin grandchildren at the mourning period following the murder of the prime minister, that "I would prefer that my children would be Arabs rather than orthodox Jews." This fawning capitulation hinted that she hated Jews more than she loved Arabs.

Israeli self-hatred took a step further when Itai Gordon, member of kibbutz Hatzor, directed his HaShomer HaTzair youth to wipe their feet on the national flag and burn a bible. In 1985, youth from the upper Galilee kibbutz Shomera violated the grave of Herzl in Jerusalem. Carrying red (Marxist) flags six hundred members of HaShomer HaTzair convened in Jerusalem to consider the deepest moral and political problems confronting Israel. A fifteen-year-old youngster participating in a group discussion said, "I don't believe in the Bible" but rather in the Balfour Declaration and the UN Partition Resolution, as connecting the Jews with their Land. In 2017, some high school seniors called on their peers not to enlist in the IDF because, they said, Israel oppresses the Palestinians and rejects peace.

It is worth recalling that before and after the founding of the state, Ben-Gurion had identified HaShomer HaTzair and its patron the Mapam party "as worse than Etzel [Irgun]." He despised the Maki communist party which was a further extreme mutation of radical leftist ideology. Back in the 1930s HaShomer HaTzair saw in the possibility of a Jewish state the oppression of the Arabs in the country. However, the believers in Zionism realize that a Jewish state is a moral imperative to save us from being oppressed—and worse—by the Arabs.

All this apparently did not make an impression on Chaim Herzog who as president of Israel attended a Communist Party convention in Haifa in 1985. Then, in addressing the Canadian Parliament in June 1989, Herzog emphasized two major points: that Israel was a democracy and that the Israelis were searching for peace. This agenda was no different from that of the essentially Arab Communist Party which he had earlier addressed in Israel. For both Jewish leftists and Arab communists, the code terminology of democracy and peace signified de–Judaizing and de–Zionizing Israel in the name of unadulterated equal citizenship for anti–Israeli Arabs, and in capitulating to the Palestinians by withdrawal from the homeland. One of the controversial crusaders on behalf of the Palestinians in Israeli courts was attorney Felicia Langer, a Communist Party member.

No less scandalous was the Tel Aviv University Faculty of Law convening a conference in January 2007 that sought to whitewash and define Palestinian terrorists as political prisoners. Ben Dror Yemini writing in *Maariv* compared this theme to a recent Holocaust denial conference held in Tehran. Yemini later wrote *Industry of Lies* (ISGAP— Institute for the Study of Anti–Semitism and Policy, 2017) that charged Western academia and media with promoting human rights/pro–Palestinian horrific untruths about Israel—that she treats Palestinians the way Nazis treated Jews, or that Israel carried out a massacre in Jenin in 2002. However, B.D. Yemini still carried his leftist credentials for the phony peace camp nonsense proudly on his political chest.

The sculptor Yigal Tamarkin provided his own manner of Jewish self-denial. He showed his wrath and contempt at a dedication ceremony of a new wing at the Israel Museum in Jerusalem in 1985 when the Hanukkah holiday candles were lit. He stormed out in protest declaring that Hanukkah, celebrating the Maccabee victory over Greek occupation of the Land of Israel, is the holiday of "backwardness and reaction." On another occasion Tumarkin said openly that "Raful" (retired former IDF Chief-of-Staff Rafael Eitan) and "Gandhi" (retired Major-General Rehavam Zeevi) are two nationalist figures that should be killed, but that he didn't have the courage to do it. Like Tumarkin who saw no bravery and purity of spirit in the Hanukkah drama, Shulamit Aloni who was an active leftist human rights activist considered that any alleged crime or vulgarity by a Jewish religious person was necessarily embedded with calumny in Judaism and its rabbinic leaders. The leftist war against religion was of a piece with its war against Zionism. Artist-author Yair Garboz caused a tsunami of political uproar when, prior to the March 2015 general elections, he erupted in a tirade of blistering ridicule at a political rally in Tel Aviv against what he considered the racists in Israeli society. He derided those Jews whose cultural baggage included "kissing talisman charms, and idol worshipers stooping and beseeching at sacred graves." That those harmless folklore expressions of religiosity could evoke a venomous assault points to the cultural abyss of acrimony that gripped the Left in Israeli society. Yet that same Garboz had said in an interview in September 1996 in *Yediot Aharonot* that he would prefer a traditional religious burial, and added that a religious wedding ceremony is preferable than a reform one which he labeled "pathetic." Israel was full of secularists who did not give a final divorce to Jewish tradition.

Guy Maayan in his essay "Exile in Eretz Israel" analyzed three young Israeli artists who showed severe signs of estrangement from Israel where they were born. The singer and song writer Eran Zur, photographer Adi Nes, and writer and journalist Uzi Weil, each in their particular cultural idiom gave voice to the helplessness facing the Zionist fate and future. Israeli and Zionist symbols were found wanting for them, and it was only a step away for them to exit and dismiss Israel as a temporary phenomenon. The malaise on the Left was far deeper than just unease with the political issues of settlements and territories.

Nevertheless, the leftist war against the settlements and Israel's presence in the territories continued unabated while the yearning for peace with the Palestinians carried a sense of urgency. For that purpose Labor parliamentarian Yossi Sarid called upon the United States, already in 1982, to recognize the PLO. David Krivine, writing in the pages of *The Jerusalem Post*, referred in mid–1984 derisively to the "bearded [settler] enthusiasts" and their hostility to the Arab population. A few decades later author Meir Shalev was proud to recall that as a leftist he was not drunk with the 1967 victory and maintained over the years his great disdain and disgust for the settlers. A special target for vituperative hatred by the Left was author Naomi Frenkel after she moved to Kiryat Arba/Hebron. Matti Peled, Yoram Kaniuk, and Michael Harsegor, denounced her as a racist and deserter from the peace camp, a victim of Beginism. Writing in July 1993 in *Yediot Aharonot*, A.B. Yehoshua proposed a Palestinian state while wanting to limit (ghettoize?) Israeli settlers to two urban centers in the West Bank. These Jews would become citizens in the state of Palestine, which was an untenable proposition knowing, as we do, that a Palestinian state was destined to be judenrein (empty of Jews). Yehoshua's plan would be more than sufficient to enrage the Jews and yet insult the Arabs. In an interview in the same year Yehoshua explained that indeed there should be a Palestinian state; however, if the Palestinians violate the agreement and fire katyusha rockets against Israel, then they should be expelled across the Jordan River. When the Palestinians in Gaza witnessed the end of Israel's rule in 2005 and established a de facto Palestinian state, they fired rockets and mortars. But Israel did not expel the Palestinians into the sea or to the desert.

Abba Eban, acclaimed dovish foreign minister, urged the Likud government to abandon settlement projects in populated Arab areas, considering such a policy inimical to any authentic Zionist purpose. He called upon Israelis to return to reason in an article in *The Jerusalem Post* in February 1984, while opinion polls foresaw a future Labor Party victory which indeed proved quite correct in July that year. Eban also called upon the United States to increase pressure on Israel in order to convince her to return to the pre–1967 borders—the very borders which he himself coined as "the Auschwitz borders." Eban's political betrayal never somehow tainted his international image of being a statesman-like voice. At the January 1985 International Book Fair in Cairo, the Egyptians appeared unconvinced by Eban's esteemed reputation, and callously threw out his books.

In addressing a New Israel Fund conference in 1988, Eban bemoaned that it is "morally wrong to subject one and a half million Palestine Arabs to Israeli rule." He asserted simplistically that one people "cannot possibly impose and maintain rule of one people over another, except by methods of coercion and by ideologies of self-assertion and ethnic superiority . . ." Abba Eban, the noted Oxford scholar, was unable to come to terms with the implications of the Arab war against Israel and readjust his moral compass. The highly educated Eban made his unsavory contribution in consecrating the jargon of "the occupied territories" as in an article in *The New York Times* on September 28, 1989, spreading this anti–Israeli household spiel around the world.

Raanan Weitz, chairman of the Settlement Department of the Jewish Agency, was shamelessly comfortable by specifically labeling Judea and Samaria as the West Bank (the Hashemite Jordanian term), while regarding the "occupied territories" as a curse and disease. Mordechai Bar-On, Knesset member for the leftist Citizen's Rights List, referred in the 1980s to the strengthening of PLO moderates as a sign that negotiations should be undertaken. The call for recognizing the PLO in the 1990s and negotiating with it was vindicated by the Labor Party.

Meanwhile, Professor Yoram Dinstein, Dean of the Faculty of Law at Tel Aviv University, proposed offering the bulk of the West Bank to Jordan. This would not threaten Israel's security because Israel "managed to survive 18 [sic. 19] years without the territories." His magic wand would assure that the past, though it had been marred by Palestinian fedayeen terrorist infiltration in the 1950s, would automatically dictate the future. The Shiloah Institute at Tel Aviv University offered its professional opinion to justify retreat from Judea, Samaria, and Gaza. In his book *West Bank: Line of Defense* (Praeger, 1985), Aryeh Shalev argued in favor of withdrawal back to the 1949 Armistice Lines with the establishment of a demilitarized Palestinian State. He and other reputed security experts with military experience regurgitated a mouthful of self-deception, humiliating submissiveness, and political folly, divorced from centuries and volumes of history and reality. General Giora Island, who served as Director of the National Security Council, considered that Israel needed only 12 percent of the West Bank. Reserve-General Amiram Levin stated in 2017 that Israel should give the Palestinians a state, adding that if they make problems—like shooting at a plane landing at Ben-Gurion International Airport—Israel then should expel them from the West Bank. Neither military science nor political science could rationally justify conceding essential territory to an enemy who will very conceivably continue to be an enemy thereafter.

General Avraham Tamir, whose jobs included head of the strategic planning branch in the IDF, wrote in *The National Review* on June 25, 1990, that "it is no longer possible to argue . . . that the establishment of a Palestinian state will inflict a disaster upon Israel . . . or that the uprising in the West Bank and Gaza Strip can simply be suppressed, or that it is possible to maintain the separate peace with Egypt indefinitely . . ." He added that Syria and Iraq are seeking peace. So much dribble and nonsense and misunderstanding and failed forecasts. Check for yourself and see that he was wrong then and for decades thereafter about everything: the Palestinians, Egypt, Syria, and Iraq. Political fairy tales filled the pages and airwaves in Israel as the experts are foolishly considered full of infallibility.

The ideological confusion even penetrated the Youth and HeHalutz Department of the World Zionist Organization where a seminar series with educational materials bore the neutral title of Israel and Palestine: Whose Land? Such political equality was a symptom of abject moral relativism. The Israelis, because of the ongoing leftist brainwashing, provided a platform for questioning the singular rights of the Jewish people.

And while the leftists were conducting their ongoing assault against the settlers and the Right, the idea was percolating that Israel was not going to leave the territories. Once deputy-mayor of Jerusalem Meron Benvenisti, of whom Daniel Pipes wrote that he "despises his own country," believed that six years of pro-settlement Likud rule from 1977 to 1983 had created "the point of no return." The Jewish population in Judea and Samaria (and Jordan Valley) rose during that period of Likud rule from 3,200 to 22,800; so Benvenisti thought that de facto annexation of the West Bank was a fait accompli. In that case the Left would concentrate on assuring Arab civil rights under Israeli rule, though other voices like David Twersky of kibbutz Gezer refused to succumb to the denial of Palestinian national rights. Mentioning far more radical Jews, we recall Israeli–born Uri Davis whose anti–Zionist position called for a revolutionary political struggle to define Palestine–Eretz Israel the home for two peoples. His political biography included joining the Fatah terrorist movement; and the necessary implication pointed to the eradication of the state of Israel. And then there is Leah Tzemel who employed her legal skills to defend Palestinian terrorists in Israeli courts. It is quite astounding that terrorists from the territories, not Arab citizens or residents of Israel, yet enjoy a right to legal representation and a trial in an Israeli court. Tzemel was a notorious pro–Arab attorney in a time when her state, Israel, was at war with the Palestinians.

A very noteworthy but atypical Jewish sympathizer with Palestinians was Rabbi Menachem Fruman of Tekoa, in Judea. He was known to meet with Muslim religious leaders, also with Arafat himself, in seeking inter-religious rapprochement. His sentimental and romantic peace vision led him to cheerfully declare in November 1989: "I would be happy to dance with the Palestinians on their independence day." He had also blithely advocated for an Arab president alongside a Jewish one in Israel. Rabbi Fruman was a Torah scholar but not a political savant.

For film writer and polemist Kobi Niv, the occupation was a violent crime which justified Palestinian actions of any kind against the settlers. In 2017 Avi Gibson Bar El, the artistic director of the Akko Fringe Theater Festival, resigned because a play about Palestinian prisoners (terrorists), "Prisoners of the Occupation" by Einat Weitzman, was disallowed by the event's steering committee. Freedom of expression is not a license to do a hatchet job on the state.

The Oslo Fiasco

The leftist passion for making peace with the Palestinians is legendary and folkloric. But it is far more than that in its philosophic and epistemological meaning. In his famous work *Novum Organum* from 1620, Francis Bacon wrote of the delusion of ideas by calling them idols imposed by words. One case refers to "names of things which do not exist." There is no more appropriate example of this in the reality of the Middle East than the word peace. This is a name but not a thing at all. There is no peace between Israel and Arabs that radiates trust and friendship. Israel's "cold peace" with Egypt and with Jordan is in a category of its own; a kind of extended cease-fire, but not a people-to-people or politically authentic peace whatsoever. There may be things without names, but peace is a name without being a thing. We are back to the shadows of illusions in Plato's cave.

The Palestine Liberation Organization (PLO) was founded in 1964 with the goal of destroying the Jewish/Zionist state of Israel, considered a colonialist and interloper proxy of imperialism occupying the Arab land of Palestine. Its revolutionary doctrine of armed warfare found its expression in an array of terrorist operations, from airplane hijackings and bombings to stoning and murdering Israelis. From the 1970s, the PLO adopted a diplomatic and propagandistic approach by feigning peace overtures, as in the 1974 Phases Strategy. In 1988 it issued its nuanced Declaration of the State of Palestine. By employing a rich panoply of stratagems, Palestinian politics, in tandem with the popular and violent uprising (intifada) that exploded in Gaza and the West Bank in 1987, sought to sow discord within the Israeli public by cultivating its left-leaning elements in dialogue.

In 1990, four Israelis of public standing—MK Dedi Zucker, former Foreign Ministry Director-General Avraham Tamir, Tel Aviv University professor Yochanan Peres, and former *Jerusalem Post* editor Ari Rath— were scheduled to meet with four well-known PLO-affiliated Palestinians. Among them was Faisal Husseini who would following the Oslo Accord admit in an interview in June 2001, that the agreement was a Trojan Horse ruse to destroy Israel. Zucker argued that meetings with an academic ambiance were not forbidden by the law banning meetings with the PLO. A policy of appeasement became the mark of leftist fraudulent peace-makers over the decades—before and after Oslo. For them the conflict was resolvable despite the overwhelming reality that Arab rejectionism generally and Palestinian hostility specifically were insurmountable.

The Israeli run-up to the Oslo Accord, so meticulously delineated by Raphael Israeli in *The Oslo Idea* (Transaction, 2012), was filled with illegality, machinations, and duplicity. The two professorial political matchmakers, Ron Pundak and Yair Hirschfeld, were presumably emissaries of Foreign Minister Shimon Peres who sought to obscure official contacts with the PLO. During this period in 1992 and into 1993, it was still an infringement of Israeli law to meet with members of a terrorist organization. The behind-the-scenes manipulation of talks in Norway was hidden from no less Prime Minister Rabin himself. Even before the beginning of a series of talks between Israelis and Palestinians, Peres had his deputy Yossi Beilin pass a note in Cairo to Mahmoud Abbas, a senior PLO official, that contrived a deal: Arab citizens in Israel would vote for the Labor Party in the 1992 elections, thereafter a Labor government would propose a territorial withdrawal from the territories and agree to a PLO-led autonomous entity in the West Bank.

Shimon Peres, who played a critical role in many Israeli diplomatic and strategic endeavors, was an elusive type despite, or because of, his blown-up rhetoric. After a public career that placed him at the center of Israel's political map, Peres veered to the Left after 1977. He strove for peace with the Arabs at every turn and fork in the road, he cultivated and cajoled the Palestinians, and dreamed of a New Middle East. While he acquired a global reputation for statesmanship and idealism, at home his message was a matter of controversy, and at times he appeared more the buffoon and loser than a man of solid judgment. His peace-mate Arafat was hardly a fool as he kept his eye on the political ball, pushing it forward in the long-term war until it would (Arafat imagined) travel the distance "from the river to the sea" to include all of Palestine.

On September 23, 1993, the Knesset voted with only 61 of 120 members in favor of approving the Oslo Accord. The "Gaza–Jericho First" Israeli withdrawal installment followed. In the parliamentary vote on October 6, 1995 to approve the Oslo 2 Accord, the vote was also a bare 61 of 120 in favor. Razor-thin majorities on a fundamental and highly contentious national policy did not conform to the need for national consensus. It would have been far more appropriate in Israel's case for such unparalleled parliamentary votes to require a "super-majority," the likes of which exist in the United States for constitutional amendments. Labor Prime Minister Yitzhak Rabin rammed through the Oslo Accords with five votes from non–Zionist non-coalition Arab party MKs. He had mocked the parliamentary opposition, especially Likud, whose leader Benjamin Netanyahu accused Rabin with lacking a Jewish majority and endangering the Israeli people for such a radical policy change that recognized the PLO. Rabin also scorned the Gush Emunim settler movement which for him was, already back in 1976, "a cancer in the social and democratic flesh of the state of Israel" (a statement documented in a video by Erez Laufer); and he insulted popular street protesters to Oslo whom he derisively dismissed as "they spin around and around like propellers." Rabin, who had changed political course in dealing with the PLO, chose a partisan policy which, in his eyes, was necessary to bring about a cessation of Palestinian terrorism in Israel. This irresponsible flight into fantasy was detailed by David Makovsky in *Making Peace with the PLO: The Rabin Government's Road to the Oslo Accord* (Washington Institute for Near East Policy, 1996). Rabin didn't hear the people's pain and anxiety, he ridiculed their futile protests, he risked civil strife.

A festival of peace burst upon Israeli society with the signing of the Oslo Accord. Euphoria put reason in the cold freezer. The novelist David Grossman was a leading peace enthusiast who forecast, witnessing the photographed signing ceremony on the White House lawn on September 13, that the "occupation" would end, a consequence of which would be the inability of Israelis to define themselves in their native spirit; as if the occupation was necessary to give Israelis a cultural reference-point. There would then be an opportunity to sharpen the distinction between the Jews in the diaspora who chose not to come to Israel and the Jews living in Israel. For Grossman, the Law of Return was problematic because it diverted attention from the need to rectify the situation of Arab citizens of Israel who did not enjoy equal status. Here was a leading cultural figure exploiting the Arab question for de–Zionizing the state.

In the spirit of his outlook, Grossman found the work of B'Tselem, an organization that fiendishly castigates Israeli soldiers for their treatment of Palestinians in the territories, "a real source of pride." In 2017 the esteemed author received an honorary doctorate from the Hebrew University of Jerusalem that allowed him, in his address at the ceremony, to bemoan the "occupation" with its cells of "ultra-nationalism and racism" and messianic zeal.

For B. Michael, writing in *Yediot Aharonot* in December 1993, the settlers were of three kinds: evil, naïve, or greedy. All were to be removed from the West Bank and resettled in the Negev. For him, individual human rights and Jewish national rights counted for nothing. Among the libelous attacks against the Gush Emunim settlers was one from noteworthy songwriter Haim Hefer, who sarcastically proposed that the settlers organize a festival that would celebrate smashing Arab windows, murdering their donkeys, burning their cars and other such violent actions. Uri Avneri, notorious anti–Zionist, slandered the settlers by calling them Cossacks—those plunderers, rapists, and murderers in southern Russian history. In 2014 Amos Oz posited a comparison between the adventurous hilltop youth in Samaria with neo–Nazis. In response, Dr. Gabi Avital, the chief scientist of the Education Ministry, deplored the fact that Israel's leading authors, rather than bolstering the spiritual backbone of the people, were actually showing solidarity with the enemy. In early 2018 Israeli leftists—the likes of Avram Burg, Yael Dayan, Tzali Reshef, Naomi Hazan, and Uri Avneri—signed a letter that appeared in *The Irish Times* to advocate the boycott of products from Judea and Samaria, and the Golan Heights. This was orchestrated in tandem with political steps initiated in Ireland to criminalize any commercial transactions with Israel across the Green Line.

Israel's academics were not to be outdone in their war against the Ariel College (later University) in the largest town in Samaria. Two professors from Tel Aviv University, Dan HaCohen and Anat Bilski, urged colleagues abroad not to attend a conference at the college because this would imply recognition of the settlement enterprise. Back in 2004, HaCohen, who teaches comparative literature, offered a comparison between Nazi Germany and the state of Israel. For him, Israel's pin-point murder of arch-terrorists like Hamas leader Sheikh Ahmed Yassin was an act of barbarism rather than an act to eliminate barbarism. HaCohen ignored the fact that Israel applied to IDF military operations stringent norms of avoiding collateral civilian damage when targeting a terrorist.

The rabid de-legitimation of Israel in many circles around the world, in the sophisticated halls of universities and in public marches, would seem to have been, at least in part, a home-grown Jewish malady in Israel itself. From Zion burst forth the virus of self-hatred. Amnon Lord writing on the *nrg* site in March 2017 leveled the sweeping but validated charge that the Israeli Left, as represented by the *Haaretz* daily, was moved by anti–Semitism. Charging Israel with racism was standard and stereotypical fodder. The mendacious accusation that Israel was racist ignored some essential facts: the presence of an Arab justice on the Supreme Court, 13 Arab MKs, thousands of Arab university students, an active Arab press, an Arab professional class of lawyers, physicians, professors, and people in the arts. The leftists shut their minds while more and more doors were opening up to the Arab citizens of Israel.

While the Jews were demonized, the Palestinians were glorified. Israeli television crews were present at Rafiah in the Gaza Strip zone in the spring of 1994 when, in accordance with the Israel–PLO Agreement, Palestinians headed by Arafat himself were able to return to Palestine. The Israeli crew were as jubilant as the returning and smiling Palestinian terrorists themselves.

Two leading Israeli journalists Nahum Barnea and Smadar Peri had interviewed Arafat in Tunis earlier in November 1992. Their report in *Yediot Aharonot* seemed to be designed to humanize the arch-terrorist and overcome Rabin's hesitation to seek a peace agreement with the PLO. Barnea and Peri wrote in intimate detail about Arafat's handshake with them, as if this was an important datum in evaluating the viability of peace with the Palestinians. This recalls Defense Minister Ezer Weizman, who had been instrumental in 1978 at the Camp David Summit negotiations, admitting that he was virtually hypnotized when he met Egyptian President Anwar Sadat.

The ideological decline of the Left was mixed with muddled strategic thinking. Writing in *Haaretz* in June 1994, Ran Kislev charged Israel with an insatiable territorial appetite in expanding Jerusalem's southern approaches to Gush Etzion. Certainly the Arabs would refuse to negotiate a political settlement if Jerusalem extended also eastward to Maale Adumim; for only cosmetic territorial changes, according to Kislev's reasoning, would perhaps be agreeable to them. Haim Asa, a strategic adviser to Prime Minister Yitzhak Rabin, wrote in an op-ed piece in the canonically leftist *Haaretz* newspaper in 1995 the following twaddle: "An independent and democratic Palestinian state is an Israeli strategic asset." That daily's international English–language edition, by the way, had become over the years the eyes and ears for readers around the world who were interested in Israel; and they were handed, not doses of fair journalism and pride in Israel, but a constant bashing of the country and the delegitmation of its national Jewish narrative.

What emerged from Oslo was a tyrannical rogue Palestinian Authority regime in Judea and Samaria and a repressive Islamic state—let in the Gaza Strip. The march of Israeli folly, hallucinating about Palestinian democracy and good government, rolled on relentlessly for the Labor Party and the Left. The Arab residents suffering under these regimes of fear were the immediate losers from Israel's peace adventure.

Following the assassination of Rabin in November 1995 Yasser Arafat, as noted above, came to the Tel Aviv apartment of the prime minister to pay his condolences to the Rabin family. Yossi Ginosar, a senior security official who was a central figure in negotiations with the Palestinians, was photographed sitting beside Arafat. Ginosar was later suspected of criminal actions, perhaps money laundering and tax evasion, in handling Arafat's $300 million bank account in Switzerland in collaboration with Muhammad Rashid, a close confidant of the PLO/PA chairman. Caroline Glick and Dan Margalit, two noteworthy journalists/authors, raised serious questions about Ginosar's conflict of interests regarding money and security. Others, like Rami Tal writing in *HaAyin Hashviit* in 2009, claimed that Ginosar would never compromise Israeli interests. As for the legal apparatus in the Ginosar affair, Attorney-General Elyakim Rubinstein and State Prosecutor Edna Arbel ordered the police in 2002 to investigate only possible economic crimes. The case fizzled out and Ginosar was never indicted. He died in 2004.

The security holes in the Oslo cheese, far more severe than personal financial corruption, were outrageously glaring from the start. In April 1994, just a little more than six months after the Oslo accord, a Muslim suicide bomber exploded on a bus in Afula killing eight people. In October, a similar act killed 22 on Dizengoff Street in Tel Aviv. Through 1995 suicide bombers from Hamas, Fatah, Palestine Islamic Jihad, and The Popular Front for the Liberation of Palestine, murdered Israelis at the Beit Lid Junction, in Ramat Gan, Jerusalem, and elsewhere in Israel. The Left, however, was in denial, as Palestinian terrorists pursued the spree of murdering and maiming citizens of Israel. Uri Orbach, journalist and satirist, writing in an article titled "On Arrogance" which later appeared in his book *Religious as Normal* (Yediot Aharonot, 2018), challenged the smug Left to admit they erred in their delusion of a New Middle East. Arafat's war against Israel didn't stop with the Oslo Accord.

The far-Left's strained feelings toward the army was of a piece with its alienation from the Zionist ethos and its overt sympathy for the Palestinians. Singer Yaffa Yarkoni, who was a folk legend by entertaining the troops on the front lines, incensed many with an IDF–Nazi analogy. Yarkoni more than suggested that Israel carried out a holocaust (!) on the Arabs, when the army responded to a wave of Palestinian terrorism with a major military operation in 2002 in Jenin and other West Bank cities. Other singers were no less pro-peace and pro–Arab. Ahinoam Ninni maintained a stubborn consistent political line. She resigned in January 2016 from the Israel Artists Association over an award given to song-writer Ariel Zilber; she took part in an Alternative Remembrance Ceremony for Israelis and Palestinians, at least twice, that commemorated Arab terrorists killed by Israeli security forces; she also declared that Abu Mazen (i.e. Mahmoud Abbas) wants peace but Netanyahu doesn't; and she supported the refusal of Professor Rivka Carmi to participate in a Knesset committee discussion of the BDS movement that focused on the suspicion that Ben-Gurion University is a hotbed of pro-BDS agitation. Political geographer Oren Yiftachel, also from the same university, denounced Israeli governments as racist and urged Jews to participate in the Arab Land Day March that was an annual anti–Israeli fest on March 30. It was ironic that an article that he submitted, co-authored with an Arab academic from Haifa University, was rejected by the English periodical *Political Geography*, with the editor explaining that the decision was based on the fact that the authors were Israeli.

To add one other example of the post–Zionist/pro–Oslo academic atmosphere in Israel, we mention a research study conducted by the Institute for Zionist Strategies in 2011. It found, naturally, that there was no political balance among faculty views in sociology departments in the universities of Israel. The Right was under-represented, or just not there.

The charge that Israel conducted a South African–style racist apartheid regime against the Palestinian population in the territories was gathering international attention and support. The BDS movement was a major propaganda vehicle to delegitimize the state of Israel and not just her policies. The ideological imprimatur of the white apartheid model from Pretoria was thrust upon Zionist Israel. The Pretoria regime based on the baneful role of a white, colonialist, supremacist ideology had collapsed, and so would that of Tel Aviv. It is more than interesting that the PLO's use of negotiations and agreements to propel Israeli capitulation in the name of ostensible peace and reconciliation approximated the African National Congress's successful strategy of negotiations with the White regime, beginning in 1990 and culminating in the dismantling of apartheid in 1994—the year which witnessed the first step in Israel's withdrawal. It was singularly appropriate for Arafat to say to Nelson Mandela when they had met in Cairo in 1990: "We're in the same trench." In this spirit South Africa's parliament passed a motion in February 2018 that could lead to the seizure of land from white farmers without even paying them compensation. The comparable Palestinian narrative charges the Zionists with the crime of seizing land in Palestine; and inspired and encouraged by the South African step, the Palestinians deftly manipulate the jargon of justice and peace to divest Jewish settlers of land they acquired in Judea and Samaria. Arab sovereignty in the soi disant disputed territories could launch Jewish ethnic cleansing of a few hundred thousand residents, which would begin in Judea and Samaria, but not necessarily end there.

Israeli academics, as we have noted, were a corrosive element in defaming Israel in the eyes of the world. Professor of Linguistics Tanya Reinhart of Tel Aviv University wrote a letter in the name of her comrades in November 2001, in praise and support of the decision taken by the Ann Arbor Council in Michigan, which decided to divest from investments it may hold in companies or funds which did business in Israel. In 2009 Professor Rachel Giora of Tel Aviv University wrote in agreement to a group of lecturers abroad regarding their work to make the boycott more comprehensive and effective. Dr. Anat Matar from the same university was set to visit SOAS in London to explain her support for BDS. Other Tel Aviv University BDS advocates against Israel included philosophy professor Adi Ophir and history professor Gadi Algazi. However American Jewish professor Alan Dershowitz, when speaking at Tel Aviv University upon receiving an honorary doctorate in May 2010, castigated academic dissenters from that very university who campaign to boycott Israeli universities. Intellectual leftist renegades were at war against Israel, and themselves.

Veteran television personality Yaakov Ahimeir wrote that "these [leftist] academics had no moral qualms about continuing to receive their salaries from what they considered to be the apartheid state of Israel." This fit the agenda of Israeli human rights activists advocating for the Palestinians against the Israeli government and its military "occupation" in the territories. Bear in mind that the BDS anti–Israel apartheid campaign never concealed that its defamation of Israel signified the delegitimation of Israel. BDS demonstrations in the West brandished posters that declared "Israel Hitler," "Stop the Holocaust in Gaza," "Confront Zionism;" while the piece de resistance being "From the River to the Sea, Palestine Will be Free." Not only Judea and Samaria were in the dock but Tel Aviv and Haifa. We might be somewhat less outraged by the BDS activists in America when at home in Israel the radical Left was maligning Israel to death. In the view of Professor David Bokay at the University of Haifa, Israel must stop funding the leftist academia.

Charges of Nazism and fascism were bandied about by the Left as nonchalantly as tossing bubble gum wrappers in the air. Gideon Samet writing in *Haaretz* in October 2002 identified proto-fascist tendencies on the Right and as manifested in the settlement enterprise. For him, the sanctity of land, homeland, and the state, were part of "the ugliest trends in Israel over the last generation." Shulamit Aloni compared former Minister of Defense Moshe Arens to the Nazi propagandist Josef Goebbels. Radio anchorman Natan Zahavi labeled well-known attorney Yoram Sheftel "Hitler." Zahavi was later charged by the court to pay a 45,000 NIS fine. Journalist Dan Margalit called Likud MK Yariv Levin a fascist because he wanted to promote reforms in the choice of justices to the Supreme Court.

The Left saw only darkness, intrigue, manipulation, and demonic behavior. In August 2010, journalist Gideon Levy from *Haaretz* derided the Jewish state when speaking abroad for a BDS Scottish Palestinian Solidarity campaign in Dundee. Meir Shalev, another leftist author, continued to love flowers and sheep, but despise mitnachalim (pioneer settlers), babbling on in 2017. Writing in *Haaretz* in April 2017, Yossi Klein bashed the national religious camp as "more dangerous than Hezbollah." This was of a kind with an earlier remark by Yair Tzaban from Mapam who called the national camp "a Hamas twin." The leftist loose cannon was shelling with abandon.

The poet Natan Zach in 2014 considered the charge by Mahmoud Abbas that Israel's military operation "Protective Edge" in the Gaza Strip constituted "genocide" to be true. Overall the guilt for the absence of peace, he thought, lay with Israeli Prime Minister Benjamin Netanyahu. Accordingly, Knesset Speaker Avrum Burg, who advised American Jews in 1993 to terminate their aid to Israel, stated in 2003 that the end of the

Zionist enterprise was at hand. He had declared himself to be a post-national as he fondled his French passport.

Shimon Peres is worth more coverage in this survey. He was after all the primary architect of the Oslo surrender, acting as the de facto defense attorney and fundraiser for the PLO in the world. In August 1993, just a month before the signing ceremony in Washington, Foreign Minister Peres flew to Oslo for the purpose—he revealed with a wink to his aides—of raising money for the Palestinians. After Ahmad al-Hindi, among the Fatah who masterminded the Munich massacre of 11 Israeli athletes in 1972 was appointed by Arafat to a senior position in his Gaza regime, Peres denied this step infringed upon the 1993 Oslo and 1994 Cairo accords. He said of al-Hindi that "he didn't have blood on his hands." Decades earlier, Mapai Foreign Minister Moshe Sharett had written that if Shimon Peres becomes a minister in the Israeli government, this promotion of Peres would represent "a malignant moral corruption." Peres' political machinations had been employed against PM Begin regarding the 1981 nuclear bombing in Iraq (which he opposed), and against PM Shamir concerning the 1987 London Agreement with Jordan (which he unsuccessfully concocted).

The relationship between Peres and Arafat was a conundrum of intrigue and collaboration. When Arafat was asked in May 1996 at the National Press Club in Washington, "whether the PLO has given up its dream of taking all of Palestine," he suddenly became angry and shouted: "this is an unfair question." Arafat, noted for his shamanic yelling jihad, jihad, jihad at Palestinian rallies, tried to conceal—before Western audiences—the strategy to pulverize Israel with terror and diplomacy to the end. Aware of this forgery of making peace while both intending and conducting war, we cannot forget the photo of Peres smiling gingerly, holding on to Arafat's sleeve as they together took the stage in a moment of political exhilaration. They were partners in peace and recipients of the Nobel Prize for their foul political theater. Peres' boundless enthusiasm combined with his political myopia actually brought him to the point of declaring that, once peace is achieved, Israel's next goal would be to join the Arab League. In response to this bizarre statement in 1994, the Secretary General of the Arab League advised Peres "to first Islamicize." Peres just never got it.

The Left did not limit itself to merely promoting a Palestinian state, stable and prosperous no less. The Israeli fascist government, wrote

Professor David Enoch, must be seen for what it is; author Eyal Megged claimed in 2002 that a fascist atmosphere had descended upon Israel. The end of democracy was at hand. This was reminiscent of Avraham Katz-Oz, once a Labor Minister of Agriculture, who gave voice to the outrage and derangement that struck the Left when Likud came to power back in 1977, and warned of a new version of Israeli fascism. No evidence, no data, no rationale; just that uncontrollable hysteria that struck the Left when Begin came to power in the elections of 1977. How these charges skirted the reality of Israel as a free society—to speak, write, assemble, protest, vote—we do not know how to explain. The leftist litany continued: Israeli draftees to the IDF should refuse serving in the "occupation army" in the territories, preached Shulamit Aloni in 1996, and perhaps refuse to serve anywhere in the view of Dan Ben Amotz; Israeli settlements must be removed. Negotiations must be renewed. The wise men of the Left signed a statement in this spirit that featured in November 2000 in *Haaretz*, and they included Shlomo Gazit, David Grossman, Natan Zach, Emmanuel Sivan, Amos Oz, Sami Smooha, David Kimchi, Menachem Klein, Eli Amir, Arieh Luba Eliav—they and others from an array of fields including politics, the military, academia, culture and the arts. Of course, their record or specialization in peace-making registered a resounding zero. Nor was "know thy enemy" part of their instruction manual. Amos Oz, with his international reputation, as in writing in the pages of *The New York Times*, contributed his hollow insight that, thanks to Hamas terrorism, Likud is saved from confronting the possibility of peace with the Palestinians. Drawing upon the tasteless notion of moral equivalence, Oz identified "the Hamas–Likud Connection" in an op-ed piece from April 1995.

However beyond the obvious political character of the Oslo charade, its cultural dimension was probably even more significant in historical terms. The Left understood that their political campaign was an expression of a cultural struggle over the identity of Israel and its future path. Ron Pundak stated in 2013 that he wanted peace in order to assure "Israeliness." He believed that the struggle was a matter of assuring that Israel be a normal state, separating religion from the state, and guaranteeing full equality for the Arab minority. This prescription overlapped and fit the territorial parameters of Israel withdrawing to the pre–1967 lines. The failure of Oslo as a political plan represents therefore the failure of Pundak's vision to "normalize Israel."

But the normalization of Israel in a deeper sense is the banalization of Israel, detaching it from its ancient Jewish roots, and shaping the state like all other states and the Jewish people as all other peoples. This would not be a liberating moment at all, but the death of Zionism and the spiritual and political annihilation of the state of Israel. Keeping Jerusalem united and under Israeli sovereignty remains a litmus test for the vitality of Jewish nationhood in these days. For the Left, Jerusalem presents a dilemma and a burden. They pine for devolving the eastern Arab parts of the city into the hands of the Palestinians. Haim Ramon of the Labor Party founded a group "to save Jewish Jerusalem" by abandoning Arab Jerusalem outside of the Old City, where there is a small but growing Jewish presence. Yet conceding the eastern part is to endanger the Jewish western side of the city from demographic flooding and terrorism. The Arabs would push their way from east to west given the signal that Israel's collapse on the question of Jerusalem will occur in stages. They will smell blood, justifiably so. A people without respect for its national treasures cannot contend or survive the assault of an enemy mesmerized with its claims to truth and power.

A compelling but not incredible symptom of leftist reality-denying in this regard was the proposal made in 2007 by the Academy of Sciences in Israel to terminate archaeological research in Jerusalem until there will be peace in the region. The unearthing of findings from ancient Jewish history serves to strengthen Israel's hold on Jerusalem and aroused deep sentiments of rootedness. Therefore, science strengthening patriotism is to be demeaned as an obstacle to a fawning reconciliation with the Palestinians.

History was also botched in leftist hands. Sammy Shalom Sheetret, principal of the Kedma High School in Tel Aviv, changed the national rituals for Holocaust Remembrance Day by commemorating in addition to the Jewish Holocaust that of the Armenians, the Indians, the gypsies, even the homosexuals. Fleeing from the truth, trivializing or mangling it, while deconstructing the Holocaust, were not morally taboo deviations in déraciné leftist ranks.

Politics continued to be a refuge for leftist manipulations. It was reported that prior to the 2015 general elections in Israel, Zionist Camp/Labor Party leader Yitzhak Herzog visited with Mahmoud Abbas, head of the Palestinian Authority and the PLO in Ramallah. Hungry for votes from the Arab citizens in Israel, Herzog, it was reported, made an extravagant political offer to the PLO: a total withdrawal to the pre–1967 lines with East Jerusalem becoming the capital of a Palestinian state. Herzog couldn't do enough politically to ingratiate himself and his party to the Arabs. An election victory with the help of anti–Zionist Arab votes was the ignoble scheme.

In summary, we have encountered the de–Zionization of Israel's leftist elites. A Jewish state had become for them a racist state. To be a Jew for them was analogous perhaps to being a racist. Leftists could not sense the stench of the swamp of self-hatred they were stuck in—in the Jewish state.

A last gloss on this appalling state of affairs demands emphasis. The leftists hated Jews more than they really loved Arabs; and their compassion for the so-called suffering and victimized Arabs was only an excuse and ruse for their odious revulsion from the religious and the Right. The Left, in order to justify its war against the Right, against Zionism and against Judaism, needed to embrace the Arabs with love and sympathy. They posed as being animated by a high moral purpose. In the Left's banishing of the Jewish ethos and smothering the saga of the modern Jewish liberation, Israel becomes "normal"—and no more.

A personal and powerful testimony on the leftist crack-up was provided by former leftist Irit Linor, who was weaned on dogma that was fed to Israelis from a young age. She co-hosted a radio program on the army station, then became a regular panel member on the weekly *The Patriots* on TV channel 20. She eventually found her way back home to her Jewish selfhood. Irit posted the following item on social media in 2014:

> Let's say I wanted to return to be a classic leftist as I was. I couldn't, because the Left has raised the bar and the entrance fee. Once, in order to be a leftist, it was enough to favor the return of territories, and whiff an aroma of socialism. Today you have to "understand" Hamas, take a subscription for *Haaretz* newspaper, believe your gender is not something you're born with but something you choose, that a mother is an option and a father is just a conventional social norm, that the state was founded essentially to absorb Sudanese, to support the international boycott of Israel, to demand the state provide apartments as gifts to the citizens; and if all that is not enough: to be a vegetarian. Wow—this is too much for me.

Irit fortunately liberated herself from the loony Left.

Israel Shapes Palestinian History

After the Six Day War, Israel employed both Esau's hands and Jacob's voice on behalf of the Palestinians. Imagining a Palestinian people, shouldering its burdens and dreaming its dreams, became an Israeli obsession and moral mission. Israel seemed to believe that it had attained its own goals, it was thus the turn of the Palestinians to achieve theirs. Leftist altruists blinded themselves to the hard realities of geography, history, ideology, religion, and nationalism, that featured in the Palestinian war against the Jews and Israel. Ignorance may be bliss but it can also be lethal.

There were at least five stages in the creation story of the Palestinians:

> ~ Israeli rule in the West Bank and Gaza Strip provided a geo-political framework to define the Arab population as Palestinians different from the Arab peoples in the region;
>
> ~ Israel facilitated the development of a Palestinian society with the attributes of universities, the press, and general social advances;
>
> ~ Israel's hesitant and less than resolute response to the 1988 intifada helped forge the Palestinian revolutionary myth of a national struggle for freedom;
>
> ~ Israel accommodated a Palestinian/PLO delegation at the 1991 Madrid Peace Conference which elevated its diplomatic visibility and status;
>
> ~ Israel's Accord with the PLO in 1993, when Arafat entered the White House as a guest of President Clinton, established the political counter-stroke to Israel by coloring the Palestinian struggle as worthy and legitimate in American and international eyes.

Over the years the Arabs imitated the Jewish narrative by imagining a Palestinian People, a Palestinian Exile, a Palestinian Diaspora, a PLO Covenant, and hoped to replace the Jews as the people of the land. When Ruth Wisse wrote about this in her book *If I Am Not for Myself: The Liberal Betrayal of the Jews* (Free Press, 1992), she was cognizant that Israelis would come to believe in the veracity of the Palestinian narrative and then doubt the validity of their own.

Israel mobilized its energies and creativity—through the virtuosos in the arts, academia, media, and literature—to administer the birth and evolution of the Palestinian people. The Left's self-inflicting madness was at war with life and common sense.

At the Camp David Summit in July 2000, President Clinton, Prime Minister Ehud Barak, and the terrorist Yasser Arafat, failed to arrive at a final status agreement of the Israeli–Palestinian conflict. The keen observer would not find this surprising considering the PLO's poor track record in fulfilling its Oslo obligations: not preventing terrorism; not outlawing terrorist groups; not seizing illegal weapons; not extraditing terrorist suspects; not denouncing anti–Israel violence; encouraging its people to call Israel "the Zionist enemy;" maintaining friendly relations with Hamas; enlisting terrorists into the Palestinian Authority police forces; not amending the PLO covenant; promoting hate speech against Israel; and smuggling weapons into the territories. Yet after Arafat rejected Barak's outlandish generosity to reach an agreement—by an almost full Israeli withdrawal, a Palestinian Jerusalem capital, and some Palestinian refugee return—the Israeli team still refused to grasp the essence of the Palestinian stance. Arafat's mystifying maneuverings and aspirations were unfathomable to Ehud Barak and Danny Yatom, his political chief-of-staff and adviser. The Left's policy of appeasement was relentless. According to journalist Raviv Drucker, writing in *Haaretz* in June 2018, Barak had been courageous at Camp David—maybe, I wonder, like Chamberlain at Munich—rather than delusionary and treasonous. Barak could not comprehend the Palestinian war; he always seemed to think that peace was around the corner, with Syria as with the Palestinians. It led him to see peace clouds on the political horizon as when he proposed a small lean army for Israel, with budgetary cuts for the IDF. Assad and Arafat, two of the major assassins and international predators in our times, were seen by Israeli Laborites and other leftists in the 1990s as partners in peace. Thoughtless leaders must be reined in or deposed before they bring total disaster upon us.

The Left had an obsessive habit of always promising the arrival of the dove of peace. Yigal Sarna, writing in *Yediot Aharonot* just prior to Israel's withdrawal from southern Lebanon in May 2000, predicted a safe border for Israel; immediately after the withdrawal Michal Kafra believed that Hezbollah would dissolve. Hezbollah did not disappear, rather was supplied by Iran with tens of thousands of missiles, and war erupted on the Lebanon border in 2006. Ari Shavit writing in *Haaretz* believed that the legitimacy of the international border between Israel and Lebanon protected the northern part of our country. The Left mocked the prophets of doom. So too the disengagement from Gaza in 2005 aroused the infantile optimism from the Left. Anchor Gabi Gazit speaking on *Reshet Bet* radio derided Netanyahu who foresaw missiles that would be fired from Gaza into Israel. But fly they did against Sderot and the kibbutzim across the Gaza line! No less myopic was the political prediction by Labor MK Ofer Shelach in March 2006 that Netanyahu's days were numbered as leader of Likud. Really? The year is now 2018 and Netanyahu is still the prime minister and the leader of Likud.

***

Based on ill-founded optimism, the "Oslo syndrome" served to organize the psychological morass and political illusion that characterized the Left from 1993. Meetings between Israeli and Palestinian leaders and officials continued through the 1990s while Palestinian terrorism continued to strike Israeli civilians all over the country. No final settlement was reached, and a second intifada exploded in September 2000. The Left's shameful appeasement of the Palestinians proved to be a political failure, a security catastrophe, and a step toward national demoralization.

When I would leave Hebrew University on Mount Scopus after work, and begin to drive home to my northern Jerusalem neighborhood, the frequency of bombings in the city sensitized me to the imminent danger of attacks. When one occurred, as in the French Hill area on March 3, 2001, which left 28 people wounded, my immediate worry was whether any of my children were at the spot at the time. In June, a suicide bomber blew himself up in a crowd of young Russian immigrants at the Dolphinarium Disco in Tel Aviv: 21 were murdered in that brutal attack. In August, a suicide-bomber attack in the Sbarro restaurant in downtown Jerusalem left 15 dead, among them parents from the Schijveschuurder family who themselves were Dutch holocaust survivors and three of their young children. They left five orphans. In response to this tragedy the Belzberg family established the One Family Fund to provide assistance to victims of terror attacks against Israel.

In 2002, 238 Israeli civilians were murdered in bomb attacks. The most heinous one took place in the Park Hotel in Netanya where Jews came to celebrate the Passover holiday. During the seder meal a Palestinian entered the hotel and detonated the explosives on his body, murdering thirty Jews in cold blood and turning the holiday into a nightmare.

Over the years of the new millennium Israeli security tightened and succeeded to preempt would-be jihadists. Yet one of the more horrific terrorist attacks hit the Samarian community of Itamar. On the Sabbath eve of March 11, 2011, two Palestinians entered the home of the Fogel family, slashed the throats and stabbed to death the two parents and three of the family's six children. The youngest victim was a three-month infant. This slaughter came at a time when the Netanyahu government had distanced itself from the Oslo charade. The freeze on negotiations didn't solve the problem, but it did preserve the dignity of Israel and at least in part clarified that the Palestinians could no longer murder Jews and have a prime minister call them "peace offerings." The Palestinians continued throughout the years to praise and honor savage terrorists (shahids) who murdered Jews/Israelis—as with the massacre of three members of the Salomon family at Halamish-Neve Tsuf on Sabbath eve July 21, 2017. More cold-blooded murders of Jews struck in 2018. Despite Leftist concessions, Oslo did not instill in the Palestinians a desire for peace with Israel. The very idea that this would happen is so politically absurd that only the Left could even conceive of this buffoonery. Once the Jews stole and occupied Palestine—this according to the Arab narrative—why would the Palestinians ever forgive such a crime? But we could also ask: why would the Jews as the carriers of civilization be willing to accommodate the purveyors of heinous cruelty? One of the most horrific examples in history of Palestinian savagery in the land was the wanton massacre of 67 Jews in Hebron in August 1929. Pierre Van Paassen, correspondent of the *Evening World* in New York, offered this Jewish civilization/Arab barbarism juxtaposition which, ever since, carries the shrill cry of truth.

Indeed, all those leftists who whitewash Palestinian barbarism either do so from fear or ignorance, or both. Few Israelis heard about Palestinian savagery against the Christians in Lebanon in the 1970s—tearing limbs off children, desecrating churches, murdering priests; if they knew, perhaps they would be realistic about Palestinian propensities against non–Muslim enemies. The enfeebled Lebanese were unable to defend themselves as their state collapsed; the state of Israel is the barrier to out-and-out Palestinian mass murder of Jews. Yet the otherworldly Left imagines it can conciliate the Palestinian Muslims by capitulation.

The language of reality cannot but describe withdrawal as defeat. There is no political alternative or strategic compensation to controlling the ground and ruling the territory. In each of the three withdrawal cases—Oslo beginning in 1994, Lebanon in 2000, and Gush Katif in 2005—the military consequences for Israel were deleterious and became the staging ground for further attacks against the country and its citizens. The Arabs are savvy to the conduct of long-term conflict, and they saw Israel's withdrawals for what they were: the product of a tired and delusional political leadership—that of Yitzhak Rabin, Ehud Barak and Ariel Sharon—that broadcast a loss of will. Israel's endurance was tested and found wanting. In trying to avoid the battle Israel strengthens its adversary for future warfare. This has been demonstrated when Fatah, Hezbollah, and Hamas, in their unrelenting campaign continued to whittle away at the national fiber of the Israelis.

It is morally imperative to note that the withdrawal from south Lebanon in 2000 constituted, in addition to a political and security miscalculation, a betrayal by Israel of allies and friends who had fought together for 25 years. In the years of military operations, some 700 South Lebanese Army soldiers were killed. The IDF fled in two days in late May, traumatized SLA fighters with a cruel abandonment, compelled their flight to Israel, ruined their lives and broke their spirit. This was an act of faithlessness and a breach of trust. Approximately 6,500 Lebanese citizens, overwhelmingly Christian, entered Israel as virtual refugees. Ever since, Hezbollah has been hot on Israel's heels from southern Lebanon.

The Hebrew University of Jerusalem

Let me preface this discussion about my university with a personal clarification. I have no intention to show ingratitude to the Hebrew University or smear its academic and national reputation. But as much as I respect the institution, and enjoyed decades of employment there, I have unmitigated respect and concern for my country and its welfare.

On July 31, 2002, a Palestinian worker in the university entered the Frank Sinatra restaurant on campus, leaving a backpack filled with explosives on a chair, and left. The blast that followed killed nine people, both university students and staff. Although I often ate in the restaurant, on that particular day I unexplainably had a feeling not to go there, and was spared.

The first President/Chancellor of the Hebrew University, Dr. Judah Magnus, set the political tone which resonates today as it did back in 1925. In his idiosyncratic non–Zionist view, Magnus proposed to the 1937 British Peel Commission that the Jewish component of the country's population remain a permanent minority not exceeding 40 percent, leaving the Arab majority in tact. This formula for a bi-national state was rejected by Jews and Arabs alike. In 1947 Magnus disapproved of the founding of a Jewish state as proposed by the United Nations, in order to avoid causing injustice to the Arabs. Some esteemed professors of the Hebrew University, like Natan Rotenstreich, were politically to the left of Ben-Gurion.

A display honoring Albert Einstein, whose personal papers became the property of the university, greets students and visitors when entering the Forum of the Hebrew University on Mount Scopus in Jerusalem. The first entry highlighting the great man's life reads: "The Birth of a Pacifist." Einstein's science contributed to discovery and humanity, his pacifism contributed nothing.

The Hebrew University as a prestigious and internationally-recognized Israeli academic institution is not accountable for the political views of its teaching staff. Yet the obscenity of remarks by its professorial staff defies intellectual decorum. Professor Yeshayahu Leibovitz called Israeli soldiers "Judeo–Nazis" and the IDF a Judeo–Nazi organization; History Professor Moshe Zimmerman compared Jewish youth in Kiryat Arba/Hebron to the Hitler youth; and Dr. Ofer Cassif teaching Political Science labeled Minister of Justice Ayelet Shaked a "neo–Nazi scum" and likened legislative initiatives in 2017, designed to recognize Israel as a Jewish nation-state and to deny foreign funding to NGOs who smear the country, as signs of Nazi Germany in the 1930s. Such men of letters were unable to make elemental distinctions and examine issues in their historical context. A Jewish state had become a political sin for the elitist Scopus intelligentsia. Bassam Abu Sharif, a PLO representative who participated in a Palestinian–Israeli peace dialogue in the Hague in early 1999, said that the conduct of the Israelis in the detention centers [prisons] for Palestinians was "worse than that of the Nazis in

Auschwitz." The Palestinian surely did not want to be outdone by some stray Israeli Israel–bashers.

Professor Zeev Sternhell provided his own colorful imagery in assaulting the nationalist settlers when he referred to tanks that would mow down the Ofra community north of Jerusalem. In an article he wrote in *Haaretz* in May 2001, Sternhell stated that most Israelis believe that the Palestinian armed resistance in the territories is legitimate, and if Palestinians were sensible they would concentrate their struggle against the settlements and avoid harming women and children, or avoid shooting at the Gilo neighborhood in southern Jerusalem or the Nahal Oz kibbutz facing the Gaza Strip. The state prosecution refrained from charging the Hebrew University professor with incitement to murder Jews. With Israeli hesitation to withdraw from the West Bank and expel the settlers, only heavy American pressure, wrote Sternhell in 1993, could bring about the desired results. For his peace illusion Sternhell was prepared to undermine Israeli independence and expose the country to international intervention. Moreover, Sternhell considered Israeli democracy on the verge of collapse against the background of the Protective Edge Operation in Gaza in 2014. He could not of course provide any evidence that human liberties had been infringed upon in the public domain of Israeli life, though had he looked harder he would have noticed that the human rights of Jews were trampled on by the Israeli government in the Gaza disengagement operation of 2005. Ever consistent and persistent, Sternhell wickedly accused Israel of "racism akin to early Nazism" in an article he wrote in *Haaretz* in January, 2018.

Professor Yehoshafat Harkabi, an early proponent for the establishment of a Palestinian state beside Israel, also summoned the United States in 1988 to force Israel to realize that this was the optimal solution. Harkabi advocated a Palestinian state when it was still a fledgling and radical idea. For him, the Palestinian question was the crux of the Arab–Israeli conflict, though wasn't the Arab war to destroy Israel the actual crux of the matter? Harkabi diagnosed what he called the hubris of Israel, for flouting international norms which included, he surmised, self-determination for the Palestinian people; and this charge came from a professor and former head of IDF Intelligence who was more versed than almost everybody else in the Arab goal of destroying the Jewish state—politicide he called it—and "liberating Palestine" as an ideological, national, and political campaign to the end. Political Science

Professor Shlomo Avineri was advising Arafat in 1989 in the pages of *The New York Times* to convince the Israelis that the PLO condemns terrorism and is open to a political settlement. He further claimed that the PLO has "gained new respect for the sacrifices of the Palestinians since the Intifada [from December 1987] began." Avineri taught Israelis at the Hebrew University and advocated for the Palestinians around the world.

Jonathan Livny, representing the Hebrew University as executive vice-president of overseas programs, addressed a McGill University student audience in March 1983 and implicated Israel's undemocratic character. He portrayed Arafat as moderate, Jews in the West Bank as a provocation. Abe Harman, president of the Hebrew University, had declared before Israel was established that he was first of all a human being, then a Jew, and thirdly a Zionist. But the essential, contemporary, and revolutionary modern story of the Jewish people was about Zionism, Abe.

The question of university lecturers expressing their political opinions in an academic environment was and remains a vexing controversy. The eminent sociologist Max Weber was categorical on this question in his noteworthy lecture in 1918 on "Science as a Vocation." He asserted that "politics is out of place in the lecture-room." It requires just a general familiarity of the intellectual environment to know of the conventional leftist slant that has historically permeated the halls of learning at the Hebrew University. Professor Naomi Chazan, the daughter of Abe Harman, was confronted with the charge that she shares her political opinions in the classroom and she could hardly deny the fact, as reported in the university student newspaper *Pi Haaton* in December 1992. From his experience as a student at the university, Erez Tadmor reported that the academic staff was singularly monolithic in its political inclination, and he found himself arguing with his professors from the first day of classes. Later he helped found the extra-parliamentary nationalist group Im Tirtzu to investigate and disclose the leftist bias in Israeli academia, as at Ben-Gurion University in Beersheba, and elsewhere.

My own encounters with mean-spirited bias included unpleasant personal incidents with a few Hebrew University professors, who were my ostensible colleagues. Galia Golan, Hava Lazarus-Yaffe, and Moshe Ma'oz, demonstrated adversarial demeanors; while with a number of others in the field of Arabic and Islamic studies I had very positive experiences.

As we have reported, there were no few Hebrew University stalwarts of infidelity to our tiny Jewish state, who paraded feelings of solidarity with the Palestinian enemy. Professor Yaron Ezrahi believed that Arafat's leadership, despite the blow it suffered in the throes of the Persian Gulf crisis and war in 1991, was of value for a future settlement with Israel. Professor Emanuel Sivan participated on the Committee for Bir Zeit (University), north-west of Ramallah, considered by the Left a groundless victim of Israeli oppression, when in fact it was a notorious hotbed of Palestinian militancy and violence against Jews and the army in the area. Sivan argued in June 1980 in an article in *Haaretz* that Fatah, the senior faction in the PLO, had gone through a process of moderation. I proved the opposite in my research essay in 1976 that was published in the first issue of *The Jerusalem Quarterly*, which had been established and edited by none other than Emanuel Sivan himself.

A respected intellectual-philosopher at the university was Rabbi David Hartman who admonished the Palestinians for not appreciating the spiritual ties between the Jewish people and the land of Israel. At the same time he was full of empathy and sentimental platitudes that the Palestinians regain their dignity after decades of misery. In a *Times* magazine interview in 1990, Hartman said: "I will not be at peace in Israel until the Palestinian has achieved his dignity." Perhaps his conscience was jolted somewhat when riding in a taxi up the Mount of Olives in Jerusalem, and an Arab youth threw a rock the size of an avocado at the vehicle. Fortunately Professor Hartman was not injured. Hartman was incessantly calling for Israelis to be sensitive to Palestinian refugee homelessness and wary of Jewish force used against the Palestinians in the territories. Hartman psychologized the Israeli soldiers as "alienated from everything normally identified as Jewish behavior." In an article "A Religious Perspective on the Conflict," Rabbi–Professor Hartman tried to teach and mend the souls of Jews and Arabs; he yearned to remove the resentment dividing the two peoples. When I was a young man in Montreal, David Hartman had been my rabbi who made a fundamental and powerful impact on the direction of my life. I will always remain indebted to him; later in Jerusalem we parted company.

Hebrew University professors were among the signers of The Inter-University Movement for a Political Solution titled: "Forced Rule in the Territories Endangers Israel." Among them were Yitzhak Galnor, Claude Klein, Elhanan Yakira, Avishai Margalit, Mordechai Kremnitzer, and Dan Patinkin. Professor of Sociology Baruch Kimmerling, who was irked by the conceptual marginalization of Arabs in Israeli social science studies, was adamant in blackening Israel's name for its "colonization of the Palestinian territories." For the Arabs, the Givat Ram campus of the university on the western side of Jerusalem was known by its pre–1948 Arabic name, Sheikh Badr. This too was therefore a Palestinian territory occupied by Jewish colonizers—Hebrew University professors in fact!

Reuven Kaminer, holding an administrative position in the university, was a devoted advocate of anti–Israeli views. When Israeli leftists demonstrated in Ramallah against the closure of Bir Zeit University as a form of collective punishment, Kaminer was the spokesman for the demonstrators of whom fifty were arrested by the Israeli authorities. He was also a member of a delegation that met with PLO officials in Romania. One of the PLO participants, Abd el-Razzaq Ahye, spoke there, and Israeli participants described his remarks as "containing no new message." But the meetings were warm and open that November 1986. In defiance of the law, Professor Naomi Chazan, MK for Meretz, met with PLO figure Nabil Shaath in August 1992.

Benjamin Netanyahu was elected in a direct election for prime minister in 1996 and, after a hiatus of four years, Likud returned to power. Netanyahu was invited to attend the graduation ceremony at the Hebrew University in 1997 on Mount Scopus. Twenty-three professors wrote to the president of the university Professor Hanoch Gutfreund that Netanyahu was not worthy of this honor because in their opinion, the PM harmed the values and institutions of an enlightened society with its democratic tradition. Among the signers were Moshe Lissack, Moshe Idel, Zev Sternhell, Moshe Ma'oz, Emanuel Sivan, Menachem Brinker, Mordechai Kremnitzer, Nachman Ben-Yehuda, Yaron Ezrahi, Yisrael Bartal, Yoram Bilu, and Nissan Oren. The professorial guard politicized academia and poured their disrespect on the elected prime minister of Israel. Fortunately most of the voters in the country were not professors.

Some Hebrew University presidents set the political tone which echoed throughout the corridors of the institution. In 1990, when Professor Yoram Ben-Porat was president, the radical iconoclastic and fervently anti–Zionist Sons of the Village group took control of the Arab Students Committee. The Arabs customarily chanted: "with blood and fire we will redeem you Palestine." At that time there were 1,150 Arab students at Hebrew University. The Arab students association traditionally wanted to commemorate the Palestinian Nakba tragedy from 1948: the Jews celebrated Israel's independence and the Arabs mourned it—at the Hebrew University. In 2010, ex-president Hanoch Gutfreund was out demonstrating on behalf of Arabs in the Sheikh Jarrah neighborhood in East Jerusalem to protest the Jewish presence in houses that were Jewish property before the Arab attacks in 1929. The illegal Arab dwellers/squatters had friends in high places.

The student newspaper *Pi Haaton* was frequently in the editorial hands of the Left. Articles denigrating the IDF in its war against Hamas in the Gaza Strip were part of the overall thrust which saw in the second Palestinian Intifada from the year 2000 a righteous response to Israel's occupation. Bear in mind, it erupted after Prime Minister Ehud Barak in July that year offered Arafat over 95 percent of Judea and Samaria. When the Student Association of Hebrew University was in the hands of the leftist Ofek faction, it decided to remove the Israeli flag from its logo. When this occurred in 1996, and again thereafter in 2001, following an interim period when the nationalist Gilad-Aviv student group restored the flag, it was reported that Ofek had made a deal with the Arab student association—and the logo would be removed. The *Pi Haaton* issue from March 29, 2009 reported that the editor Eli Oshrov expressed his opinion that "the government's policy is directed to kill Palestinian civilians." The only thing correct in this sordid antipathy was that there was a government and there were civilians. The impression was that a sympathetic pro–Palestinian approach characterized the university's Center for Human Rights headed by Professor David Kretzmer.

The university's unwillingness to convey pride in the state of Israel was reflected in its decision for the second year in a row not to play the Hatikva national anthem at the graduation ceremony in May 2017. The reason was to avoid offending Arabs who do not identify with the majesty of the lyrics that the Jews "be a free people." The Hebrew University recognizes the right of the Arab students to veto Hatikva.

And this is the point. The pro-peace pro–Palestinian university agenda, if it could be called that, is only part of the picture whose flip-side is an anti–Zionist agenda. According to historian Israel Bartal, who chaired the Jewish History Department and was one of the most influential figures on the Education Ministry's curriculum committees, "the Zionist narrative has disappeared from the academic world." Jewish history, Jewish nationality, Jewish culture, love of the homeland, and loyalty to the Jewish state, had served as the themes in the state education law of 1953. Now with the primary input of Hebrew University professors, other agendas are addressed. The academic Left committed itself to destroying the myths that underpin the national renaissance. Perhaps Israel's version of the "treason of the intellectuals" will end one day.

In 2017, the Hebrew University continued to pursue its post–Zionist or anti–Zionist agenda. Its thematic components included diversity and relativism, pluralism and multi-culturalism. The university promotes programs for students and staff to enhance inter-religious Jewish–Muslim–Christian dialogue, Jewish familiarity with Arab society, and the presence of the Arabic language on campus. Yet the university's investment of thought and good will, energy and funds, on behalf of the Arabs in Israel, who continue to loathe Zionism and feel no loyalty to the state of Israel, is an exercise in self-abasement. As explained by the esteemed scholar G.E. Von Grunebaum in his book *Islam: Essays in the Nature and Growth of a Cultural Tradition* (Routledge & Kegan Paul, 1961), the Arab culture code highlights group solidarity and not civic virtue. The university's effort will likely intensify Arab arrogance and catalyze Arab demands.

As one would have it, on November 9 the same year radical Arab students at the university demonstrated in the Forum area spouting political expletives against the state of Israel. The most resounding slogan was "Zionists out!" Now here was a basis for some Jewish–Arab collaboration at the university. The Hebrew University administration issued a statement thereafter that all demonstrations require a permit, but the organizers hadn't requested one. Certainly one of the most weird and morally staggering innovations at the Hebrew University was a student's sociological research on Israeli soldiers who, despite the alleged wicked occupation of the territories, refrain from raping Palestinian women. The researcher concluded that Jewish soldiers were racist and exclusivist in refusing the opportunity to exploit Arab women as sex plunder. This was a mind-blowing new Israeli twist to an old anti–Semitic theme.

The Truman Institute for Peace

Conceived in 1965, established at Hebrew University on the liberated Mount Scopus campus in 1970 soon after the 1967 War, the Truman Institute serves as a formidable academic forum on behalf of the Palestinian people, its suffering and struggle, and the fostering of its identity, nationality, and political aspirations. The Truman mandate for peace became a platform for the Palestinian narrative.

Following is a partial list of events at the Institute: workshop on the Palestinian Media in January, 1985; lecture by Dr. Hatem Abu Ghazaleh on "The Past Suffering: A Palestinian View From Gaza;" workshop on Human Rights in the West Bank and Gaza Strip; workshop on the social-psychological and non-violent aspects of the Intifada in November, 1988. Dr. Edy Kaufman, executive director of the Truman Institute, removed in 1988 both the Israeli and Hebrew University flags from the stage of the Truman Auditorium and put them on the floor at the demand of Yosef Abu Samra and Nafez Asaeili, Arabs who were participating in a conference.

Here's more: a conference in May 1993 on "Israel's Arabs as a Political Community in Formation;" a conference on "The PLO and Israel: From Armed Conflict to Political Settlement," May 1994, with the participation of Ilan Pappe, a known post–Zionist historian, and Palestinian scholar Muhammad Muslih. The Middle East Unit conducted a seminar in 1994–5 titled "The Problem of Eretz Israel/Palestine;" the Institute's 1994–1995 Annual Report featured on page 36 a photo from a visit to Gaza by Truman staff that included Academic Director Moshe Ma'oz meeting with PLO chairman Arafat; on September 13, 2000, a discussion convened on the prospects of a permanent settlement between Israel and the Palestinians, chaired by Dr. Adel Manna with the participation of Dr. Azmi Bsharra.

Truman News reported on April 1, 2001 the sponsoring of a course on "Palestinians in the 20th Century: A Look from Within," whose lecturers included Dr. Adel Manna, Dr. Khalil Shkaki, and Professor Yazid Sayigh; the Truman Annual Report 2003 devoted a story to the Israeli–Palestinian Relations Project that dealt with Israeli–Palestinian peace education activities, Palestinian textbooks, human rights, grievances of Palestinian citizens in Israel, and rights of Arabs as a national minority. A June 2001 conference on "The economic-social hardships among the Arab

Israeli population" featured six speakers, all Arabs, to set forth the ills of Arab life in Israel. The platform is theirs!

A symposium on the political discourse of Palestinian citizens in Israel was held in January, 2002 with Arab participants; The Truman Research Institute Annual Report for 2004 reported a workshop conducted on January 28, 2004 dedicated to Fadwa Tuqan, the late Palestinian poet. Participants spoke of her life for women's liberation and the homeland. I wonder if the participants chose to mention the cannibalistic statement of Tuqan wanting "to eat the livers of Jews" at a time when she developed a warm relationship with Israeli poetess Dahlia Ravikovitch after 1967.

Truman News 2006 reported workshops on peacekeeping, featuring Israeli Professor Galia Golan and Dr. Sufian Abu Zaida, a member of the Palestinian Fatah movement who spent 12 years in Israeli prisons. The *Truman News* of 2008 related that Professor Ma'oz conducted a series on the dilemmas faced by Israel, Palestinians, Lebanon, and Syria in the Middle East conflict. He considered "the chances for agreement" to be fairly good; and that an Israeli peace agreement with Syria could lead to a political settlement with Hamas and rein in Hezbollah. Ma'oz explained that "Syria could lean on Hamas to negotiate a political settlement with Israel, cease Syrian military aid to Hezbollah, and downgrade its relations with Tehran." Quite a mouthful of utter nonsense! Marking the fiftieth year of the Six Day War, and Israel's liberation of East and Old Jerusalem, the Truman Institute was scheduled to hold a conference on "50 years of Occupation." At the last minute university authorities canceled the event.

The Institute, its professors and cohorts, were engaged in building Palestine and its Arab people. One voice for reason, sobriety, and academic excellence at Truman was Professor Raphael Israeli for whom Zionism was a legitimate reality. Hardly anybody else from the Right was there.

Institutions and Organizations

Human Rights organizations are notorious for their left-wing politicization of investigation and advocacy. They are zealously anti–Israel. Their foil has been uncovered, and a poll from 2016 as published by the Israel Democracy Institute revealed that a majority of Israelis do not believe in the integrity and honesty of these bodies. They are exposed for their bias and the harm they cause the IDF and Israel. They are nothing less than bands of traitors in wartime who don the garb of idealism.

~ *Peace Now* emerged with a predominant role of professors and lecturers at the Hebrew University, with Avishai Margalit identified by *The Jerusalem Post* on March 10, 1989 as "the ideological guru of the peace movement . . . the intellectual leader of Peace Now." Economics professors the likes of Omri Padan, Yoram Ben-Porat, Michael Bruno, Eitan Shashinsky, Menachem Yaari, and Gur Ofer, are cited as members of the outfit. When Likud came to power in 1977 Ben-Porat appealed to Professor Herbert Stein, an adviser to the American president, that the United States apply economic pressure on Israel to conduct negotiations for withdrawal from the territories. Mimicking the American model of anti–Vietnam War demonstrations, Peace Now organized demonstrations in 1982–83 against the War in Lebanon. PLO terrorists had a long history of infiltrating and attacking Israel across the porous Lebanese border, striking Nahariya and Maalot; the Vietcong in southeast Asia could only dream of such a geo-strategic circumstance for attacking Manhattan and Miami.

The Israeli Peace Now could draw upon a precedent from the United States in the early 1940s when a Peace Now Committee promoted American accommodation with the Nazis and the Fascists—Germany, Italy, and Japan. The committee blamed Roosevelt for the war. The goal must be peace and not victory because a victory will prevent peace. In Israel Peace Now founders like Janet Aviad, Yuli Tamir, and Amir Peretz, adopted an appeasement approach toward the Palestinians as the way to avoid war and deny Israel a victory on the battlefield, or elsewhere. Janet Aviad, in one Peace Now statement, claimed "we know that true security will be achieved only with the advent of peace." This sermonizing dribble was beyond cure. Israeli withdrawal from the West Bank and the cessation or dismantlement of Jewish settlement activity was the self-flaggelational formula for peace. In April 2017, Palestinian flags waved in the wind alongside Peace Now placards at a demonstration in the area of Michmash–Rimonim on the Allon Road in Binyamin, north of Jerusalem. Radical Jews traveled ideologically to join with Arabs against the Israeli settlement enterprise.

In a brochure from January 1983, Peace Now voiced its fear that the expansion of Israeli settlement activity, which it monitored and then tattled on, and the increase in the number of Jews in the territories, would catalyze the Israeli government to expel the local Arab population. Regardless of this unfounded assessment, the fact that leftist Jewish Israelis were committed to the Palestinians was typical of a loss of solidarity and commitment with the Zionist return to Judea and Samaria. In April 1984, a Peace Now delegation, like a subversive anti–Israeli front, went to Egypt to meet with senior Egyptian officials.

Blaming the government for the enemy's hostility and for the absence of peace had been standard demagoguery. The Reserve Officers' letter to Prime Minister Begin on April 24, 1978 had expressed that view. Demonstrating against the new community of Efrat south of Jerusalem in 1983 illustrated that Peace Now diverged from the national consensus that supported settlement in the Gush Etzion enclave. Peace Now chairman Yariv Oppenheimer tried to embarrass Likud by leaking a report of Jewish acquisitions in East Jerusalem.

After the first intifada erupted in late 1987, and Jews were being murdered, the dogmatic Peace Now gang confidently declared prior to a march in Jerusalem in December 1989 that "a Palestinian state will be established." But the Palestinians wanted a Palestinian state in all of Palestine, not a pygmy Bantustan entity beside Israel in the West Bank. Amiram Goldblum, heading Peace Now's settlement watch team, disclosed in May 2001 that "construction in the settlements has always been an act of provocation."

The persistent Peace Now campaign against the nationalist camp was complemented by overlooking and excusing Palestinian violence, breaches of trust and agreements. Yet we can note one occasion in August 1990 when in an Open Letter to the Palestinian Leadership in the Occupied Territories, Peace Now expressed its disappointment "by the enthusiastic Palestinian support for Saddam Hussein." Iraq had conquered Kuwait, and the Palestinians hoped that it would help them conquer Israel. Palestinians danced on the rooftops when Iraqi missiles struck Ramat Gan and other Israeli localities in early 1991.

Peace Now served as an agency for foreign governments whose hostility to Israel and the settlement enterprise led them to fill the coffers of this active NGO. An item from 2006 divulged the generous contributions made by the British Foreign Office, the Norwegian Foreign Ministry, and the Finnish Embassy in Israel. Collaboration opened creative avenues for the Peace Now group.

Dror Etkes was responsible for monitoring settlement construction in the West Bank. The Peace Now goal was to convince the Israeli public to support disengaging from the territories and dismantling settlements, as indeed was carried out in Gaza and part of Samaria in 2005. Yariv Oppenheimer, the secretary-general of Peace Now, admitted that the public is not sufficiently informed about what transpires in Judea, Samaria, and Gaza. Clearly foreign funds gave a boost and assured that Peace Now will continuously pursue its educational campaign and surveillance in the territories.

Collaborating with Arab enemies and betraying Jewish brothers was the modus operandi of Peace Now. It demonized the Right—beginning with Menachem Begin—and blamed him for the absence of Israeli–Palestinian peace. Already in a demonstration in Tel Aviv in June 1980, after the 1978

Camp David Accords and before the 1982 War in Lebanon, Peace Now placards screamed out, "Democracy and Not Fascism." Begin was the pristine liberal in Israeli political history, before becoming prime minister and after, but the radical Left could not muster up respect for this political opponent (except when he agreed that Israel withdraw from the Sinai). Begin was popularly and nationally seen as grandfatherly, courteous, and as dignified as "a European gentleman."

~ *The Jaffee Center for Strategic* Studies at Tel Aviv University, in a 1989 report by ex–Mossad employee Yossi Alpher and former Military Intelligence chief Aharon Yariv, stated that Israel should not negate the possibility of a Palestinian state as the PLO was on a moderate course. Here is a glaring paradox between so much Intelligence but yet so little . . . intelligence. Mark Heller at the Center also wrote a book advocating the same message—*A Palestinian State: The Implications for Israel* (Harvard University Press, 1983).

~ *The 2003 Geneva Initiative* was devised by former government minister Yossi Beilin, and it proposed a Palestinian state in virtually all of the West Bank and Gaza Strip, an East Jerusalem capital, and some refugee return to pre–1967 Israel. The strong desire for peace led leftists like Beilin to engage in repetitive advocacy.

~ *East for Peace* appeared in 1983 led by Oriental Sephardi Israeli Jews, especially Shlomo Elbaz lecturer in Comparative Literature at the Hebrew University, and poetess Shelly Elkayam. They combined communal pride with a vision of building a bridge of peace to the Arabs. However, their origin from North Africa and their familiarity with Arab culture did not arm them with a keen sense of politics. They feigned an acumen to make peace with an enemy steeped in anti–Jewish, anti–Zionist, and anti–Israel muck. But the Arabs could be a useful foil for the leftists' vengeful instincts against Ashkenazi–European domination of Israeli national life since the state's inception. This noted, a Sephardi–Leftist is a virtual self-contradiction; Mizrahi/Eastern Jews, historically experiencing dhimmi humiliation and insecurity in Muslim lands, should have had little inclination to trust Arab adversaries of Israel. The generally politically right-leaning Sephardim little forgot or forgave Labor-Left discrimination and abuse suffered in the formative years of the state, this in contrast to the epochal Likud electoral victory in 1977 which catapulted non–Ashkenazi communities into prominence. A penetrating article by Tom Mehager in January 2015 in *Oketz* systematically analyzed why Mizrahim don't vote for the Left, generally speaking.

~ *The Van Leer Institute* served as an intellectual entrepôt for a potpourri of leftism, tolerance, pluralism, with conferences, publications, and words, words, words. It aspired to "deepen Israel's democracy" and diversify cultural expressions in Israel, no less promoting the rights of the Palestinian citizens. This drivel was a way to cloud its post–Zionism deviation.

~ *The Council for Peace and Security*, with its 800 members, 70 of whom are reserve-generals, wrote in an ad in 1994 on the heels of the Oslo Accord that "we [Israel] are leaving Gaza and Jericho—one step for peace . . ." In the army the officers are courageous, deliberate, and patriotic; when they leave the army, all intellectual hell breaks loose. The dumb dogma that withdrawal is the path to peace with the Palestinians refused to die.

~ *Shimon Peres Center for Peace*, whose name said it all, was forged with the friendship of Terje Roed-Larsen, UN special coordinator for the Middle East peace process. His Norwegian credentials along with those of his wife Mona Juul were lined with financial transactions: Norwegian government money went to the Center and a cash payment of $100,000 to Juul. Terje was known to have been a key player in the sleazy backroom Oslo talks, he no less a notorious slanderer of Israel's 2002 military operations—war crimes said Terje—in the West Bank. Attorney-General Elyakim Rubinstein said Larsen's mendacious remarks were cause for declaring him persona non grata. Peres responded saying that Larsen had made "a special contribution to peace in our region for years." In 1998, the Center workforce numbered 35 employees. Working intensely with Arafat and the Palestinian Authority, Peres and his Center were financed by European countries just as the Oslo Accord itself was a joint Israeli Left–European political scandal.

~ *B'Tselem*, a virtual arm for Palestinian propaganda and disinformation, exposed in a June 2001 report the detrimental effects of Israel's so-called siege in the occupied territories, with soldiers delaying ambulances transporting Palestinian patients from getting to an Israeli hospital. In fact, thousands of them were treated by Israeli medical personnel. Israeli security sources responded to the odious accusation by pointing to the tightening of closure following terrorist attacks in Tel Aviv. B'Tselem "armed with cameras" workshops were conducted for Palestinian women to take the camera and film soldiers and themselves under the occupation. Theater replaced truth in the ugly war against Israel. In 2016, the executive director of B'Tselem, Hagai Elad, led his campaign against his country by addressing the UN Security Council, calling upon this nefarious body to act against Israel's settlement enterprise. He wasn't squeamish to cross the lines in front of the whole world.

~ *Breaking the Silence* was an especially servile servant of the Palestinians by concocting distorted evidence of soldiers' violence and mistreatment of Palestinians in the territories. This avant-garde agit-prop band set out to disseminate falsehoods about the Israeli army and to destroy Israel's reputation abroad. Oddly enough, Dean Issacharoff, the organization's spokesman in 2017, revealed that he physically beat up an Arab in Hebron in March 2014 when serving with his military unit. Yet when an investigation was carried out, it seemed the story was a fabrication. Issacharoff, strangely enough, incriminated himself in order to illustrate that the "occupation" necessarily is the incubator for violence. Dean was actually willing to sacrifice his own personal reputation for his higher cause of defaming his country. With all due attention to the absurdity of this odd report, did Breaking the Silence have its own culprit right in its own ranks? Here was the crack-up of the Israeli Left in all its perverse and convoluted colors.

We add an additional list of leftist political moles and the ideological malevolence in anti–Zionist circles:

~ *Yesh Din* was established in 2005 by women who had been active in Machsom Watch beginning in 2001 that monitored, like enemy spies, how the Palestinians were treated at army check-points in Judea and Samaria. Yesh Din also played a pivotal role in locating dubious and illegally-grounded Palestinian proprietors of land with the goal of expelling Jews from their homes, as in the case of Amona in 2017. Financed by the European Union, and specifically by Norway, Ireland, Germany, Britain, and Belgium, the organization effectively works in tandem with the High Court in Jerusalem which has demonstrated a readiness to accept tendentious Arab claims to land ownership where settlements were established and thriving. On the issue of Israeli communities in the territories, Migron north of Jerusalem and Netiv Ha-Avot south of Jerusalem, the court declared the rule of law necessitated the destruction of these communities considered illegal. Not only was Arab evidence of proprietary rights quite debatable, the court could have after the fact recommended Israeli compensation to the Arabs rather than the destruction of Jewish homes in place. Yesh Din was also active against the high-school Ulpana campus in Bet El and the "nine houses in Ofra," that the High Court ordered destroyed. Dror Etkes is the mover and shaker in seeking out Palestinian landowners.

Other organizations include:

~ the self-explanatory Enough of the Occupation (Dai Lakibush);
~ Remembering (Zochrot) plays on the theme of lost Arab lands in the 1948 Israeli borders;
~ The Committee Against [Arab] House Demolitions headed by Jeff Halper;
~ City of the Nations (Ir Amim);
~ Gush Shalom (Peace Bloc) with spokesman Adam Keller that gathered information on officers and security personnel, and Ministry of Interior officials, to incriminate them for crimes that will send them to trial at the International Criminal Court in the Hague;
~ Yesh Gvul that seems to oppose the military draft in Israel and opposed army service in Lebanon in the years the IDF was engaged there;
~ The Association for Civil Rights in Israel conducted visits to the Arabs in Gaza and the West Bank, and monitored trials in military courts on behalf of the Palestinians;
~ the Women's Peace Coalition and the Israel's Women's Network;
~ Brit Bnei Shem that sponsored Jewish and Arab youth encounters in the belief that children from enemy peoples would embrace peace;
~ Adala committed to Palestinian justice for the "internal" Arabs from 1948;
~ Shatil promoting equality and tolerance between Jewish and Arab citizens;
~ Israel/Palestine Center for Research and Information (IPCRI) that despite its egalitarian name works to advance Palestine at the expense of Israel;
~ Women in Black who regularly held an anti-occupation protest at Paris Square in Jerusalem;
~ Mesarvot (Women Conscientious Objectors) against military service led by Dr. Anat Matar from the Philosophy Department at Tel Aviv University;

~ Doctors for Human Rights—for Palestinians only;

~ Rabbis for Human Rights that regularly monitored purported mistreatment of Arabs at army checkpoints;

~ Physicians for Human Rights on behalf of security prisoners (terrorists) from the Occupied Palestinian Territories (sic.) and their detention and incarceration in Israeli jails;

~ Akeyvot (Tracks) funded by the Swiss government, Rockefeller Brothers Fund, and the Euro-Med Foundation, traced the signs of Palestinian victimhood at the hands of Zionism;

~ the religious Oz Ve-Shalom and Netivot Shalom among whose spokesmen was Professor Uriel Simon;

~ Taayush that called for Jewish–Arab co-existence to defend Palestinian shepherds and farmers in Judea and Samaria from Zionist youth provocations;

~ Anarchists Against the Fence, one of whose activists, Yifat Doron aged 40, actually delivered a sweeping slap on the face to a military prosecutor in the court case of Ahed Tamimi from Nebi Salah who herself slapped an Israeli army officer. Leftist violence was running free and wild.

That said, the number of unreported Arab provocations and attacks against Jews in the territories would fill the stacks of the Library of Congress.

So we continue with the Left:

~ The New Israel Fund, whose budget was reported to reach 125 million dollars in 2017, defined its purpose with a base in its Jerusalem office, "to strengthen and cultivate Israeli democracy;" it established Shatil as an Israeli conduit for (Arab) citizen rights; to train lawyers specializing in citizen rights and to create an enlightened society; to finance the ACRI (Association for Civil Rights in Israel), which received seven and half million dollars from 2008–2014, which promotes Bedouin rights in the south, illegal African migrant workers' rights in Tel Aviv, and Arab rights in Haifa; to fund the radical anti-religious anti-settlement Molad organization and a plethora of other leftist outfits some of whom we mentioned above (East for Peace, Oz Ve-Shalom, and more). The NIF is also active in the IDF promoting its liberal agenda and in the Ministry of Education bringing a new progressive-left language to education. The motive was to mobilize pressure to create a public tumult, while redefining the lines of discourse that would bring down Netanyahu and Likud. Talia Sasson, Israeli president of the NIF, unabashedly referred to Israel engaging in "ethnic cleansing" of Palestinians, while the only people who as a community have been expelled from their homes have been Jews—not Arabs—from Rujeib, Yamit, Katif, Homesh, Sa-Nur, and Amona.

~ The Israel Democracy Institute, with an air of academic objectivity and serving Israel's national interests, transparently reveals by its name that it is partial to democracy rather than to an integral and buoyant Jewish Israel. It is not because the democratic underpinnings in Israel are endangered, or that there has been an erosion of the democratic process and values. In fact the rise of Likud proved the vitality of Israel's democratic system and culture. The democratic catchword used by the Left is designed to pulverize the national and Zionist priority of Israel's collective identity. I have nothing against democracy and in fact definitely want to live in a liberal country—and a Jewish state.

The Israeli Left, sadly alienated from the nationalist shift in the country's political orientation, vegetates in "the disenchantment of the world," the phrase coined by sociologist Max Weber. Its fetish for peace is invalidated by the matrix of Middle East political affairs; and its magical formulas for reconciliation with the Palestinians resembles imploring the spirits but not learning the facts. After the Left or far-Left set out to drain Israel of its drama, idealism, and patriotism, the Right struggles to keep the dream and reality of Israel alive.

A Commentary

The Socialist Workers Party was formed in Jaffa in 1919. It opposed the slogan of Hebrew Labor in favor of an economic bond with Arab workers. It denounced Zionism as reactionary and bourgeois, and opposed Aliya. Under the name of the Palestine Communist Party, the Jewish Reds exalted Arab pogroms and the massacre of Jews in 1929 as the national awakening of the exploited Arab masses. Jewish communists incited the Palestinian fellah (peasant) to violence and terror against the Jews in the country. The same approach, though attenuated somewhat, is part of the more recent history of the Left. It bemoans Arab suffering and encourages their struggle, assisting them politically, recognizing the PLO diplomatically and befriending its terrorist leadership from Arafat down; there are those who advocate negotiating with Hamas; then demonizing Jewish pioneers and calling for withdrawal from territories, clamoring for the dismantlement-destruction of Jewish settlements; then supplying the Palestinians with arms, forgiving their lies and ignoring their violations. This humiliating and transparent treason is a natural outgrowth of the original poison in the early days of Zionism. That poison has unfortunately not been extracted from the body politic.

Shmuel Dotan, in his volume *Reds: The Communist Party in Palestine* (Shevna Hasofer, 1991), recognized the need for a psychological analysis of Jewish alienation and self-hatred that was disguised as noble values of equality and progress. On the ideological periphery of Zionism teachers from Hebrew University established Brit Shalom (Peace Covenant) in the 1920s, and sympathized with the communists. They provided them with an intellectual and public defense. Jewish auto-anti–Semites collaborated with Arab haters of Jews in the Land of Israel.

The Israeli daily *Haaretz* is the epitome of journalistic distance from the people and fawning infatuation with the enemies. For them, the Israeli government, certainly one led by Likud and Netanyahu, can do no good—and the Arabs can do no bad. The "occupation" is the cause of all ills and evil. Israel is guilty of the political freeze on the Palestinian question. Articles by Gideon Levy, Akiva Eldar, Amira Hass, Yoel Marcus, and others, pay homage to the Palestinians and defame Israeli nationalists. Uri Tuval wrote about the loss of army captain Eliraz Peretz in a Gaza military operation by defaming Miriam his mother and her ideological community as "jihadic fascists." He ridiculed soldiers "sent to their death" as if combatting Hamas and defending Israel were capricious choices rather than a national imperative against an unrelenting Islamic enemy.

Journalist Aluf Ben called Syrian president Bashar Assad "a good neighbor," so why not bring the butcher of Damascus to the shores of the Kinneret (Sea of Galilee) with an Israeli withdrawal from the Golan Heights? But then out of the blue, the Arab Spring struck Syria with thunder in 2011 and the good neighbor decided to massacre half a million of his citizens. Aluf Ben forgot to take into account that Bashar's father Hafez butchered the Lebanese and imposed foreign occupation over the land of the cedars. For decades, the Assads were always getting their hands into Israeli affairs by hosting and arming their proxy Palestinian terrorists—Hamas and the Palestine Islamic Jihad (PIJ). But the Left felt exasperated that Israel did not somehow yield the Golan and make peace with Damascus at any price, regardless of the consequences.

Leftist antipathy toward the Right emerges from its disconnection from Zionism. This is really the source of the malady of hatred. A people in war for so many years requires a special idea to persevere and sustain its faith in a state of permanent adversity. Zionism has its myths: the courage and tragedy of Yosef Trumpeldor at Tel Hai in Upper Galilee, the Exodus ship bringing Jewish Holocaust survivors to the Promised Land, and Meir Har Zion from the 101 crack combat unit. Draining the swamps of the Jezreel Valley for Jewish settlement is another myth. When two Haifa University geographers, Yoram Bar Gal and Shmuel Shamai, debunk the pioneering myth of reclaiming and draining the marshes of the Jezreel Valley, anti–Zionist propagandists might exploit their research for political purposes.

Other very substantive dangers lurk in the arsenal of the leftist camp. A confused government, like the one led by Ehud Barak in 2000, is not incapable of agreeing to Palestinian refugee return in order to arrive at a final status peace agreement. The state could collapse under the impact of a misguided political decision camouflaged as the peace camp's resolution of the conflict. Another daft scenario would be Israel agreeing —in the interests of peace and reconciliation in the region—to dismantle its nuclear arsenal. A non-nuclear Middle East—finally a New Middle East— is a formula to expose Israel to destruction after her modern-day miraculous redemption.

Natan Alterman, poet and publicist, wrote words that are a legacy in the struggle for normalcy in the Jewish soul of Israel: "Satan said: How can I overcome him [Israel]? He has strength and talent, and weapons of war ... I will make his brain numb and he will forget that justice is on his side." The Left has unraveled the code: Israel can be undone from within, by breaking her unity as a nation at war, sowing dissension and controversy, raising doubt and guilt.

The noteworthy socialist leader Berl Katznelson, who died in 1944, wrote:

> Are there among the peoples whose sons have come to such mental and emotional distortion, that everything their people do, its creativity and suffering are denigrated and mocked, and everything that their people's enemy does, every theft, murder and rape, fills their hearts with the feeling of admiration ... ? So long as it is feasible that a Jewish child can come to Eretz Israel ... and here he will be afflicted with the germs of self-hatred ... and they will make him crazy to the extent that he will see in the Palestinian Nazis the Socialist redemption, who succeeded to concentrate in the country the zoological antisemitism from Europe with the savor of the dagger in the East—our conscience will never rest.

Many decades later and the germ of self-hatred still infests the minds of Jews in Israel.

In Mapam kibbutz circles and its HaShomer HaTzair youth movement the distance from Judaism created, as one from the far-Left admitted, a spiritual fatigue and "Red assimilation." The Soviet–inspired mind-set strangled free thought, later convincing the socialist leftists by the 1970s that the Palestinians are really conducting a legitimate national liberation struggle against the illegitimate state of Israel.

From the early beginnings of modern Zionism a debate erupted in the national renaissance, whether Judaism and traditional Jewish life were to be extirpated from the new community (yishuv), or whether they would provide the historical or spiritual foundation for it? Novelist Yosef Haim Brenner, who was murdered by Arabs in Jaffa in 1920, felt revulsion for Jewish life in the shtetels (rural villages and towns) of Eastern Europe and Russia, for what he saw as a life of parasitism, life disconnected from anything larger than the immediate environs, for coveting money and cheating the gentiles. His was a cruel indictment which disregarded the circumstances of Jewish poverty and powerlessness—the scourge of exilic life and disarray in the diaspora. Zionist author Ahad Ha'am countered Brenner's vicious charges and defended the vitality and creativity in Jewish culture for the revival of Jewish life in the homeland.

After the Six Day War the Left basically decided to divorce from Zionism. The war was interpreted as the breaking moment, the point when Israel—which won the war—had twice sinned: causing the death of hundreds of Israeli soldiers, and causing the oppression of a large defeated Arab population. The Israeli enterprise was considered morally bankrupt. Among kibbutz soldiers returning from the war were those who referred to "the tragedy of being victors" and who revealed that "our generation looks askance at Zionism." One identified with Palestinian refugees fleeing on the Jericho road. In the soldiers' volume *The Seventh Day: Talk about the Six-Day War* (Andre Deutsch, 1970), there were nonetheless references to the power of Jewish history which was felt with the physical return to Jerusalem and Hebron.

Professor Hillel Weiss of Bar-Ilan University summarized the direction of Israeli literature after 1967 in particular, as with authors Amos Eilon and Tzvi Luz, in demonizing the Israeli military hero, raising moral inquietude, heading for a certain and futile end in battle. Without peace with the Arabs, life loses its significance. This is the crux of the leftists' existential crisis in Israel for the last fifty years. Both life and death are meaningless. Liddell Hart, eminent military historian, wrote that the downfall of civilized states tends to come not from the direct assaults of foes but from internal decay and exhaustion in war.

Jewish hatred of Jews and Judaism is a colossal conundrum in human history. Maybe there lurks a small anti–Semite in every Jew, who has imbibed from the poison wells of disfiguring and defaming Jews throughout history. We have been injected with the virus of seeing the negative images and stereotypes. We have seen Jews who at times conform to those awful stereotypes—corrupt, money-grubbing, deceitful, and haughty. The overwhelming numbers of Jews are able to put this in context and maintain a healthy sense of proportion. They know the truth about the essential goodness and righteousness of Jews whose decency, generosity, and kindness are legendary. There are of course the exceptions, and there are the villains in the anti–Semitic script, enemies of their people, haters of anything concerning things Jewish. Playwright and theater director Hanoch Levin had an especially derisive view of

Jews as portrayed in *The Patriot* written in 1982. Vulgarly anti–Semitic in tone and substance, the play had a small Arab boy in a forlorn scene that was inspired for Levin by one of the saddest of pictures from the Holocaust of the small Jewish boy, expressing abandonment and dread, about to be sent by the Nazis to his death. Dror Feiler, a naturalized Swedish citizen and active in organizing the Gaza Freedom Flotilla to break the allegedly inhumane Israeli blockade of Gaza in 2010, created an obscene artistic exhibit of Jewish blood to highlight Palestinian terrorist bombings in Haifa in 2003 which left 21 Israelis dead. Feiler the ex–Israeli disguised as a humanitarian, was gorged full of hate for Jews and Israel. Of similar notoriety was Moshe Machover, a naturalized British citizen, whose anti–Zionism went the full ideological course to denying the right of Israel to exist. Israeli author and novelist Aharon Applefeld had written that "anti–Semitism directed at oneself was an original Jewish creation. I don't know of any other nation so flooded with self-criticism ..." Early in the days of the reconstituted Jewish state, Applefeld had proposed that a synagogue be built in each school in order to give all Israeli–Jewish children a taste and touch with the tradition of their people. A Jewish soul without Judaism is impaired, thought Applefeld.

Novelist A.B. Yehoshua continued to outdo himself in reaching new heights of betrayal of his country. In September, 2017, a fifth-generation descendant of James Balfour visited Israel and, like his namesake from World War One days, expressed sympathy and support for the Jewish Return as a biblical prophesy fulfilled. Yehoshua, rather than gratefully appreciating this righteous gentile, berated Lord Balfour for promising the land in 1917—not to the majority Arabs but to the minority Jews. Foreign Minister Balfour then intended his Declaration for the Jewish people as a whole and worldwide, not just for the then small Jewish population in the country. Strange that a non–Jew believes in Zionism and its moral mandate, while a Jew believes in Palestinian rights. This Yehoshua–Balfour verbal exchange in Jerusalem was an embarrassment to any self-respecting Israeli.

Just to put an added historical touch to Jewish self-hatred. Rosa Luxembourg, a Jewish German communist, cared for the Negroes of Africa, not for the Jews in the ghettos. Leon Trotsky (born Lev Bronstein), a notorious Jewish communist, cared for the Russian peasants, not the helpless Jewish poor. Pogroms against Jews left Luxembourg and Trotsky cold; later both were murdered by gentile assassins. Today in Israel, Palestinian bombs, guns, and knives strike mercilessly and viciously against Jews and Israelis. Without the IDF and police, there is no Israel; not a Right nor a Left one.

The Army

Symptomatic of the prominence of the Left in the army was the appointment of Professor of Philosophy Asa Kasher to write the moral code for the IDF. His essential purpose was to elevate the moral conduct of Israeli soldiers toward the enemy. Perhaps victory was not for Asa Kasher the essential moral objective of the state of Israel.

Major-General Yair Golan, serving as the Deputy Chief-of-Staff, more than insinuated in a speech given on Holocaust Remembrance Day in 2016 that Israeli society showed signs of intolerance and violence reminiscent of Nazi Germany in the 1930s. This outrageous analogy should have led to his immediate dismissal from the army. A subdued mini-debate ensued with inane salutes to the right of freedom of expression. But General Golan could rely on Justice Barak as a reliable reference who, addressing an audience of ambassadors to Israel in 2010, remarked that "if it [totalitarianism or genocide?] could happen in Germany, it could happen everywhere in the world" (reported in *Israel Hayom*, Feb. 24, 2010). Author Arieh Stav, writing in *Hayarden* on August 12, 1988, did not mince his words in stating that anyone who considered Jews to be Nazis, or that Zionism is racist, removes himself from the Jewish people and joins the ranks among the haters of Israel.

Other perverse developments infiltrated into the army. Military courts released terrorists prior to the end of their sentence. Forty-three reserve duty soldiers serving in the elite 8200 intelligence unit of the army wrote a letter to the prime minister and chief-of-staff in 2014 refusing to take part in any assignment that is against Palestinians. Intelligence/information gathering is, in truth, an instrument of Israel's military rule in the territories through surveillance of potential or actual terrorists. Needless to say that military personnel in whatever unit are legally and morally committed to assure the country's security, regardless of their personal political views. In another weird twist, Elor Azarya, serving with his infantry unit in Hebron, was put on trial in a military court in 2016 after he shot and perhaps murdered a wounded terrorist who had earlier attacked a soldier. Israel's surrealistic "purity of arms" doctrine was allegedly violated by a soldier assuring that a Palestinian terrorist be definitively neutralized. Elor was found guilty by a military court for misconduct and given an eighteen-month jail sentence, later released in May, 2018.

A military court in 2018 provided a bizarre example of the abandonment of the Jews. A Palestinian knife-wielding terrorist had assaulted a Jewish woman in Gush Etzion in 2015. The blade penetrated and was lodged in her body, then the terrorist fled. The judges considered that there was no murderous intent because the length of the blade was not in their opinion adequate to inflict a lethal crime. They concluded that the Palestinian wanted to injure but not murder—when every Israeli knows that all Arab terrorists want to murder Jews. The accused yelled the Allah Akbar war cry, but the judicial panel would only agree to charge him with a lesser crime than intent to kill.

There were other unsavory affairs in the IDF which touched upon Chief-of-Staff Gabi Ashkenazi. He dismissed from service two highly commended brigadier-generals, Imad Fares and Moshe (Chico) Tamir, for petty non-military misdeeds. He chose the cold letter of the law rather than the spirit of things and broader considerations. Then there was the instance of Ashkenazi's own suspect behavior in interfering in the constitutional decision-making process conducted by the Defense Minister regarding the appointment of his successor. Ashkenazi, the darling of the political Left, patronized by Shimon Peres, and ambitious to become a Labor Party prime minister, got off scot-free publicly and legally. This noxious subject was exposed in an investigative book, titled *The Pit* [Ha-Bor] (Kinneret, Zmora, 2011) by the reputable journalists Dan Margalit and Ronen Bergman.

The army was suspected of adopting policies designed to blunt the increasing influence of the religious Zionist sector in combat units and the cultural nuances attending its prominent presence. This related to the role of the Bina Organization and the Hartman Institute as outsourcing educational platforms to provide lectures and courses for IDF officers. Their prejudice was tilted heavily in the direction of the New Israel Fund, which indeed was financing both outfits, in anti-nationalist, pro-peace, and double Israeli–Palestinian narratives. The army, though its mandate is defense and warfare, was promoting democracy and advocating feminist, egalitarian, and progressive values, wrapped in Jewish pluralism. In brief, a mélange of soft maudlin civilian and leftist ideas. Traditional Judaism and Zionism, the cultivation of patriotism and love of the Land, were values challenged or marginalized by a new agenda. Fortunately, in 2016 Minister of Defense Avigdor Lieberman, new in office, learned of this deliberate attempt to warp the fighting spirit and focused mission of Tzahal; and so he canceled the contracts with Bina and Hartman. Meanwhile, no less disruptive of morale and clear-thinking, IDF soldiers were engaged in social activities with children of illegal African infiltrators who posed problems for south Tel-Aviv residents. Hopefully, the IDF will return to its full senses.

Rabbi Yigal Levinstein, who heads the pre-army academy at Eli in Samaria, delivered a blistering verbal attack in March 2017 against the army's policy of forming male-female combat units. In his view this was part of a post–Zionist feminist agenda, itself the result of propaganda and ideological agitation, to undermine the moral backbone of the IDF. The army was taking a position on social issues which had nothing to do with its responsibility for the defense of the country. The Left mocked Rabbi Levinstein and called for his resignation. Avigdor Lieberman, the Minister of Defense, demanded a review of the rabbi's statements, but the controversy seemed to have ended with that.

Haredim / Ultra–Orthodox Anti–Zionists

The Israeli Nobel laureate author Shmuel Yosef Agnon provided a scathing portrait of the ultra-orthodox haredim hassidim in Jerusalem in his monumental novel *Shira*. What message was given to the readers about haredim? They make the city ugly with their clothing and ways. They don't work or contribute to society, they are idle, lazy, acrimonious. Agnon was not willing to overlook the exploitative and parasitic features in the haredi sector in comparison with the productive energy and national commitment that featured in the renaissance of pioneering Jewish life in the Land.

The ultra-orthodox minority has aroused animosity within the country. Haredi extremism, regardless of its alleged halakhic basis, set the country in turmoil in the domain of public discourse. Separating the sexes in public transportation, denying female singers' participation in public events, invading and altering the ambiance in a number of towns and neighborhoods throughout the country, are examples of tension and conflict in the cultural divide as it widens in Israeli society.

The Rabbi who leads the Hassidic flock of the Belz sect stressed in speaking to his followers in 2014 the importance of learning Torah and that they, the students, are the essence of the Jewish people. He added: "We have no need for a state or a government. We need halls of learning and yeshivot [academies] ..." The rabbi was unable to appreciate the security provided by the state's army that made possible a safe and free environment for all Jews in the country. The haredim rejected the moral principle of equal military service for all Israeli Jews. No financial sanctions were imposed upon the AWOL culprits and their rabbinic leaders; thus secular Israeli society was financing a significant part of the population which adamantly refused to share the burden of military service. The temporary exemption from recruitment had been exploited and expanded exponentially since 1948.

All the while, haredim aroused exceptional abhorrence. Horrific language has been hurled at them, but physical attacks have not ensued. TV personality Amnon Dankner wished to set aflame the beards of those "weird Shas [Sephardic political party] rabbis," and Uri Avnery savored the thought of machine-gunning them down in Meah Shearim—a haredi neighborhood in Jerusalem. Yet actual violence came from the ultra-orthodox themselves. The more extreme and violence-prone among these sectarians were incorrigibly active in physically assaulting any soldier in uniform passing through their environs. Special violent treatment was meted out to haredi soldiers who dared to enlist, and do a mitzvah (a good deed) by sharing responsibility in defending the country.

In April 2017, Rabbi Zvi Feldman of Rabbi Orbach's Jerusalem faction forbade his adherents serving in the army. He called upon the young men to face the alternative of prison where delinquent recruits are being held for not appearing for draft procedures: "Let every mother know that if her son goes to the army ... death is preferable." It wasn't love for Torah that motivated this impudent and troubling rebellion. Haredim teach their children hostility toward Israel, and the extreme haredim teach their children hatred for the state.

Convicted Leftist Traitors

While the lists are lengthy for intellectual and political traitors, we cannot overlook the security traitors who were arrested, investigated, charged, and sentenced to prison terms.

Israel Be'er, personal military adviser no less to Prime Minister Ben-Gurion, was arrested in 1961 having visited communist East Berlin and was suspected of passing security secrets to enemy countries, like Egypt; Moshe Sneh, of Mapam and then Maki (Israel Communist Party), suspected of being an agent of Soviet Intelligence; Marcus Klingberg passed on information about Israel's biological secrets to the Russians; and Shabtai Kalmanovitz spent seven years in an Israeli prison after found to be active, not only in the Labor Party, but also in transferring information to the KGB. Other spies, who veered not to the Russians but to the Arabs, included Udi Adiv, member of the anti–Zionist Matzpen group who had met with PLO members in Damascus, then jailed in Israel in 1968; and Mordechai Vanunu befriended PLO-supporting Arab students at Beersheba University, while photographing 57 times at the high-security nuclear site at Dimona where he was employed as a technician. He was imprisoned in 1986.

We must not forget to mention one very critical point. Aside from ideology and morality as incentives, it is good business to be a leftist. You get funded from foreign anti–Semites, you get to travel around the world, speak on distinguished panels, enjoy extensive media coverage, and receive praise from a variety of prominent people and noteworthy organizations. Fame, though short-lived, is an attractive commodity, though tarnished by infamy forever. For the chronicles of history will endure to record that Breaking the Silence accused the IDF of war crimes; B'Tselem censured Israel for apartheid; the Negev Coexistence Forum incited the Bedouin against the state; Rabbis for Human Rights condemned Israel for ethnic cleansing; and ASSAF and ARDC (African Refugee Development Center) undermined Israel by striving to enfranchise illegal African workers in the country. Woe to them who stood not with their country in times of danger and threat—in years of glory and triumph. We have thus deposited our indictment of the Left in the metaphorical or mythical court of the Jewish people.

Chapter Seven

FOREIGN JEWISH LEFTISTS AND OTHERS

Israel is both a Jewish state and the state of the Jewish people. Its substantive national ethos is rooted in Torah and history, mediated in the life, identity, and spirit of the country; the Hebrew calendar, the Sabbath day, the Hebrew language, and the continuity of memory of the land of Israel. Israel's mission as the state of the Jewish people, anchored in the Law of Return and active concern and responsibility for the Jews in the world, assigns it the political definition of being a Jewish nation-state. The Jews of Israel as a national community are part of the global Jewish people, as the Jews of the world can and do rightfully claim that Israel is their spiritual homeland regardless of living beyond its borders. All Jews everywhere are potential citizens of Israel and can actualize their return to the ancient land any day.

There have been Jews who since the appearance of modern Zionism showed great enthusiasm and extended generous support for the national rebirth. Some came on aliya, others were active due to bonds of solidarity and pride in being part of Israel's restoration, yet others provided financial support. However some preferred to distance themselves from Israel, alienated from or indifferent to its rebirth. There were Jews in communist countries who believed that the wave of the future was colored by socialism and cosmopolitanism, that would allow Jews to melt within the confines of an egalitarian society, and disappear.

Jews of a liberal-leftist stance in America estranged themselves from Israel beginning in the period after the 1967 war. They demanded that Israel live up to their political expectations and not to Zionist ideals or

Middle Eastern realities, but conforming to their American values. They would metaphorically abduct the prophet Isaiah and mongrelize his prophesy into the spirit of abstract humanitarianism. Nationalism as the ideological core of Zionism was for some Jews an alienating idea.

Mainstream organized American Jewry traditionally supported Israel and its government at any point in time. This was broadly the case for the American Jewish Congress, American Jewish Committee, Presidents of American Jewish Organizations, B'nai Brith, and the American Israel Public Affairs Committee (AIPAC). The Zionist Organization of America (ZOA) and Americans for a Safe Israel (AFSI) were firmly identified with the nationalist Right in Israel. A public opinion survey conducted in 1995 indicated a convergence between American Jewish opinion and Israeli government policies concerning the so-called "peace process" in the Middle East. A majority of the respondents supported peace initiatives regarding the specific Palestinian, Jordanian, and Syrian tracks. Over time trust in the PLO declined and opposition to a Palestinian state increased.

Organizations against Israel

CONAME (Committee on New Alternatives in the Middle East) was established in 1970 by Bob Loeb; a year later MERIP (Middle East Research and Information Project) appeared. The political era was reverberating with the leftist anti–Israel onslaught by radical Jews. The political atmosphere was suffused with the anti–Vietnam War campaign and invigorated by the Palestinian revolutionary élan against Israeli rule. Anti–Zionism was on the rise in youthful Jewish circles. In America CONAME sponsored Arie Bober, a leader of Matzpen, a small Israeli group which advocated the dissolution of the Jewish state.

Breira (Alternative) was founded at the end of 1973 and one of its founding members, Gershon Hundert, wanted to change the focus of American Jews from the centrality of Israel to local communal welfare in the diaspora. But that was just a cover for Breira's true political objective. It called for negotiating with the PLO and recognizing Palestinian national aspirations in a PLO-dominated state in the West Bank and Gaza. With its activist orientation drawn from the spirit of the civil rights movement, Breira depicted Judaism as a social revolutionary manifesto. It expectedly opposed American policy in Vietnam. Reform Rabbis were especially affiliated with Breira and they expressed their unease with

Israel's military image and performance which for them was divorced from a moral compass. Arthur Waskow, advocating war against the American Empire while seeking universal messianic redemption, opposed buying products from Israeli settlements in Judea and Samaria. Hillel Foundations were incubators of Breira and their conventional sensitivity to civil rights made them sympathetic to the self-declared plight of the Palestinians. At root, Breira was explicit in its scorning of Israel and its support for the Palestinians.

The New Jewish Agenda was founded in 1979 by two Hillel rabbis— Gerald Serotta and Albert Axelrad. It highlighted a progressive Judaism, a radical cultural agenda for gays and lesbians, and advocacy for a Palestinian state. In 1982 NJA called on Israel to recognize the PLO. It cooperated with radical anti–Israel groups like the Arab–American Anti-Discrimination Committee. It sponsored Uri Avnery, founder of the Gush Shalom peace movement and author of *Israel without Zionism* (Collier, 1971); opposed U.S. aid to Israel; called for a settlement freeze in the territories; and cavorted with anti–Semitic personalities and organizations. Leftists from the NJA aggressively occupied offices of the Jewish Federation in Seattle and brandished placards denouncing "Israeli genocide" of Palestinians with the outbreak of the Intifada in 1987.

Americans for Peace Now, as it affiliated with the Peace Now organization founded in Israel, maligned Israel and promoted a Palestinian position. If Israelis are anti–Israel, why not American Jews? In Israel, Peace Now demanded in its founding in 1978 flexibility from Prime Minister Begin, which indeed characterized his decision to withdraw from all of Sinai for the sake of a peace agreement with Egypt. Realizing that Begin would not be conciliatory or capitulate on the West Bank front, Peace Now turned its hostility against Likud and claimed that the conflict with the Palestinians could be resolved if only Israel would dismantle settlements in Judea and Samaria and return to the June 4, 1967 lines. In an Open Letter from November 1983, the Chicago Friends of Peace Now warned that Israel's settlement policy endangers the country and stymies a peaceful solution to the conflict, while corrupting the soul of the people of Israel and isolating her from the democratic community. This cheap slander was off the mark: settlements enhanced Israel's security and sadly did not prevent the wacky Oslo peace effort. Israel's international standing—despite the ongoing settlement enterprise—was enhanced with both Western nations and Asian countries during the following decades. Israel was vital and rejuvenated, confident and proud, and moved forward on all domestic and foreign fronts. The settlement enterprise flourished and deepened its roots in the heart of the homeland. Daniel Greenfield, in his essay "Liberating Our Jerusalem" posted on his *Sultanknish* blog on May 13, 2018, passionately called for Jews to liberate themselves from the lies of diplomacy which never did anything good for Israel. The ethnic cleansing of Jews and the Islamization of Jerusalem were ever-present dangers and partial realities in Israel's modern life.

Prominent Jews in America supported the Peace Now movement and published a letter in that spirit in *The New York Times* in the summer of 1978. Its signatories included Saul Bellow, Irving Howe, Seymour Martin Lipset, Martin Peretz—mainly from the Trotskyist, socialist, and New Left. This was Breira under a new name. The Samuel Rubin Foundation was financing the emerging American Peace Now branch, and the leftist *New Outlook* magazine was a link with (the Israeli) Peace Now's activity in the U.S. Satisfying the PLO was a major theme that was promoted with an eye to influencing Washington's policy toward Israel and the conflict. The inane mantra that American Peace Now was pro-peace was supposed to ingratiate it with all peace-loving peoples and justify all nefarious anti–Israeli actions. In 1996 Leonard Fein and other APN ideologues traveled to Gaza for dinner with Yasser Arafat. Fein enthusiastically reported that Arafat "cut some schnitzel from his own plate, put it on mine, encouraged me to taste it, and then mentioned to the waiter to bring me a fresh plate." The politics of the Arab cuisine cast this liberal Jew as a political fool. Arafat continued to promote terrorism against Jews and never changed the PLO Covenant whose unshakable dogma is the destruction of Israel.

Professor Michael Walzer was a member of Peace Now in America who later put pen to paper to support boycotting Israeli settlement products. In 2014 he called for personal sanctions against prominent rightist Israelis, like Naphtali Bennett leader of the HaBayit HaYehudi Party, whose crime lay in preserving the "occupation." Walzer, who had acquired an academic reputation writing about peace and war, was still the naïve sieve for the ridiculous notion that the Arabs could be pacified and satisfied and live side-by-side with a Jewish state—in Palestine.

The New Israel Fund, founded in 1979, was dedicated to equality for all the inhabitants of Israel and to securing minority rights in a changed democratic framework. It granted more than $300 million to more than 900 organizations on the far radical Jewish Left, Arab outfits, and outwardly anti–Israel organizations. Examples include B'Tselem and Breaking the Silence, and Adala and Mossawa of the Arab community in Israel. While somewhat shying away from explicitly endorsing the BDS movement, yet at other times accommodating it on university campuses, the NIF provided funding for groups that want to turn Israel into a pariah state. Machsom Watch and Yesh Din are two glaring examples of this. CEO Daniel Sokatch declares that the NIF opposes the occupation and settlements, but the fallout and spinoff of this position extends much further into the domain of delegitimizing Israel at its root. As is known, Reform Jews are exceptionally skewed to the Left as exemplified by Rabbi Rick Jacobs, the president of the Reform Movement in America, who is also a member of the NIF international council.

J Street was founded in 2008 by Jeremy Ben-Ami whose statement, that he favors a Jewish democratic home in the state of Israel, was revelatory of his fundamental and nuanced denial of Israel as a Jewish state. His dishonest, ambiguous, and subtle text or sub-text refuted the existence of Israel as constituted in 1948. The stated themes of *J Street* as "pro–Israel, pro-Peace" included a Palestinian state, pre–1967 borders, and probably Palestinian refugee return. Most pointedly *J Street* was an arrogant front to undermine the democratically-elected Netanyahu–led government in Israel. Co-founder Daniel Levy called Israel's creation "an act that went wrong." For this organization, a warped moral equivalence was the criterion of judgment when Israel faced Palestinians in warfare, as in the Cast Lead Operation in 2012. Both sides are to blame. To be neutral toward Israel was only a mask for being positive toward the Palestinians. But *J Street* in its spiritual conceit was, as David Weinberg wrote in 2009, colored with an array of progressive types and women rabbis, inter-religious leaders, and diversity facilitators, all of whom provided a halo of purity to the organization. *J Street* bashed Israel and tried to save the Jewish soul—but not the Jewish state. With Saudi money and a blessing from MK Likud–renegade Tzipi Livny, *J Street* convened its annual conference in February 2011 to continue its political assault against Israel and against the mainstream pro–Israel AIPAC political lobby in Washington. Scholar Barry Rubin and lawyer Alan Dershowitz scorned *J Street's* pro–Zionism as a masquerade and a fraud. Associating with pro-BDS activists, the organization campaigned the

Obama administration to not veto an anti–Israel resolution at the UN Security Council in 2011. David Friedman, who was later appointed ambassador to Israel by President Trump, earlier pulled out the heavy guns calling *J Street* worse than Kapos—those Jews who collaborated with the Nazis in the mass genocide of Jews in the Holocaust. *J Street* was most definitely a major part of the anti–Israel American Jewish Left.

***

Jews, especially students, were actively campaigning against Israeli security and national rights in a host of left-wing anti–Zionist organizations. Anti–Israel Jewish political apostasy was like a new religious current. A typical example of this was the Progressive Zionist Caucus located in New York that could fool people to infer that no inner contradiction marred its elastic name. It called for an "end to the occupation of the West Bank and Gaza," areas central to the biblical Jewish homeland; and incidentally, a close reading of the biblical boundaries will confirm that the Gaza area is indeed within the Land of Israel. Other anti–Israel agencies included Jews for Boycotting Israeli Goods (JBIG), and the Jewish Voice for Peace that advocated on behalf of BDS and lined up with the Palestinian war against Israel to end the occupation. The campaign of Return the Birthright called on young Jews to boycott Birthright, which provides a free trip for Jewish youth to visit Israel, and to support the right of Palestinian refugees to return to their homes in Israel. So-called Rabbi Ellen Lippmann, so-called married to a woman, and an activist on social issues, led the progressive Kolot Chayeinu congregation in Brooklyn, and invited members to join with her at a protest outside the Israeli Consulate in New York against "50 years of occupation." Nothing new in this betrayal as the Jewish people have known, long ago intimated by the prophet Isaiah in chapter 49, that the enemy is not only from the outside but also among and within our nationhood.

Leftist radical Jews have projected their impulse for social activism and commitment to justice in America on to the Israeli political playing-field. They are energized by the moral instinct packed away in their Jewish identity. About Israel they know little, about the Arabs very little, about the Middle East and Islam nothing. They are carefree poseurs, entrepreneurs of ideals, and terribly self-satisfied with their generosity. But all this cannot hide the glaring fact that they are irresponsible buffoons causing public damage to Israel and the Jewish people. The state we prayed for and worked for became for these ego-drunkards a victim of their puerile arrogance. Their forebears—grandfathers, grandmothers, and the generations before them—in the ghettos and mellahs, who were bashed and battered and persecuted as powerless Jews, would have given their all to live even one day in the armed, free, independent Jewish state of Israel.

Jewish organizations which did not malign the Jewish state, yet adhered to the Oslo peace rhetoric of the 1990s, were comfortably aligned with the Labor Party position. This necessitated silencing the Right from voicing its political opposition. As an example, *Midstream* magazine published by the Theodor Herzl Institute in New York, under the capable editorship of Joel Carmichael, was obliged—as he wrote to me in a private correspondence in December 1999—"not to attack the peace process [with the PLO]—in principle." Carmichael, an independent thinker, was gagged from generating debate in his monthly Jewish review. Free academic and public discussion was also smothered when the illiberal pro–Palestinian Alliance of Jewish Progressives and Allies in collaboration with the campus Hillel House prevented Israeli Deputy Foreign Minister Tsippy Hotovely from addressing an audience at Princeton University in November 2017. Reform Judaism, unable to unearth its Jewish self, opposed President Trump's December 2017 declaration that recognized Jerusalem as the capital of Israel.

Prominent Jews against Israel

It is far from surprising that very accomplished Jewish academics and artists, intellectuals and writers, have been far off the mark regarding the subject of Israel. Factors other than cogent thought and empirical data are replaced by personal agendas in shaping their political opinion. They use their credentials to give weight to their views on matters far from their talents and specializations, but close to their political sentiments. I recall how the famed symphony conductor Leonard Bernstein proclaimed his leftist-liberal views regarding Israel and the Middle East as if he could wave his baton to create musical harmony among the cacophony of voices and melodies in the region. So too theater producer Theodore Mann who on his off–Broadway locales stated that he regards "the efforts to make the borders of Eretz Yisrael [including Judea and Samaria] coterminous with the borders of Medinat [the state of] Israel, repugnant." Just like no reasonable person would take medical advice from a carpenter or hire a psychiatrist to build a bridge, it is absurd for a symphony conductor and stage manager to sign petitions for pro–Palestinian peace plans in the Middle East—a region ravaged by Islamic fanaticism, Arab butchery, and Palestinian terrorism. In August 1993, the Jewish Theological Seminary supported Project Nishma in Washington that lauded Yitzhak Rabin's military credentials, placing a full-page ad in this spirit just a month before the Oslo signing in September. Among the signatories were folk-singer Theodore Bikel and Rabbi Irving Greenberg, author William Novak, Albert Vorspan a leader of Reform Judaism who criticized Israel in the first Palestinian intifada when Rabin was Minister of Defense, and Philip Klutznick who opposed Israel's siege of Beirut in 1982 and proposed Israel negotiate with the PLO terrorists. Liberal blabberers are quite a nuisance and hazard to Israel's body politic.

Seymour Martin Lipset, after writing "I Love Israel," promised in a letter to those of similar political orientation in The Committee of Concerned American Jews that the experience and expertise in non-partisan citizens' organizations in America should be channeled to assist the Peace Camp in Israel. Alan Dershowitz, who identified as a Jewish liberal, had been in his own words "urging Israel to end its occupation of the West Bank." He went on to say in the pages of *The Jerusalem Post* in August 1990 that when "the Arab nations recognize Israel's right to exist and make real peace with the Jewish state, Israel will relinquish control over the critical military buffer it continues to occupy for security reasons." This advice formulated as forecast from a Harvard law professor living in America assumed that there is some alchemic substance that can be identified as "real peace."

Journalist Thomas Friedman, somewhat of a Jewish liberal know nothing, magisterially declared in 2002 that the settlement policy was "going to lead to the demise of the Jewish state." He was moreover out of his statistical element in predicting that by 2010 there would be more Palestinians than Jews in Israel, the West Bank and Gaza combined. As of 2017 the Jewish majority margin is over 60 percent and Gaza, under Hamas rule since 2007, is generally no longer included in the demographic equation. Fellow journalist Peter Beinart favored boycotting the settlements and drew a certain parallel between South Africa—a truly apartheid state until 1994—and liberal Israel fighting for its existence. Beinart's books, like *The Crisis of Zionism* (Times Books, 2012), scorned the American Jewish establishment's consistent support for Israel, blamed the "occupation" as inimical with liberal values, and heaped praise on Obama as "the Jewish president." By inference, the Palestinians were helpless victims rather than perpetrators of violence and practitioners of rejectionism. Palestinian human rights rather than Jewish national rights became the hallmark of liberal discourse.

The idea that leftist Jews provide political ammunition to the general American and world public is illustrated by the vitriolic editorial that graced the pages of *The New Republic* on May 2, 1988, titled "Israel's Mad Settlers." Editor Martin Peretz prattled with animus against "right-wing fanatics" and "mystically motivated" settlers who established Elon Moreh near Shechem. Curious how Peretz would define Abraham the Patriarch who came alone to Shechem nearly four thousand years ago with its existing Canaanite population in the land; Joshua who had to fight his way into the land and conquer it for Israelite settlement; and David who became king in Jerusalem populated by Jebusites. Mad Jews and not just the "mad settlers."

Then there is Richard Falk from Princeton University, an assimilationist Jew, who served as the UN Special Rapporteur on Human Rights in the Palestinian Territories. He rejected the two-state solution in order that a one-state solution be the political vessel in which Jewish Israel dissolves. As an enthusiast of the Ayatollah Khomeini in 1979, forecasting that an Islamic republic would respect human and minority rights, this sycophant also bowed before the idol of Arafat and Palestine. For Falk Israel was on the path toward executing a Palestinian holocaust, certainly engaged in Arab ethnic cleansing. When he tried to enter Israel in May 2008 as a UN representative, he was refused.

Marie Syrkin, a noteworthy Zionist voice from Labor ranks, berated Prime Minister Menachem Begin in an article in the *Los Angeles Times* that was picked up by *The Montreal Gazette* in May 1982, for "his obsession with the biblical patrimony in Judea and Samaria." But dear Marie, was it not Jewish "obsession" with the biblical patrimony which gave rise to modern Zionism and the return to Eretz Israel, which Syrkin definitely believed in? She considered building settlements in Judea and Samaria "provocative." Professor Ian Lustick scolded Israel, including Labor Party governments under Golda Meir (1969–74) and Yitzhak Rabin (1974–77), for having "rebuffed several Arab peace feelers." In so doing the Palestinians, the Egyptians and the Jordanians, could no longer be blamed for the state of war. Israel, unlike Lustick, was at times sensitive to the deceitfulness of so-called Arab peace offerings and vigilantly refused to fall into the trap.

As early as 1989 left-wing Jewish leaders like Alexander Schindler, Arthur Hertzberg—who bemoaned the fact that Israel won a great victory in the Six Day War—Balfour Brickner, Philip Klutznick among others, had supported negotiations with the PLO. Here were Arafat's Jews prodding the Washington administration and the Israeli government to capitulate to a terrorist organization whose declared purpose was the destruction of the Jewish state. The PLO covenant in its 33 articles was explicit on this score. Henry Siegman, executive director of the American Jewish Congress, when writing from some distant planet in the political orbit surmised that Israel would be "free to pursue its Jewish vocation without the burden of a permanent occupation and repression of nearly two million Palestinians" once peace is realized with them. Later, in early 2018, with no Palestinian state in the offing, Siegman shifted to advocating Palestinian rights in an article in *The National Interest*, and accusing Israel of practicing a policy of apartheid—presumably because the Arabs and their allies told him so. Edgar M. Bronfman, who headed the World Jewish Congress, wrote in 1980 that he and his family disagree with Begin on the settlement issue "as a matter of principle." Jewish establishment organizations were also opposed to the settlements as when the Jewish National Fund and the United Jewish Appeal in America refused to financially assist Jewish projects beyond the Green Line, in Judea and Samaria. An extraordinarily wealthy person of Jewish descent, Holocaust survivor George Soros, was notorious for supporting a host of anti-Israel organizations—Adalah, Breaking the Silence, B'Tselem, and many others—through his Open Society Foundations.

Fawning was part of the radical Jewish repertoire. An outfit called Jews for Peace in Palestine sent a delegation of American Jews to visit Arafat in his headquarters in Ramallah in December 2001. The Jews spoke with Arafat about "a just peace," undoubtedly unaware that this phrase carried the implication for the Arabs of Israel's disappearance in order that justice be done for the Palestinian people. In Paris, sociologist André Glucksmann with his Maoist credentials and pro–Palestinian orientation called for Israel's unconditional withdrawal from the territories because "human rights cannot be divided." While Israel contended with a violent intifada in 1988, Glucksmann and other French intellectuals broke ranks from their people and its struggle. Author Bernard Avishai , after a brief stint as a Canadian immigrant to Israel, decided to choose democracy in the West rather than Zionism (and democracy) in Israel. Although he later returned to Israel, Avishai's priority for western liberal values, as evidenced in his book *The Tragedy of Zionism* (Helios, 2002), colored his phobia with Israel's occupation. The nuances and circumstances in the juxtaposition of Zionism and democracy were ignored in this tome.

The Washington Post columnist Richard Cohen put it succinctly when he wrote in 2006 that Israel was a "mistake." Yet Israel's tenacity and resourcefulness, that included a hard military punch, had turned the "mistake" into a reasonable wager. Michael Lerner, editor of Tikkun Magazine, advocated the cause of the PLO while never failing to blame Israel. He had developed a close relationship with Hillary Clinton and no doubt provided a moral license for her Palestinian sympathies. This court Jew put his progressivism before his Judaism with a swirl of cosmopolitanism and spiritualism. Needless to say he knew nothing about the dark sides of the Middle East. When so-called Palestinian intellectuals began to discuss the idea of Israeli sovereignty over the West Bank as a springboard for the emergence of a Jewish–Arab binational state, Lerner was encouraged by this strategy to democratically undo the Jewish state. At *The New York Times*, a number of Jewish liberal columnists, the likes of Thomas Friedman, Roger Cohen, and Michelle Goldberg, set the political tone for the anti–Israel charge concerning Jewish settlements and military operations in Gaza. Professor Yakov Rabkin, speaking at a panel discussion at a Canadian Jewish Federation meeting in Montreal in 2001, called for the dismantlement of Israel as a Jewish state, arousing the anger of the local audience.

While Reform, Conservative, and Reconstructionist rabbis were actively affiliated with the leftist capitulation camp, there were Orthodox rabbis who also jumped on the rickety peace bandwagon. Chief Rabbi Emanuel Jakobowitz of the United Kingdom once said that if the Israelis could not get the Arabs to make peace, Israel should abolish itself. It was probably this kind of outrageous statement that endeared the rabbi to the Queen, as he was later appointed to the House of Lords. Rabbi Binyamin Walfish of the Rabbinic Council of America was comfortable with the Peace Now deviation. The Shultz Peace Initiative in 1988 earned the support of prominent Jews such as Isaiah Berlin, Isaac Stern, and Saul Bellow. Unlike perhaps Stern and Bellow, Berlin knew who Montesquieu and Marx were, but aside from that, his expertise in political philosophy provided him with no advantage in understanding the Palestinians and the politics of the Middle East more than an esteemed violinist and a noteworthy author. Henry Kissinger as American Secretary of State during the October 1973 Yom Kippur War is remembered for the alleged statement that "he wanted the Israelis to bleed," denying them a military airlift in the early days of the fighting.

Certainly one of the most notorious anti–Israel Jewish quislings was Norman Finkelstein who depicted Israel in a demonic fashion. His anti–Semitic tirades included referring to Jewish leaders as gangsters and Elie Weisel as "the resident clown for the Holocaust circus." Somewhat less vicious but nonetheless playing the role of "useful idiots" were those long standing anti–Zionists who signed an ad in *The New York Times* in 1989 that called on Israeli Prime Minister Yitzhak Shamir to negotiate with the PLO. These signers, based in Manhattan and other upbeat environs, knew little and experienced none of Palestinian terrorism and the savage murder of Jews. Let us remember therefore that Woody Allen, Philip Roth, Arthur Miller, Betty Friedan, Allen Ginsburg, Abie Hoffman, and I.F. Stone, will be remembered for their abrasive intrusion into the political domain and the Middle East morass that were far beyond their intellectual reach and artistic vocation. It was the work of two Jews, Alan Rabinovich and Rachel Goldstein, who produced a film for the PLO called *Revolution until Victory*, which described Zionists as bestial creatures.

Sometime around the turn of the twenty-first century a certain glimmer of sanity and honesty peeked through the leftist prism. Leonard Fein, founder of America for Peace Now, Reform leader Alexander Schindler who had alleged Israel was betraying the Zionist dream, Labor Zionist Menachem Rosensaft who visited Arafat in Stockholm in 1988, and a few others, later admitted their error in having promoted the PLO and supporting the Oslo Accords. Earlier Rosensaft was lecturing Arafat to renounce terrorism and work together with the Israelis for the common good. For Arafat there are no Palestinian terrorists but only freedom fighters and holy jihadists; and he incessantly harangued his devotees to become martyrs in the struggle—not for a nuisance-like silly peace with Israel but to liberate all of Palestine.

Noam Chomsky of MIT was undoubtedly one of the most malicious (Jewish) haters of Israel. For beginners, he predicted that Israel's end would come either through military defeat or on a drift towards internal social, moral, and political degeneration. Soldiers coming home from the occupied territories, he believed, are old in spirit and guilt-ridden— neither of which is true. Peres, Begin, and Shamir were, in his opinion, terrorists. Chomsky himself was tolerant of neo–Nazis, saying he defends their freedom of speech. A dissident intellectual, a blistering anti-American, a fellow-traveler with Holocaust–deniers, Chomsky fits the bill as an anti–Semite and enemy of the Jewish state.

A coterie of anti–Israel Jewish professors at the Berkeley branch of the University of California is a telling instance of west-coast detachment and libertarianism. Judith Butler, Daniel Boyarin, Chana Kronfeld, and Martin Jay, are among the progressive, pro-BDS advocates. Terror, which Professor Edward Alexander understood to be "the very essence of Palestinian nationalism," did not seem to trouble these free-thinkers, who apparently believe that Arab aggression is Israel's fault. Meanwhile, in cozy Ontario, three women of a radical feminist and anti–Zionist bent—Jennifer Peto, Judy Rebick, and Naomi Klein—fulminated against the exploitation of the Holocaust for contemporary Israeli purposes. And across the ocean in England, Jews calling to boycott Israel organized in 2002 under the leadership of academic Steven Rose and his wife Hilary to parade their progressive credentials. A noteworthy American Jewish progressive, the 2015 presidential hopeful Bernie Sanders, delivered a message on the fiftieth anniversary of Israel's victory in the 1967 War by calling for an end to Israel's occupation, and propounded the need for real peace. Poor Bernie, unbeknownst to him is the fact that in the real world of names and things there is no Israeli "occupation" and there is no "real peace"—with Arabs.

Real life did not exist in the ethereal firmament of Jewish leftist/ liberal academic and political musings. It existed elsewhere. It existed in Palestinian political quarters where Fatah/PLO executive council member Abbas Zaki declared deep in the Oslo years that "the greater goal cannot be accomplished in one go." He was referring to the Palestinian strategic stages theory of step-by-step to total victory against Zionism. Israel will come to an end, Zaki believed, when Israel will withdraw from Jerusalem and evacuate 650,000 settlers; moreover Allah is gathering the Jews in one place and then the Palestinians can kill them. We can add that pitiful Jews plead for peace, proud Arabs pray for vanquishing Israel and conquering Palestine. Jewish U.S. State Department employees serving as diplomats and advisers, showing support for Palestinian positions like statehood, included Daniel Kurtzer, Martin Indyk, David Makovsky, and Dan Shapiro.

A primary consideration for diaspora Jewish liberals-leftists-progressives was to disassociate themselves from the nationalist-conservative current that came to dominate Israeli politics. The U.S. foreign policy establishment was notoriously scornful of Likud and Netanyahu, until Donald Trump became president. Israeli policies had been branded as illegal, expansionist, and an obstacle to peace. Feeling uncomfortable and anxious to maintain their status and role in America, the liberals chose sides against Israel. How certain gentile circles viewed them was a greater psychological and social concern than demonstrating solidarity with the Jews in Israel. This exilic complex was unresolvable and loyalty to America was the Jews' first priority. Regarding Israel Jews looked to the left, and this fit in with their Democratic Party preference.

At the Holocaust Denial Conference in Tehran in December 2006, members of the Jewish hassidic Neturei Karta sect from America were present. One was photographed kissing Iranian president Ahmadinejad.

An Addendum: Non–Jewish Anti–Israel Foreigners

Compassion for our dedicated readers convinced me to offer just a short, sketchy, and unsystematic citation of other villains. For example: the United Nations and its agencies, labeling Israel an apartheid country while denying the Jewish people's heritage in the Land of Israel:—via the pro-BDS Human Rights Council, the UN High Commissioner for Human Rights, the UN-organized Durban Conference of 2001 that was attended by 1,500 anti–Israel NGOs accusing the Jewish state of war crimes and proposing boycotting Israel; UNESCO rejecting any Jewish connection to the ancient Western Wall in Jerusalem or to Abraham's city of Hebron; the United Nations Relief and Works Agency (UNWRA) whose Palestinian educational materials in refugee camps promote jihad, the Nazi ideology, and Israel's destruction; and UNICEF—oPt [Occupied Palestinian Territories] blackening the IDF at the level of Al Qaeda and Boko Haram for grave violations of children's rights; Human Rights Watch ideologically biased against Israel and supporting the BDS campaign; Amnesty International with its BDS campaign to delegitimize the Jewish

State; American Friends Service Committee with its historic Palestinian credentials; the Arabist U.S. State Department which as Israel's traditional adversary intervened, according to a Senate Investigatory Committee report, through the V15 association to (unsuccessfully) influence the 2015 Israeli elections by funneling funds to conduct a smear campaign against Netanyahu—and it, the State Department, audaciously referring in 2017 to the Israelite/Hebrew King Solomon's Pools south of Bethlehem as a Palestinian heritage site; EU and USA funding to the tune of $300 million for One Voice that opposed the Israeli law requiring transparency from all organizations active in Israeli public affairs to divulge foreign funding; Democratic Socialists of America whose national convention in 2017 not only advocated the BDS policy but members burst into a chant of From the River to the Sea/Palestine will be Free; and a variety of anti–Zionist churches like the Presbyterian Church; and the Church of Scotland and the Church of Sweden as hostile to Israel's very existence.

In one year the government of Norway and Finland, the EU and the British Embassy in Israel, together contributed millions of shekels to Peace Now, as reported in 2007 from an official government source in Israel; Sweden through its International Development Cooperation Agency funds NGOs that support BDS, are anti–Semitic, and delegitimize the Jewish state; while NGOs working on behalf of illegal African infiltrators into Israel were supplied from 2012–17 with close to $13 million from foreign entities that included Scandinavian countries in particular. The Berlin film festival is notorious for praising anti–Israel propaganda movies against the "occupation" and standing with the BDS movement. Israeli film-maker Udi Aloni, son of the late Shulamit Aloni, was a favorite of the Germans. And a large section of German public opinion thought Israel was acting like Nazis against the Palestinians. Such was the result of a historic bad German conscience and a massive propaganda campaign against the Jewish state. We recall the Swedish social democrat Prime Minister Olof Palme who, friend of Castro and the PLO, accused Israelis of being Nazis. Norwegian newspapers ran anti–Israel and anti–Semitic caricatures; Norwegian leaders visited Hamas in Gaza. The Anti–Israel Movement in the United States, sloganeering with Free Palestine, came to include Black Lives Matter as an expression of an Afro–American/Arab alliance against Israel's very existence; in Canada the largest private sector labor union (Unifor) adopted an anti–Israel

BDS position in 2017; and at Montreal's esteemed McGill University (my alma mater) a pro-BDS student group, Democratize McGill, purged Jewish or pro-Israel students from the University's Students Society. Signs of anti-Semitism on campus, as at UCLA, merged smoothly with its anti-Zionist pro-Palestinian ideological twin; and the World Council of Churches was active financing illegal Arab construction in Area C in the territories and trampling on Israeli sovereignty. In early 2018, the Israeli government issued a detailed list of foreign pro-Palestinian organizations to be denied entry into the country: included were BDS Italy, Palestine Solidarity Association in Sweden, the Palestine Committee of Norway, Ireland Palestine Solidarity Campaign, and in the United States—Code Pink, American Muslims for Palestine, and National Students for Justice in Palestine; and vicious campaigns were conducted on university campuses which included attacks against Jews, vandalizing their property, and silencing the voice of pro-Israel students, as at Columbia University and New York University. There is in this anti-Israel assault a mixture of anti-Semitism and anti-Zionism dedicated ultimately to the destruction of the Jewish state.

Most odiously prominent was Israel Apartheid Week that began at the University of Toronto in 2005, and spread to become a global movement to defame and delegitimize Israel as an apartheid racist state. Anti-Zionist and pro-Palestinian, this anti-Semitic and propagandistic hate-group targeted Israel on university campuses around the world. While Israel's citizens of all identities and denominations enjoyed the public space for a most liberal political and cultural life, the country was yet locked in the conundrum of dealing with Arab-Jewish tensions, the Palestinian issue, and the territories. This did not at all turn the Jewish state into an apartheid state, but rather presented her with challenges to manage in an ongoing precarious state of conflict and violence.

Chapter Eight

THE RABIN ASSASSINATION:

A LEFTIST PLOT?

Political assassinations sometimes leave lingering questions unanswered many years after the event. Winding trails of suspicions and suspects are covered in darkness. Conspiracy theories abound. Sometimes the real assassin is unknown, or his motives unclear, and the organizational or underground network hardly exposed. The political assassination of Prime Minister Yitzhak Rabin on November 4, 1995, was no exception.

Rabin and Oslo

The political context of the Rabin assassination is the period of the Oslo Peace Process whose goal was reconciliation and rapprochement between Israel and the Palestinians, to be realized by the Labor-led government of Yitzhak Rabin and the Palestine Liberation Organization led by Yasser Arafat. The Oslo I Accord was signed on Sept. 13, 1993 and Oslo II on September 28, 1995. The former agreement was implemented by Israel when it withdrew its forces from most of the Gaza Strip and the Jericho area near the Jordan River. The latter agreement delineated a further Israeli territorial withdrawal from Judea and Samaria, specifically from seven Palestinian cities to be transferred to the Palestinian Authority's unilateral rule designated as Area A; while Area B designated rural areas under Palestinian civilian authority and Israeli security authority; and Area C totally under Israeli control. Of apparent significance is the fact that only six weeks separated Rabin's decision to authorize Oslo II and his subsequent murder.

From the start, the Right and the Zionist religious camp considered Oslo an act born of poor political judgment and manifesting national treason. The Jewish settlers, who interminably faced danger as a daily way of life, now felt betrayed by their government and their life's work lay in the balance. Palestinian villages reverting to PA-PLO rule within Area B would be threatening to the vulnerable Jewish communities. Any future Oslo III political map would enhance the possibility of forming a Palestinian state that could be accompanied by the dismantlement of Israeli settlements and the expulsion of the Jewish residents. Rabin had earlier differentiated between security settlements and political settlements, considering the latter an unacceptable ideological provocation of the Right, and therefore slated to be destroyed somewhere down the line.

Mendacity, machinations, and maneuvering were the hallmark of Arafat's political conduct. He was the quintessential arch-terrorist and political rogue. But the Left looked aside. Immediately after the Oslo Declaration of Principles signing, Arafat in an address in Arabic revealed that this was the first step in accordance with the PLO's 1974 plan for Israel's destruction. When the Palestinian terrorist campaign accelerated in 1994, as suicide bombers exploded themselves on buses and in restaurants murdering hundreds of Israelis, Rabin persisted with the Oslo farce. He labeled the victims "peace sacrifices" rather than having the courage and honesty to admit they were victims of war. We recall Arafat's speech in a mosque in Johannesburg on May 10, 1994, where he called for Holy War to liberate Jerusalem, and referred to the Islamic precedent of the Hudaybiyya agreement by Mohammad in 628. Just as Mohammad chose to tactically adopt a limited cease-fire with his enemy, so Arafat signaled he was using the Oslo Agreement as a temporary and phony truce in the jihad against the Jews. On September 19, 1995, on the verge of signing Oslo II, Arafat admitted in an interview in the Jordanian newspaper *Al-Dustour* that "Oslo is nothing more than the execution of what our Palestinian National Council decided upon in 1974," that is, the phased or incremental strategy to erase Israel from the map. In a secret speech in Stockholm in February 1996, Arafat would later divulge that his intention was "to eliminate Israel and establish a purely Palestinian state." In the course of these developments millions of Israelis, he said, would leave the country.

The Israeli government never held Arafat accountable for his violations by word and deed of the Oslo Accord. This heedless policy lasted until Prime Minister Sharon sent the IDF in April 2002 back into the Area A Palestinian towns to destroy the terrorist infrastructures in Operation Defensive Wall. From then until his death in 2004 in France, Arafat was virtually made a prisoner in his Muqataa headquarters in Ramallah.

Straight-talking native-born sabra that he was, Yitzhak Rabin was not particularly prone or inclined to engage in political deception. Yet he did slip up in one very important instance. In a phone briefing to the Conference of Presidents of Major Jewish Organizations on August 10, 1993, the Prime Minister declared that Israel will maintain its policy of not negotiating with the PLO. Secret meetings and political negotiations had by that time been underway for many months in Norway between Israeli and Palestinian officials. The two sides were on the verge of signing an agreement when Rabin nonetheless declared that Israel would not negotiate with the PLO. Rabin, unlike Foreign Minister Shimon Peres, was uneasy about dealing with Arafat, and his awkwardness was apparent at the Washington ceremony of the Oslo Accord in September a month later. If Rabin thought that the Palestinian negotiators of the Oslo Accord were not senior figures in the PLO or subservient to Arafat's authority, then he was foolishly ignorant of the political constellation in Palestinian circles. But if he knew the identity of the negotiators, he was simply lying to the American Jewish leadership.

In another encounter with the Conference of Major Jewish Organizations at the end of September 1995, Malcolm Hoenlein, the executive vice-president, reported that Rabin's tone "was harsh" in the meeting. He was upset that Jewish leaders expressed political views inconsistent with his own. Rabin had become frustrated with Jewish criticism of his Oslo policy and lashed out against the American Jewish leadership establishment.

At home, Rabin was derisive in talking about his domestic political rivals and putative public opponents as "degenerates." He called soldiers who fought and bled for Israel "cry babies" because they opposed his policy of surrendering Jewish land to Arab enemies. He was insensitive to the distress which struck the Right and the settlers. He would brook no discussion of his political path. He vilified the Likud Party as "allies of Hamas," as both opposed Oslo. Rabin insulted his own Labor Party members in January 1995 as "imbeciles."

Following one ghastly terrorist attack on a bus on Dizengoff Street in Tel Aviv on October 19, 1994, that left 22 Israeli fatalities, Rabin spoke on television in the evening to say that if he stops the Oslo process and dealing with Fatah, then in the end Israel will be forced to deal with Hamas. Rabin was sadly out of his political depth.

Foreign Minister Shimon Peres, by contrast, was by nature always comfortable in playing the political game. He with his associates concocted the Oslo brew. He directed his minions to forge a back-door diplomatic track to prepare for Israeli recognition of the PLO and convince Rabin to approve this démarche as a fait accompli. Dr. Yair Hershfeld, one of the chief negotiators on behalf of Peres, divulged in 1996 that during the understandings with the Palestinians—this during the secret sessions of 1993—the Israelis agreed to a Palestinian state at the end of the process, with its capital on the outskirts of East Jerusalem. Seemingly all this was surreptitiously, clandestinely, and underhandedly hidden—at least initially—even from Prime Minister Rabin.

Peres drew a portrait of himself as a visionary, but there were other shades to his political profile. It was suggested that the choice of Norway as the venue for negotiations was not accidental because Peres and his staff had already considered submitting his name as a candidate for the Nobel Peace Prize. It was reported by Shimon Shiffer in *Yediot Aharonot* on October 3, 1995, that Peres had preferred that Rabin not attend the signing ceremony in Washington, leaving the "glory" to him alone.

Yet marketing Oslo to the Israeli public proved to be far less successful than the Left expected. In a poll that appeared in *Yediot Aharonot* on January 27, 1995, 51 percent of the respondents favored ending the "peace process with the Palestinians" while 46 percent believed it should continue. The same newspaper reported on September 3 that a Dahaf poll showed Rabin and Netanyahu were tied at 42 percent as to who the public would vote for in the next elections. Very spirited and sometimes militant anti–Oslo demonstrations took place around the country and eroded support for Rabin and the Left.

On October 5, 1995, a month before the assassination in Tel Aviv, a large boisterous anti–Oslo demonstration took place in Jerusalem. Nationalist opposition leaders including Netanyahu, Ariel Sharon, Rehavam Zeevi, and Rafael Eitan, stood on a balcony at Zion Square and called for nullifying the Oslo Accords. Images of Rabin wearing a kaffiyeh (Arab head-dress) and dressed in a Nazi SS uniform created a diabolical photo of the prime minister. The anti-government campaign against Oslo was transformed from a political controversy to profaning the reputation of Yitzhak Rabin. He was now vilified as a traitor to Israel.

The anti–Oslo political street campaign in 1995, initiated by Moshe Feiglin and his Zo Artzeinu movement, generated civil disobedience that blocked road traffic. On one occasion 12,000 demonstrators simultaneously congregated at 78 intersections throughout Israel on August 8, 1995, from Tsfat (Safed) in the north to Kiryat Malachi in the south, burning tires and ignoring police demands to disperse. Jerusalem was among the locations of demonstrations, as on September 13, 1995, and confrontations erupted between the protesters and the police. Tensions escalated throughout the country.

On Friday November 3, a group of noisy demonstrators confronted Leah Rabin in front of the Rabin apartment in Ramat Aviv north of Tel Aviv at three o'clock in the afternoon. Yael Gevirtz, in a long article on Rabin and the assassination that appeared in *Yediot Aharonot* on September 13 a year later, described the taunting directed against the prime minister's wife and her husband. The following evening Yitzhak Rabin was murdered near Kings Square (later to be renamed Rabin Square) in Tel Aviv.

On that Saturday evening November 4, 1995 a mass rally was organized in the Malchei [Kings] Square under the theme of peace and pursuing the path of Oslo. The purpose was to mobilize popular support for the Rabin government in the city with its ample leftist-liberal pretensions. It was a songfest and political "happening." Rabin and Peres were on the stage. A good spirit abounded, Oslo must go on. Yet the textual theme of the evening was captured by the slogan "YES to Peace and NO to Violence," though it was fitting that "terrorism" and not "violence" be juxtaposed to "peace." The organizers were aiming their message against the Right, smeared as a violent camp. The word "terrorism" would have been directed against the "Palestinians" and their unrelenting and savage campaign that spilled the blood of Israelis throughout the country. But the Left focused on its political war against the Right and not on a military war against the Palestinians. The framing of the message of the Tel Aviv rally revealed the primary problem facing the Left: assuring its political power against the Right. The Palestinians' war against the Jews was a secondary problem.

A self-fulfilling scenario unfolded on the fourth of November. A nationalist Jewish militant murdered Yitzhak Rabin and this confirmed the Left's accusation of rightist violence. However, the connection between the theme of the rally and the act of murder was so complete as to arouse more than a little suspicion that there were those who fabricated the political happening and produced its results.

The peace rally, wrote Orly Azoulay-Katz in *Yediot Aharonot* on September 13, 1996, was organized by Foreign Minister Shimon Peres. It was known to all that Rabin did not like or trust Peres; their personal acrimony was a challenge to cooperating during their intertwined political careers. Rabin suspected Peres as subversive. Peres considered the unintellectual Rabin as small-minded. But together they sang "The Song of Peace" (*Shir Ha-Shalom*) on the stage that evening in Tel Aviv.

The rally ended and Rabin, without Peres at his side, descended the stairs to his awaiting car. Peres meanwhile got into his car and left the scene. Rabin's bodyguards somewhat distanced themselves from the prime minister. This gave the assassin Yigal Amir the moment he needed. Seconds later shots were heard. The video film shows a man firing at Rabin from behind, then the PM hustled toward the car while on his feet. A hand opens the car door from inside and Rabin enters. At the time of the shots someone situated in the center of things screams—"Srak, srak" (dummy bullets), as if Rabin was not wounded at all. A woman witness was immediately interviewed, and speaking in a very confident tone repeatedly confirmed that Rabin was not injured. He had put his foot into the vehicle and was not hurt. With Rabin now in the car, the vehicle speeds away to the nearby Ichilov Hospital. Menachem Damti, who replaced Rabin's regular driver, traveled the distance in ten minutes when it should have taken just two minutes. The obvious question is whether something nefarious transpired in the car during the extended drive.

Within a few minutes an official announcement informed the stunned Israeli public that Rabin died from gunshot wounds.

Questions and Suspicions

Against the advice of the General Security Services headed by Carmi Gillon, Rabin was not wearing a bullet proof vest on the night of the assassination. On the stage Rabin reportedly said to Peres that there were rumors of possible violence. An atmosphere of political tension had been felt throughout the country for many months, with suspicions that from among the settlers in Judea and Samaria violent actions could erupt.

Avishai Raviv was from the late 1980s an *agent provocateur* for the GSS. He founded a semi-underground movement of radical youth called Eyal (the organization for Jewish fighters). He had a reputation for being violent. Jews, including the head of the Kiryat Arba Council, had noted his thuggish behavior in overturning Arab stalls in the Hebron market. As reported by Revital Bracha in *Haaretz* on February 15, 1993, Eyal promoted collective Arab punishment and advocated the transfer of Arabs out of the country. It set out also to harass nationalist politicians while despising leftist ones.

When charges were laid against Raviv for his very suspicious activities, state prosecutors closed the files for lack of evidence and interest to the public. A document from the Ministry of Justice confirmed on June 16, 1996, that Avishai Raviv was "a problematic agent" of the GSS, yet his operators continued to use him. Raviv's criminal behavior and incitement to violence against Arabs were well known. At the same time one of Raviv's organizations, fictitious or not, was called "The Sword of David" and it took responsibility for the murder of three Arabs in Tarqumiyya west of Hebron. Raviv sought to raise tensions between Jews and Arabs while ostensibly focusing on his opposition to the Oslo accords and the Rabin government. When Rabin was dressed with the SS uniform on the placards at Zion Square, it was GSS operative Avishai Raviv who had orchestrated this depraved image for the purpose of slandering the Right. As Oslo was unraveling, the Left shifted public attention to the political opposition which had exposed the Left's policy as a colossal betrayal from the start. After all, Rabin spoke of Eretz-Israel not as the national homeland, but as a piece of real estate.

Part of the war against the Right led to luring ideological militant youth into extreme organizations to then justify their arrest. It was reported that Shabak/GSS operatives were active at anti–Oslo demonstrations, encouraging youth to join in, but then disappearing into a police van and fleeing the scene. The GSS set a trap for enthusiastic patriotic youngsters caught up in the turmoil of Oslo to entice them into Raviv's radical circle of followers.

One of them who at the very minimum had been exposed to Raviv's incitement and criminality was Yigal Amir from Herzliya. He was a student at Bar Ilan University who had worked for an official state security agency active in Latvia, though his work was presented as on behalf of the Jewish community. This part of Amir's biography is shrouded in mystery and secrecy. In a protest event against Oslo in which Raviv and Amir participated, someone overheard Amir say that he intends to murder Yitzhak Rabin. In response Raviv challenged and incited him: "You're just talking, let's see if you really are a man." This was reported in an article in *Yediot Aharonot* on November 21, 1995, after the assassination.

On that woeful November 4 evening, Yigal Amir did indeed fire shots at Rabin's back when the prime minister approached his car at the end of the political rally. When later Rabin was declared dead, it certainly seemed that Amir's shots were the cause of the death. However, forensic investigations would later raise doubts. Leah Rabin related that immediately following the shooting, the GSS told her that the bullets were blank. In addition a right-wing organization issued a statement to the media saying "this time we missed." Added to these suspicious revelations was the insightful comment by Moshe Feiglin that the original sin of the GSS was that its director, Carmi Gillon, had been appointed in March 1994 to his position having earlier headed the Jewish Section in the organization. One wonders if his former job became the defining feature in his new appointment. Shifting the focus to the Jews and not the Arabs, this oddly enough when a deadly spree of Palestinian terrorism hit the streets of Israel, is a strange development. Gillon, who wrote a master's thesis in 1991 at Haifa University on the subject of the extreme Right and civil disobedience, had apparently warned the Israeli cabinet three months prior to the assassination that a threat to the prime minister was real. In their book on the assassination, *Crimes d'état* (Belfond, 1996), Uri Dan and Dennis Eisenberg were sure that Gillon's appointment to head the Shabak was a political choice by Yitzhak Rabin, perhaps supported by Shimon Peres. Later Gillon would be appointed to head the Shimon Peres Center for Peace.

***

Yigal Amir was situated casually in the area defined as sterile from a security point of view; Shimon Peres who preceded Rabin down the stairs from the rally was seen circling the car as if examining it, prior to the Prime Minister's departure.

The security detail protecting Yitzhak Rabin on November 4 in Tel Aviv aroused suspicion. Gillon himself admitted in an article in *Yediot Aharonot* on April 21, 2000, that when Rabin's personal bodyguard saw Yigal Amir draw his pistol, the response should have been immediate to neutralize him. Then the back door of the car opened from within and Yoram Rubin shoved Rabin in, and the car fled the scene. Ichilov Hospital director Professor Gabi Barabash revealed that he hadn't received any alert to expect the prime minister. In fact, when the car arrived Rabin was already dead.

An air of escalating doubts clouded the presentation of a clear picture of what transpired at 9:45 and thereafter on the evening of the assassination. It was reported that three shots had been fired at Rabin's back, though a ballistics expert claimed that the bullets were not fired from any distance, but rather point blank. Interviewed that night, Health Minister Ephraim Sneh (himself a physician) said that Rabin had been shot three times—in the chest, the stomach, and the spinal cord—not in the back. In an affidavit submitted to the Supreme Court against the State of Israel by Shmuel Fleishman, a lawyer for Yigal Amir, it was claimed that one of the bullets fired was not of the same caliber as the other two. The pathology report on Rabin's body raised serious questions never satisfactorily answered.

Days after the assassination a group of nationalist organizations claimed that an investigatory committee should be established to examine the connection between the Rabin murder and the GSS. Avishai Raviv had earlier been investigated by the GSS and the police for his criminal activities, and for his alleged involvement in the murder of two elderly Arabs in Samaria. The rightist organizations that Raviv had established in addition to Eyal were now suspected to be the brainchild of the GSS. Gideon Ezra, deputy head of the GSS, revealed in November 1995 that the Shabak had Raviv move to Kiryat Arba, a center of religious nationalist sentiment. Amnon Abramovitz, the leftist journalist, revealed that Raviv's code name was Champagne. Clearly this high-profile bubbling agent was intoxicated with his official mission against the Right.

It is vital and perhaps revealing to recall suspicions concerning Shabak tactics in earlier incidents. In 1984 the Jewish Underground of 27, mentioned earlier, was uncovered and arrested; and it is more than possible that the secret services were monitoring its operations prior to the underground's murder of Muslim students in Hebron and the maiming of Arab mayors in 1980. When there was an imminent plan afoot to attack Arab buses filled with children, the Shabak preempted and foiled the operation. So a suspicion exists that perhaps Shabak knew about Amir's intended assassination operation; maybe even put him up to it; perhaps sneakily inserted blanks into his revolver; and all to use a rightist militant in a fake assassination attempt that would stain the reputation of the Right—as violent, flouting the law, and violating the sacred dictum that Jews don't kill Jews. Nahum Barnea, writing two weeks after the assassination in *Yediot Aharonot* on November 19, questioned whether as in Soviet Russia that Israeli security services co-opted and then manipulated problematic opposition elements for essentially the regime's political purposes; or perhaps, in the case before us, that Raviv misled his handlers by going too far in his role as an agent. Again: did the Shabak actually plan a pseudo-assassination which back-fired?

The police investigation after the murder presented its own bag of suspicions and a scenario for a veritable witch-hunt. A barber in Jerusalem who didn't express sadness at Rabin's passing was interrogated as a possible accomplice to the crime. Margalit Har-Shefi, a young student at Bar-Ilan University where Yigal Amir studied, was found guilty for not preventing the murder after hearing Amir declare he would kill Rabin. Although she did not share Amir's views, and could not know whether he really intended to carry out such an action, she was sent to jail for nine months. The exact opposite of the Har-Shefi case was that of Shlomi Halevi: this Bar Ilan University student did give the Shabak information concerning Yigal Amir "who intended to murder the Prime Minister." But the Shabak apparently did not follow up on this information, and Yigal Amir carried on with the normal course of his activities.

Avishai Raviv, who heard Amir saying he would kill Rabin, and spent time together with him, was spared any conviction and prison sentence after the assassination. Apparently his intimate connection with the Shabak since 1987 paid off in the end. Raviv incited Amir and took no steps to prevent the murder. The Commission of Investigation into the Murder of Prime Minister Yitzhak Rabin headed by Justice Meir Shamgar listed in a report from 1997—parts of which were never revealed according to a directive by Prime Minister Peres who succeeded Rabin in office—the series of provocations, attacks, and damages caused by

Avishai Raviv. But the commission refrained from demanding that he be prosecuted in court. Will the complete truth about the Rabin assassination ever be known?

The Right generally and the settlers specifically were targeted as guilty for the crime of the prime minister's murder. The entire religious Zionist community was denounced. The Left hounded the religious Right, demanding the closing of the *Arutz 7* Gush Emunim radio station and the interrogation of rabbis who were suspected of having given a Jewish legal opinion that defined Rabin as a threat to the welfare of the Jewish people. A political witch-hunt spread through the country but especially in the Jewish communities in Judea and Samaria. The religious Right did some soul-searching; the irreligious Left did some hammer-smashing. Leah Rabin explicitly charged the Right in a collective public indictment with the murder of her husband.

Shimon Peres chose a few months after the assassination to call for early elections. He surmised that the effect of the trauma and tragedy of the Rabin assassination would serve as a political spring-board to enable Labor retaining power in the face of the challenge of Likud from the Right. However the passing of Rabin did not make Peres more popular; and Likud leader Benjamin Netanyahu, youthful and intelligent, mounted a serious challenge to Peres that ultimately brought Likud to power in 1996. Yet both before and after the election, the Left would shamelessly continue to blame the Right for the assassination. This collective guilt accusation was from a historical perspective of a piece with the Right or Revisionists accused of murdering Haim Arlosoroff, who headed the political department of the Jewish Agency, in 1933. The Left neither forgives nor forgets; and the same can be said for the Right, rather justifiably so.

Let us summarize many murky questions never clarified nor resolved: the role of the Shabak on the night of the murder; the medical reports and the forensic evidence of the bullets; the unexplained filming of the murder by Roni Kempler from a roof-top; the presence of individuals in the back seat of Rabin's vehicle; the longer-than-needed time to drive to the hospital; the rumor of the murder of one of Rabin's bodyguards after the event; Shabak director Carmi Gillon being abroad at the time of the murder; the earlier suspicious July suicide of Mota Gur, Deputy Minister of Defense, considering his vocal opposition to the "peace" process and his sympathy, unlike Rabin's antipathy, for the settlers; prior plans and failed attempts by Amir to murder Rabin; Yigal Amir's connection with the secret Nativ state agency and his work in Latvia; the intricacies of the Amir-Raviv connection and relations with the Shabak. The investigation by Barry Chamish, who authored *Who Murdered Yitzhak Rabin?* (Brookline, 1998), concluded that the assassination was a conspiracy. Chamish later emigrated from Israel.

Peres had become Labor leader and the unelected prime minister after the assassination. He then enjoyed a healthy lead in the polls against Netanyahu for the upcoming elections in 1996. A poll from February of that year gave Peres a 24-point lead over the Likud leader. A month later two terrorist bus bombings in Jerusalem caused the death of 18 people. The country was in trauma, the government headed by Peres declared an all-out war against Hamas. Although trailing by five points in a poll a week before the ballot boxes opened, Netanyahu carried the May 29, 1996 election, edging out Peres by a tiny majority of 50.5 percent of the popular vote for prime minister.

America and the Rabin Assassination

Questions were unanswered regarding the role of foreign powers and their connections with senior Israeli figures. According to reports, Rabin had been under pressure from President George Bush in 1992 to prepare for territorial withdrawals. Meeting in September of that year at Kennebunkport, Maine, Bush pressed Rabin to agree to an Israeli withdrawal from the Golan Heights. The Prime Minister was later considered to have lost faith in the Oslo gambit, unconvinced of Arafat's willingness and ability to truly consolidate peace with Israel. Rabin was generally suspicious of Arab intentions; and he was a man whose military concerns were critical in his political thinking. Rabin was caught in the claws of multiple political predicaments.

Let us go back to Rabin's time in Washington where he served as Israel's ambassador from 1968–1973. He came under the influence of Henry Kissinger, National Security Adviser and later Secretary of State under President Richard Nixon. Nixon had met Rabin when he was the IDF Chief-of-Staff during a visit to Israel in 1966. Nixon was a Quaker by faith, and in Washington Rabin apparently sent his son to a Quaker school. With Golda Meir drained physically and emotionally from the 1973 Yom Kippur War, Kissinger wanted Rabin to replace her as prime minister. Mohamed Heikal, in his book *The Road to Ramadan* (Ballantine,

1975), dealing with the war of 1973, relates the anecdote from Donald Bergus, in charge of U.S. interests in Cairo, telling the Egyptians as early as 1970 that Washington "would arrange things so that Rabin would become Prime Minister" after Golda Meir left office. Rabin, who considered America the linchpin of Israel's strategic interests, became prime minister in 1974 and under heavy pressure agreed to a partial Sinai withdrawal in 1975. He would move from a centrist position closer to the Left and agree to withdraw from the West Bank, maybe also from the Golan Heights. Nixon, who was a strategic hawk, changed course and withdrew American troops from Vietnam. Nixon turned toward China, Rabin turned toward the Arabs.

In the domestic political arena, the Left drove Nixon mad in America; and the Right drove Rabin mad in Israel. Nixon used his staff to try and cause political damage to the Left in the Watergate escapade; Rabin used the security apparatus to infiltrate the religious settler community and cause political damage to the Right. In the early 1990s, when Prime Minister Shamir withstood American pressure and was unable to work easily in tandem with the Bush administration regarding the question of settlements and U.S. aid, Rabin emerged—and won the 1992 election.

Once Arafat demonstrated that he couldn't be trusted, even Rabin began to question the value of sustaining the Oslo process. The prime minister was returning to a national consensus position. In a Knesset speech on October 5, a month before his assassination, Rabin clarified that he opposed a Palestinian state or dividing Jerusalem. The Left and elements in his Labor Party feared that Rabin, now disgusted with Arafat for Palestinian terrorism in Israel, had become a political liability in the imaginary peace scenario. Rabin must go so that Labor and Oslo could succeed, explained Arieh Stav in the pages of his *Nativ* magazine a month after the assassination, by way of interpreting leftist Mapai–style shrewd thinking.

Kissinger, who apparently had secret meetings with Rabin after the 1993 Oslo signing, was in Hong Kong when the assassination occurred, and said he was unable to get a flight to be at the funeral in Jerusalem. The pieces of the puzzle were spread from Washington to Tel Aviv, from Hong Kong to Paris, where Carmi Gillon was visiting on the night of the assassination.

President Bill Clinton was at the funeral and left his memorable emotional schmaltzy words—Shalom Haver (Goodbye Friend)—as a testimonial to Yitzhak Rabin. Perhaps Clinton knew a thing or two about Yitzhak, like his faltering commitment to Oslo. The president's standing and political investment in Oslo required that the peace process follow its route until a final resolution of the Israeli–Palestinian conflict.

The suspicious reference for Clinton concerning the Rabin assassination would be *The Strange Death of Vincent Foster* (The Free Press, 1997), an investigative book by Christopher Ruddy. It concerns the White House deputy counsel whose dead body was found in Virginia, close to Washington D.C., in July 1993. The immediate explanation focused on Foster committing suicide because of his emotional depression, but Ruddy systematically presented a host of questions regarding the physical and forensic evidence. It looked to him to be a homicide and not a suicide. But the cover-up was near-total and the press did not demonstrate particular interest in the unanswered questions. If the Clintons had Foster murdered, that would add to a number of scandals that hit the White House during Bill's two-term presidency.

In late October 1995, just a few days before his murder, Rabin visited Washington and held talks with Bill Clinton. At a United Jewish Appeal reception with the president in attendance, Rabin blundered while intending to thank President Clinton for his efforts on behalf of Middle East peace and instead thanked "President Nixon." He corrected himself and cheers arose from the audience. Rabin's slip of the tongue, no less at such an august occasion, suggests its Freudian signification: releasing unwillingly and unintentionally a thought hiding in the recesses of one's heart. Rabin gave voice to his admiration for Richard Nixon and his identifying himself with him. The mental defense mechanism failed him, so the secret was revealed. Rabin got to know Nixon during his years as ambassador in Washington; he held the president in esteem, appreciated his military support for Israel, and probably for his resolve in the turnabout with China by opening up diplomatic relations with Beijing. That might have been, for Rabin, a kind of model to emulate when the prime minister recognized the PLO. When Rabin mistakenly referred to "President Nixon," his unconscious slip of the tongue was the way, as Freud explained, the "influence of thoughts that lie outside the intended speech determines the occurrence of the slip and provides an adequate explanation of the mistake." He spoke the name of the man who may have been a source of inspiration. In the end Nixon lost his office, and Rabin lost his life.

Of yet more personal significance for Rabin was the torrent of hatred poured by the liberal Left upon Nixon; yet he stood his political ground. Rabin also stood his ground against the torrent of animosity the Israel Right threw at him. Both Nixon and Rabin reviled their respective political opponents. Then, Nixon stood behind a felony and an act of foolishness with the Watergate break-in scandal against the Democratic Party headquarters. Nixon lost self-control, frantic for his political future, and ended up losing it all. Perhaps Rabin, without reflection, utilized his security apparatus to set a plot against the Right; but it backfired and he became the victim of an error, or of betrayal from within the ranks by senior political and security personnel. When Rabin mistakenly referred to President Nixon instead of President Clinton, his high regard for Nixon surfaced from his heart. By slighting Clinton, the host of the Oslo Accord signing ceremony in Washington on September 13, 1993, Rabin conveyed his agony over Oslo, and it crushed and confused him throughout. When Rabin erred in not addressing President Clinton, the gods would say he had an eerie feeling that Clinton, pushing him on the Oslo track, was not really a friend. Perhaps Clinton himself unconsciously dropped a clue to that effect when he ironically made a point, at the funeral, of calling Rabin his "friend." Freud said we sometimes reveal verbally what we want to hide in our heart; but as Nietzsche wrote, we have a mouth to sometimes hide what is in our heart.

Clinton spoke to President Ezer Weizman when he came to Israel for Rabin's funeral, asking him to help Peres form his own post–Rabin government. In May 1996, a few days prior to the national elections in Israel, Clinton received Arafat in the Oval Office for an intimate conversation. By appearing with Arafat, wrote Steven Erlanger in *The New York Times* on May 2, the "President was implicitly supporting the election of Mr. Peres, the Palestinian's partner in the peace process." The Labor Party had just then dropped its opposition to a Palestinian state.

The Americans through the CIA were perhaps orchestrating developments in Israel with an eye to important diplomatic steps between Israel, and the Palestinians and Syrians. The CIA, with a rich history of organizing assassinations and political coups as in Guatemala, Chile, and Iran, and attempted coups in Syria and Cuba, engineered undercover operations to serve America's interests in different parts of the world. So we wonder whether Clinton, in coming to Israel in early November 1995, was primarily motivated to honor the dead or rather to distribute instructions to the living. Washington has been managing and ordering Israel from close to day one of its modern political rebirth.

As for Shimon Peres, markedly dovish since his political transformation in the latter 1970s, he had a difficult and checkered political career. It resonated with much clamor, drama, and movement. The Israeli public referred to him as "the loser" because of his repeated electoral defeats at the polls. In the 1984 round he did manage to lead Labor to a Pyrrhic victory but was unable to form a coalition government on his own, necessitating a national unity government with the arch-rival Likud. Furthermore, Peres acquired a well-earned reputation as a devious politician. He did after all rope Rabin into the Oslo fiasco. And he did come to succeed to the premiership after Rabin was removed from the political arena. In the polls taken a month after the assassination, Peres led Netanyahu by a large margin. The initial rebound Labor received from the tragedy was apparent. Rightists were arrested, rabbis interrogated, any criticism of the Left or suspicions surrounding the assassination were silenced. The Steimatzky's bookstore chain in Israel refused to carry Barry Chamish's investigative book. Rabin became a virtual martyr for the party—but it was politically in vain.

On the political wings of Peres' Oslo deal was his letter to the Norwegian Foreign Minister Johan Jorgen Holst on October 11, 1993, in assuring Israel's recognition of the positive role of Palestinian institutions in East Jerusalem. Peres was later to deny having written this letter, but he was exposed for his duplicity. Housing Minister Binyamin Ben Eliezer divulged that in the months preceding the 1996 election the Peres–led Labor Party was interested in reaching an agreement with the PLO that would commit Arafat to preventing terrorist attacks in Israel prior to polling day. This deal was designed primarily to garner electoral support from the Arab citizens in Israel.

We do not know whether Shimon Peres had a hand in the assassination of Yitzhak Rabin. Nor do we know whether Yitzhak Rabin had a hand in planning the scam which backfired. We only know that the actors, the circumstances, and the gravity of the crime have left tracks in the political muck. But the Israeli people with their healthy political instincts figured it out, and brought Likud to power in 1996.

Geula Amir, the mother of Yigal the convicted assassin, believed that "an unsavory intrigue at the highest levels of government" is the essence of the story of the Rabin assassination. Yigal received a life sentence in solitary confinement. Geula Amir was interviewed in John Kennedy Jr.'s *George* in March 1997 in an article titled "A Mother's Defense" written by Linda Gradstein. We ponder two mysterious and controversial assassinations—that of President John Kennedy and that of Prime Minister Yitzhak Rabin. Both the Warren Commission and the Shamgar Commission failed to convince many Americans and Israelis that everything was accounted for.

John Kennedy Jr., the son of JFK, was himself mysteriously killed in a plane on July 16, 1999, when he was flying his light aircraft, with his wife and her sister aboard. The plane crashed in the Atlantic Ocean killing all three of them. John Jr. had opened up the pages of his magazine to Yigal Amir's mother: Geula Amir and John Jr. both suffered the agonizing sensation that the truth had not been revealed and acknowledged in full public view. Because of that, suspicions for both assassinations will live on.

All this cannot however erase the possibility that Yigal Amir was in fact motivated to take action against Rabin, moved by a patriotic but perverted conviction that it was necessary or permissible to murder the prime minister as a way to get Oslo off track. This interpretation of the assassination remains a central—and obvious—explanation of what transpired on the tragic night of November 4, 1995, in Tel Aviv.

Further Thoughts

Each year a state ceremony is held to commemorate the murder of Yitzhak Rabin. Those who are alienated from this commemoration deride it as "the Rabin festival." It is a strained awkward moment; many Israelis are no longer saddened. But the purpose is to maintain in the public mind the Right's guilt for the murder on November 4 in Tel Aviv. This is coupled with the mantra of Rabin's legacy, undefinable and unconvincing though it is. Was his legacy grounded in making a courageous peace with the PLO, in forging a New Middle East as Peres formulated that utopia; or in the flattering claptrap of U.S. ambassador Martin Indyk who, on November 16, 1995, declared at the University of Haifa that Rabin was "the greatest statesman of the late twentieth-century." One can only wonder how that eulogy must have peeved Shimon Peres.

Clearly the world of the Right was endangered when Rabin was elected in 1992. Labor formed a government without Likud and embarked on the Oslo political voyage. The entire settlement enterprise was in jeopardy. When De Gaulle turned the political corner and conceived of France without Algeria, the threat of the OAS Right and the colons settlers assassinating the French president became a real possibility. But Israel carries no history of military putsch, army mutiny, and popular revolution. Political assassinations and regicides of illegitimate rulers, and murders of legitimate rulers, have rocked the world, and the Middle East specifically—Iraq, Egypt, Syria, Jordan, and Lebanon, have experienced this phenomenon. But it is not an Israeli experience. However warnings were sounded that a Jew might try to kill Prime Minister Rabin.

I can say on a personal note that when the news item appeared on our television screens Saturday night, November 4, 1995, an intuitive insight struck me. With Rabin gone, Likud would win the next election. The sense of the assassination delegitimizing the Right and assuring Labor's victory in the next election round in 1996 did not seem compelling to me. I felt otherwise. Rabin was somewhat of an Israeli icon. He was profiled as pure and intelligent. Without him, I surmised, Labor would suffer from a rudderless political shipwreck on the beaches of the Oslo War. Without Rabin, Labor was finished. I shared this premonition/prediction with my family as we watched the events unfold that fateful Saturday night.

Chapter Nine

TRUTH AND PEACE

The illustrious Rabbi Avraham Yitzhak HaCohen Kook (d. 1935) explained in *Orot Hakodesh* that the masses feel naturally and instinctively in touch with past and present; they have a firm integral identity. A man in the Machane Yehuda fruit market in Jerusalem knows about life and people; intellectuals at Tel-Aviv University know more about books and theories. Donald Trump's presidential victory proved this: the miner in Pennsylvania and the farmer in Idaho know more about life, people, and the ways of the world, than the academic in New York and the journalist in Chicago, certainly more than the movie actor in Hollywood.

The great poet and polemicist Uri Zvi Greenberg was a defiant and powerful voice for the Jewish people and Zionism in Israel. He wrote that he had wanted to live in Europe where he was born, but it wasn't possible. Maybe the East will let him come back and accept him. As for the Jews in Israel, they gave up on the rebuilding and recovering the Kingdom and the Temple. Would they also give up on their nationhood and the state, Greenberg wondered. The Left had abandoned the essentials of our existence: Torah, peoplehood, Land of Israel, maybe the state of Israel. They had turned to dedicate themselves to the restoration of a Palestine that never was. The Left palestinized its being and thought. It was adrift in self-oblivion and emasculation. It was exiting from Jewish history. Novelist Dorit Rabinyan explained with relief with the initial Oslo signing: "Peace represents in my eyes the removal of the heavy burden of nationalism ... always remembering that you are a Jew." It was a moment to be seduced by the allure of forgetfulness.

In modern Zionism, truth joined with power to revolutionize Jewish life. An ancient religion now became a platform for a renewed identity and spirit among patriotic youth, religious and also for "secular" youth, who are filled with an instinctive feeling for loving their country and people for whom they will give their all. Together they filled the ranks of the army's combat units, they engage in volunteer programs, they go out to guard the fields from marauding Arab robbers. Haredi youth on the whole do little for the country and refuse to join the ranks of the IDF. Perhaps one day they will recognize their shameful behavior.

But shame is also the lot of national leaders. History should judge the degree to which prime ministers were loyal to the principles and interests underlying Israel's existence. Were their decisions and actions consistent with the bedrock immemorial values of the Jewish people? Which prime minister would head the list for wisdom, moderation, patriotism; who would be at the bottom? Rabin would not be near the top of the list, and Ben-Gurion would be thanks to decisions in 1948 and thereafter close to the top—as he chose Jerusalem as the capital, blocked Palestinian refugee return, incorporated areas into the state beyond the UN partition lines. He might really be first in line.

One wonders how Likud leaders would be judged in the earthly political court. Haim Landau, a major figure in Herut and then Likud, was an early advocate of imposing Israeli law and sovereignty over the liberated areas of the homeland after the 1967 victory. Fifty years later Likud Prime Minister Netanyahu, like his party predecessors at the helm, Begin and Shamir, refuses to take a dramatic decision to normalize Israel's military and civilian presence in Judea and Samaria—though incremental legal steps were in the offing. Admittedly, demographic Arab complications and the international constellation of forces make such a move exceptionally difficult. But we still wonder when the decision and policy will gain traction and lead to the legal incorporation of all the Land of Israel west of the Jordan River—i.e. Judea and Samaria—into the borders of the State of Israel. East Jerusalem was officially incorporated into the state in June 1967 (and reconfirmed in 1980), and so too the Golan Heights in 1981. Netanyahu declared in a settlement celebration in late August 2017 that Samaria was essential for Israel's security to assure that no Islamic jihadist force control the mountain tops and threaten the coast below; he added that his government would never uproot a settlement, a promise which demands validation after the destruction of Amona.

Israel has been unwilling since 1967 to exercise a firm, no-holds-barred, authoritative security policy in Judea and Samaria. Fifty years

later, it was still commonplace for Palestinian youth to stone Jewish vehicles and military jeeps on roads near their villages. Israelis cannot take
it for granted that they can hike and tour on the hills and valleys without
the danger of being ambushed by Palestinian predators. In 1993, Ori
Shahor aged 18 and Ohad Bachrach aged 19 were murdered hiking in
Wadi Qelt between Jerusalem and Jericho. In 2000, Rabbi Binyamin
Herling was shot dead hiking with a group on Mount Eval near Shechem.
Israelis are only partially the masters of the Land. Three murders of Jews
were recorded in the beginning of 2018: Raziel Shevach shot to death
near his home at Havat Gilad in Samaria in January, Itamar Ben-Gal from
Har Bracha stabbed to death near Ariel in February, and Adiel Kolman
stabbed to death in March in the Old City of Jerusalem. The Arab war
never heard of the Oslo peace accord.

The crack-up of the Right, if we can at all define it as that, did not
arouse nausea and disgust as that of the Left. The Right at times evoked
pitifulness and a weak backbone, lacking scope or depth. Its rhetoric out-
distanced its policies. It fought Arab criminality as if one hand was tied
behind its back. Netanyahu, deftly managing national public affairs, himself was less than a vigorous rightist prime minister: he withdrew from
most of Hebron, shook Arafat's hand, initially voted for the Gaza
disengagement, intermittingly succumbed to Obama and temporarily
froze construction in Jerusalem. However Netanyahu politically maneu-
vered with great agility, landing on his feet. He played the game within
the Oslo parameters without sanctifying them. He even stopped mentioning a two-state solution after Trump was elected president. Yet he
failed to launch any strategic breakthrough, except for the construction
of the wall to block African infiltration. The fundamental political/secu-
rity problems remained: Hamas in Gaza, Fatah in Judea and Samaria, the
Bedouin deluge in the Negev, the Arab torrent in the Galilee, Hezbollah
on the northern border. Israel had yet to bring down the harsh and necessary blow, and solve major problems. All the while the Left was relentless in trying to advance the dejudaization of Israel and promoting the
arabization/palestinization of the country—all in the name of equality,
tolerance, inclusion. Its radical elements "had un-learned the ABC of nationhood," a phrase used by Herzl for certain Jews in his novel
Altneuland (Old-New Land) from 1902. While the Left lied about its real
motives, it succeeded to partially paralyze the Right. Israelis rarely if at
all openly declared that the Arabs in Israel are a perennial enemy popu-

lation, and that withdrawal from Judea and Samaria is a veritable act of utter insanity. If you told the truth, you would be branded a racist, not a patriot.

The Left, for whom the dove of peace was fluttering incessantly in the air, existed in a state of despair and denial. Of course that did not convince them that their idealism was in fact a form of doctrinarianism. By contrast the Right was in a state of frustration. It so wanted to win the recognition, not only the power, it really deserved. The Left needed to recover its sobriety and reason, and the Right needed to understand that politics is linked to culture and not only to electoral constituencies and votes. Likud was in need of creating a counter-culture to take the moral high-ground in modern Israel. Many of its traditional supporters and voters had over time been drawn into the cultural net of liberal decadence.

And the Left needs to liberate its decades-long obsession with settlements, Oslo, and Palestinians. This congenital claptrap and utopianism is shameful coming from inheritors of the Labor movement, some of whose paramount personalities, like Ben-Gurion, Moshe Sharett, Golda Meir, and Yigal Allon, represented patriotism and principle, good judgment and honesty. Let their example guide contemporary Laborites if at all there is a future for their party.

While the Left has been in political decline for decades, it has however survived and flourished as a hegemonic cultural elite. From being a marginal and subversive force until the early 1970s, its eclectic agenda of morality, individuality, cosmopolitanism, secularism, liberalism, enlightenment, anti-militarism, and yuppie (young urban professional) culture, became part of a mainstream Israeli current. The flip-side of this balance-sheet is the Left's detachment from Zionism, nationalism, patriotism, and Judaism. In his cogent essay "The Rise and Fall of the Sombre Sons" (*HaShiloach*, April 2018), Ehud Firer explained how the pessimism and despair of the Left made them outsiders in a socio-cultural reality that saw the emergence of competing sectors, like the national-religious, Russian, and Sephardi communities, for whom Zionism and love of the country provided spiritual nutrition in the Israel of the twenty-first century. Tel-Aviv was the pulse of culture, but also a refuge for the anti-establishment authors, artists, and intellectuals. Hopelessness was especially striking when anti–Zionist academics, actually promoting an academic boycott of Israel, left the country—permanently or not—examples being professors/scholars Niv Gordon, Ilan Pappe, Adi Ophir, Haim Bresheeth, Idith Zertal, Eyal Sivan, and Merav Amir. The New Historians, as an academic expression of the radical Left, smashed what for them was the idol of Zionism; but Zionism yet resonated in the hearts of Israelis for whom the national project was a vehicle for deliverance from powerlessness and a home for our people. For the Left to yet hold the Right in contempt was a rather pitiful display of political conceit.

***

At the crux of the Israeli quandary and conundrum is the great need for reconciliation between the Right and the Left. These rival political forces each hold on to something authentic in Jewish terms. The Left cannot easily liberate itself from an ideological arrogance that it sustains morality, equality, and compassion, for the weak and the Arabs. They want to set the Palestinians—within the Green Line and beyond in the territories—free from the shackles of Israeli rule. There is a heavy dose of naiveté and blindness in this approach; but it does contain a kernel of moral sensitivity and egalitarian pathos. Now and then a flicker of optimism and a gesture of humanity appear; as when an Arab in September 2016 saved five American Jewish yeshiva students from being lynched by predatory youth in Hebron. This incident, registering a nobility of spirit and exceptional courage, cannot compensate for the Palestinian path of terrorism so embedded in many decades of savage warfare.

The Right is bound to a biblical vision of the land and Jewish national identity, cognizant of the process of redemption in the Zionist Return. This is a corrective to the shame of Exile and raises the banner for Jewish liberation. The Rightists know that not democracy was our ideal but Judaism, and Herzl had more than an inkling about this profound truth. We no longer have to dance only at other peoples' celebrations because the celebration of our independence is our gala experience in these times.

Ultimately the Left must be healed of its assimilationist tendencies and return to the people's cultural hearth. Its youth must love and learn the Bible as do religious youth. The Left must undergo an agonizing process of cleansing its tarred soul of vulgarity and self-deceit; undeniably signs abound of moral and social decadence—gay parades, same sex marriages, deviant family structures, artistic nudity paraded as creativity, disloyalty to the country cast as a moral option. For the rightist the heart is happy when a new settlement is built on a hilltop in Samaria or overlooking the Judean desert; while the leftist feels satisfaction when a settlement is dismantled and destroyed, as at Sadot in the Yamit salient in 1982 and Homesh in northern Samaria in 2005.

Ben-Gurion, who came from the socialist Left, but always a believing Zionist, is a teacher for future generations. He said at the twenty-first Zionist Congress in Basel in 1937: "No Jew is at liberty to surrender the right of the Jewish nation . . . . No Jewish body is sanctioned to do so. No Jew alive has the authority to yield any piece of the Land whatsoever . . ." This is the testimony of our people for nearly four thousand years of history. The Right will welcome the Left returning home to this elemental truth. The Jews are not rootless gypsies without history and homeland.

Most poignant is the fact that the core of ancient biblical and Jewish history, with its sites and stories, is located in the mountain heartland of Judea and Samaria. If the Left gets its way, as it implemented its first treasonous steps with Oslo in the 1990s, then withdrawing from the Land is no less staggering than the Jewish people withdrawing from its history.

Should the Left have the power to withdraw fully from Judea and Samaria, the shock and trauma could veritably destroy Israel from within. The political foundations would totter and set aflame civil strife and fierce repression. Back in power, the Left could irresponsibly undo the good the Right has done in matters of security, the economy, culture, and on the territorial and Palestinian issues. The Left cannot be trusted with the reins of government; the Israelis must deny them power and thus save the nation from catastrophe. This is so because on the Left the national idea withered. Loyalty to the Jewish people was partly replaced in succumbing to and feeding into the Palestinians' vilifying propaganda against Israel as an occupation regime, maybe since 1948, minimally since 1967.

The Arabs were unwilling to accept the results of the 1948 war as conclusive and justified; the leftists were unwilling to accept the results of the 1967 war as conclusive and justified. They have both battled the turn of the political tide with Israel's modern military performance. In the first war the Jews established the state, and in the second they recovered the core of the homeland. Arabs and Israeli leftists want to turn back the clock of history.

Let us end with an encouraging reflection. We draw upon Hegel in *The Phenomenology of Mind* and learn that "it is the nature of truth to force its way to recognition when the time comes, and that it only appears when its time has come, and hence never appears too soon . . ." Indeed, the modern Jewish redemption fits ancient biblical and rabbinic forecasts. A new spirit is emerging as Israel advances forward on all frontiers. Reconciliation between the Right and Left, or what is left of the Left, as a kind of "unity of contradictions," must be a central pillar of the New Israel once the truths of life and politics will become transparent and acknowledged by all.

Select Terms Index

- *Al HaMishmar*: far-left daily newspaper in the years 1943–1995 affiliated with HaShomer Hatzair and the Mapam Party.
- Aliya: literally "going up . . ." Jewish immigration to the Land of Israel.
- *Arutz 7*: national-religious Zionist radio station and internet news site in the years 1988–2003.
- Betar: nationalist youth movement founded in 1923 by Zeev Jabotinsky.
- B'Tselem: human rights pro–Palestinian NGO founded in 1989.
- Breaking the Silence: anti–IDF pro–Palestinian NGO established in 2004.
- *Davar*: daily newspaper affiliated with the Labor Party, appearing from 1925–1996.
- Etzel: also known as the Irgun; a para-military organization inspired by Zeev Jabotinsky and led by Menachem Begin, that evolved beginning in 1931, dissolved in 1948.
- Fatah: the Palestinian National Liberation Movement founded by Yasser Arafat in 1965, later led by Mahmoud Abbas.
- *Galatz*: acronym for the *Galei Tzahal* army radio network.
- *Galei Israel*: Zionist radio station.
- Galut: Hebrew for the Jewish exile and diaspora.
- GSS: General Security Services (Shabak/Shin Bet), the internal security services.
- Gush Emunim: nationalist-religious Zionist settlement movement founded in 1974–5.
- *Haaretz*: far-left daily newspaper founded in 1918.

~ HaBayit HaYehudi (Jewish Home): orthodox Zionist party founded in 2008, replacing the NRP (National Religious Party/Mafdal).

~ Haganah: self-defense military unit founded in 1920, affiliated with the Labor Party and dissolved in 1948.

~ Hamas: Islamic Resistance Movement founded in 1988 as an offshoot of the Muslim Brotherhood, with the aim of liberating Palestine.

~ Haredim: Ultra–Orthodox anti–Zionist Jews, re-fusing military service.

~ HaShomer HaTzair: far-left Zionist socialist young guard movement founded in 1913.

~ HaTechiya: nationalist-right party founded in 1979 in opposition to the Camp David Accords; dissolved in 1992.

~ *Hatzofe*: religious Zionist daily newspaper during the years 1937–2008.

~ Herut: nationalist party formed in 1948 to repre-sent the ideology of Jabotinsky and Betar; merged into Likud in 1973.

~ Hezbollah: Lebanese Shiite–Islamic 'Party of Allah' formed in 1982 as an Iranian proxy.

~ Histadrut: trade union with economic enterprises founded in 1920 and affiliated with the Labor Party.

~ IDF: Israel Defense Forces, known in the Hebrew acronym as Tzahal.

~ Im Tirtzu: Zionist NGO established in 2006 to strengthen the national position in general and especially on university campuses.

~ Irgun: see Etzel.

~ *Israel Hayom*: right-of-center daily newspaper dis-tributed free of charge appearing since 2007.

~ Yisrael Beiteinu (Israel is our Home) rightist party founded in 1999 with appeal to Russian immigrants.

~ Kach: far-right religious party founded by Rabbi Meir Kahane in 1971, banned in 1994.

~ Labor Party: historically Mapai (The Eretz-Israel Workers Party) founded in 1930, dissolved in 1968, later emerging as the Labor Party.

~ Lehi: nationalist underground founded in 1940 to fight British rule.

~ Likud: national party from 1973 based on merger of Herut/Gahal with other factions.

~ *Maariv*: national daily newspaper from 1948 which moved from the right to the center on the political spectrum.

~ *Makor Rishon*: religious-rightist weekly newspaper founded in 1997.

~ Mapai: see Labor Party.

~ Mapam: far-left socialist party from 1948 until 1997, merging into Meretz.

~ Member of Knesset, MK.

~ Meretz: leftist-secular party that was established in 1992.

~ Moledet: far-right party appearing in 1988, dissolved in 1999 when merging with the National Union (now part of HaBayit HaYehudi).

~ Nili: acronym for the Jewish–Zionist espionage pro–British group in 1915–17.

~ Oslo: Israel–PLO interim arrangements agreement in 1993 that launched a 'peace process'.

~ Palmach: Zionist strike force of the Haganah founded in 1941, dissolved in 1948.

~ PLO: Palestine Liberation Organization founded in 1964.

~ Revisionists: a nationalist Zionist faction from 1935 led by Zeev Jabotinsky (representing the NZO—New Zionist Organization).

~ Shabak (Shin Bet): see GSS.

~ Shas: Sephardi/Oriental ultra-orthodox party.

~ Tzahal: see IDF.

~ Yahadut HaTorah: Ashkenazi anti–Zionist ultra-orthodox party.

~ *Yediot Aharonot*: centrist left-leaning daily newspaper founded in 1939.

~ Yesh Atid (There is a Future): liberal-secular party founded in 2012.

~ Yeshuv/Ha-yishuv: the active and pioneering pre–1948 Jewish Zionist community emerging in the Land.

50244880R00126

Made in the USA
Middletown, DE
24 June 2019